FORTUNE'S
CHILD

FORTUNE'S CHILD

A Portrait of the United States as Spendthrift Heir

Lewis H. Lapham

FRANKLIN
SQUARE
PRESS

NEW YORK

To my wife

Copyright © 1994 Franklin Square Press

Published by Franklin Square Press, a division of Harper's Magazine, 666 Broadway, New York, N.Y. 10012

First Edition.

First printing 1994.

Library of Congress Cataloging-in-Publication Data:
Fortune's child: a portrait of the United States as spendthrift heir/
by Lewis H. Lapham/edited by Ellen Rosenbush.
p.cm.
ISBN: 1-879957-21-3 $12.95 (pbk.)
1. United States—Civilization—1945– . II. United States—Social
conditions—1945–. I. Title
E169.1.L357 1994
973.92—dc20
94-34123
CIP

Book and cover design by Deborah Thomas.

Cover photograph: Collection of the New York Public Library
Picture Collection.

Manufactured in the United States of America.

This book has been produced on acid-free paper.

CONTENTS

ACKNOWLEDGMENTS

The following articles first appeared in *Harper's Magazine*: "The Mandate of Heaven" (as "The Temptation of the Sacred Cow"); "America's Guest" (revision of "Victory for the Big Dumb Money"); "Deadly Virtue" (revision of "Deadly Virtue," January 1978, and combined with "The Wizard of Oz"); "The King's Pleasure" (revision of "The King's Pleasure," March 1976, and combined with "The Art of Innocence"); "A Nation of Dreamers"; "Lost Horizon"; "City Lights"; "The American Bedouin" (combined with "The Melancholy Herd"); "The Assassin as Celebrity"; "Fear of Heights"; "Hostages to Fortune"; "Confusion Worse Confounded"; "A Rake's Progress"; "The Arabian Oil Bubble"; "Notes on the View from 43,000 Feet" (as "Perspectives of Flight"); "The Leisure State" (as "Veblen Revisited"); "Guests of the Management" (combined with "Juggernaut of Words," June 1979); "The Retreat from Democracy" (combined with "The Capitalist Paradox," March 1977).

The following article is reprinted from *The Saturday Evening Post*: May 4 and May 18, 1968: "Talking to the White Rabbit" (a revision of "There Once Was a Guru from Rishikesh").

Introduction

The essays in this book make the assumption that with the victory of World War II the heirs to the American fortune got into the habit of thinking of themselves as rich kids. The corollary delusion of unlimited wealth has had the customary ill effects. For the last fifty years the widespread presumptions of divine grace and eternal credit have been as characteristic of the American democracy playing with the toys of art and government as of the spendthrift and still prodigal sons squandering the available patrimony.

During the first half of the twentieth century, the European powers twice attempted suicide, and at the end of World War II what was left of Western civilization passed into the American account. The war prompted the country to invent a miraculous economic machine that seemed to grant as many wishes as were asked of it. The continental United States escaped the scourge of battle, and so it was easy enough for the heirs to imagine that they had been singularly favored by God. In 1945, as in the seventeenth century when the founders of the Puritan enterprises accepted into their hands the blessing of a bountiful wilderness, the United States once again seemed to have received the mandate of heaven. No wonder the Americans believed themselves heirs apparent—not only of the Greek and Christian past but also of the earth and all of its creation.

As the inheritors became increasingly profligate (cf. the steadily rising levels of inflation, consumption, and debt over the last fifty years), so also the assumptions of privilege became habitual among larger segments of the population. Within a decade the presumptions of entitlement were extended throughout the whole of the society. The *droits du seigneur* had relatively little to do with something so worldly as money, and they became as commonplace among the sons of immigrant peddlers as among the daughters of the *haute bourgeoisie,* among the intellectual as well as the merchant classes. At the same time and for the same prices the rich and the not-so-rich acquired such proofs of their salvation as television sets, boats, amphetamines, a second house or mortgage, and the assurance that they could write novels no less great than those of Melville and James. Everybody was entitled to everything. The feeling of amplitude was sustained by the miracle of the reawakened consumer markets. Habits of extravagance once plausible only in the children of the rich were imitated by people with enough money to gain access to credit. As larger numbers of people acquired the emblems of wealth they also acquired the attitudes appropriate to the defense and worship of wealth. Why else had the war been won if not for the enjoyment of the heirs? Why else had the immigrant fathers made so many sacrifices (during the Depression as well as at Anzio and Guadalcanal) if the sons couldn't become whatever they chose to become—poets and statesmen as well as talk-show personalities and owners of subsidiary rights? What else does it mean to be an heir if he cannot have anything that it occurs to him to want?

THE SELF-ENCHANTMENT implicit in the assumption of privilege first forced itself on my attention at Yale University in the middle 1950s. Dwight Eisenhower was elected President of the United States during the autumn of my freshman year, and for the next eight years he administered the national inheritance like a drowsy and avuncular trustee. Occasionally there were wars or rumors of war on the frontiers (in Eastern Europe and Korea), and obviously all was not well in

Mississippi and Georgia. But these were minor inadequacies and temporary failures that surely would be corrected when somebody had the time to get around to the chore of cleaning up the premises. In the meantime, the fortunate inheritors could play in the sun of the nation's victories. All the lines on all the graphs pointed triumphantly upward. For the children of the affluent middle class an education was a necessary ornament, something that one couldn't afford to be without (like tennis clothes or dancing lessons), but not something of which a gentleman needed to take much notice. The American fortune was so great that it couldn't be counted, and it was deemed proper for the inheritors to affect a languid carelessness (a manner known at Yale as "cool") about their possessions. Nobody was expected to work too hard, as if he really needed to remember what was being said, and nobody had to "find himself" because everybody already had been found. The sobriquet of "the silent generation" thus attached itself to people who didn't feel obliged to attract attention to themselves. The happy few could concentrate their attention on questions of style and address—to wonder whether to wear white shoes or not to wear white shoes, to weigh the advantage of going into the family investment business against the pleasure of taking up the hobbies of war and diplomacy. During the summer vacations people went to Europe to inspect the newly acquired cultural properties and to see how poor were the Europeans.

COMPARABLE EXPECTATIONS of subsidy shaped the attitudes of those students who identified themselves as the rising generation of intellectuals. Assuming that they had inherited the prerogatives of sensibility, they believed themselves fit to govern, if not the United States (in which as yet they had little interest) then the Museum of Modern Art and the New York publishing emporia. Many of the apprentice intellectuals whom I heard deriding Theodore Dreiser in 1954 I later heard deriding, in much the same language and for most of the same reasons, the administrations of Lyndon Johnson, Richard Nixon, and Jimmy Carter. The political protests of the 1960s were inconceivable because nobody could imagine their having the slightest effect. The chance of a nuclear holocaust was very much on everybody's mind, and it was fashionable to say, with Dostoevsky, that nothing made any difference and that all was permissible. Wasn't that the whole point of the Weimar Republic and the writings of Camus and Brecht? What was the use of milling around with a placard in the rain (and by so doing making a fool of oneself) if the individual remained helpless against the Minotaur lodged within the labyrinth of the modern state? By ignoring all questions of politics and economics (the former being somehow connected to the latter and therefore not worth troubling about among people living on allowances) the intelligentsia could direct its attention to the great question of "creativity." Anybody judged to be creative could insult his friends, neglect his debts, and seduce as many women as might be necessary to his egoism or convenient to his lust. All would be forgiven because, like the inheritor of a trust fund worth $3 million a year, the fellow quite obviously had been anointed by God. Conversely, of the man found lacking in creativity, nothing would be forgiven. The miserable wretch of a philistine was sentenced to rot in the galleys of commerce. The harshness of this doctrine divided the faithful into fierce and embittered factions. Arguments about the legitimacy of claims to the patronage of the Muse frequently condemned the rival claimants to mutual and life-long hatred. How, for instance, could G— be taken seriously as a composer when everybody knew that he played Bach on the piano instead of on the harpsichord? What monstrous impertinence persuaded B— to proclaim himself a writer when everybody knew that he had gone to high school in Texas and had not read Proust? The disputes were theological in nature, much like the later disputes about social justice, and they had to do with the condition of grace. Creativity was something ineffable, something impossible to acquire by diligence or study; it was as much a matter of birth as an inflection of speech, and it remained forever beyond the reach of parvenus. Because creativity depended upon divine favor and therefore could not be demonstrated by published works (subject to the corruptions of the critics), the great question, like the equally great question of white shoes, resolved itself into matters of taste, style, and deportment. Candidates for admission into clubrooms of art took the precaution of dressing and behaving in a manner that would signify their acquaintance with the view from Parnassus. When not engaged in laying waste to other people's pretensions, they took as much trouble rehearsing the mannerisms of alienation as the young men of property took with the affectations of insouciance. Anybody who wore a beard or who threw things on the floor at least stood the chance of having his daubs or manuscripts accepted as works of genius. Everybody expected to write the great American novel or to make the great American movie, but nobody thought that he had to make the sacrifices necessary to accomplish these ambitions. (For what is the point of ambition among people who already own everything worth owning?) Lacking either purpose or vision, the apprentice intellectuals of the 1950s proclaimed themselves critics of one kind or another (social, political, literary, cultural), and for the next twenty years they set about the great task of awarding the patents of nobility.

WHEN I first went to work for a newspaper, nobody present in the city room would have had the effrontery to call himself "a journalist." This was a term of opprobrium, reserved for fops and Englishmen. Within a matter of a few years, partially as a result of President Kennedy's accession to the White House, the procurators of what came to be known as "the media" learned to think of themselves not only as the conscience of the nation but also as a social class. The journalists who came to prominence in the 1960s brought with them the bound volumes of absolute truth that they had collected at Yale or Harvard. Few of them had the patience for democratic politics. Educated to literary abstraction rather than to the experience of the streets or the courthouse, they measured all things in the perfect balance of what they had been told about right and wrong. The absolutism of the aesthetic disputes of the 1950s shifted into a political mode.

If much of the history of the last fifty years can be understood as a family quarrel about the division of the estate, then the bitterness of the rivalries for financial and ideological preference that defined the decade of the 1960s resulted from the suddenness with which the United States came into its inheritance. It is no more than seventy-nine years from the closing of the frontier to the walk on the moon; roughly the same span of time measures the building of Chartres Cathedral and the period between John D. Rockefeller's entry into business and his death amid incalculable riches. Most of the public arguments about social justice resolved themselves in questions of primogeniture.

The press amplified the fratricidal rivalries throughout the whole of the society, and it used the arguments about public policy as vehicles for the quarrel about the distribution of the estate. If money was the weapon of the ruthless parent, then journalism was the weapon of the angry child. Thus the willingness of the press to find occasions (Vietnam, civil rights, the counterculture, et cetera) for defending the interests of youth, beauty, innocence, truth, and justice against the villainy of a system variously identified with money, hypocrisy, greed, pain, experience, and age. The anger of the press was both adolescent and proprietary. It was the national inheritance with which the older generation was making mistakes, and the press presumed to speak for anybody and everybody who thought that the trust fund was being mismanaged. Implicit in the general criticism was the notion that if the country could tolerate a government of mediocrities and fools, then the country didn't deserve the allegiance of the governed. The moral dandyism of this attitude ignored the melancholy truth that most people are mediocrities and fools (journalists not least among them), and that laws and institutions come into being precisely because most people cannot be counted upon to behave in the manner of heroes and saints.

DURING THE early years of the 1960s the quarrel about the division of the national estate was barely noticeable. For the time being it seemed as if there would be enough for everybody. The rivals for financial and ideological preference hadn't yet separated themselves into the factions of the 1970s that formed themselves around the standards and rallying cries of environmentalism, free enterprise, big government, the First Amendment, feminism, and human rights. When President Eisenhower, as regent and trustee, relinquished the American fortune to John F. Kennedy, the prince and heir, the repressed Oedipal passivity of the 1950s gave way to the Oedipal assertion of the new decade. The boom in the stock markets coincided with the opulent idealism of Hyannis Port, Harvard, and Palm Beach.

In an earlier and more spacious age the American millionaire beset by intimations of mortality contented himself with collecting stuffed animals or objects of art. President Kennedy brought into vogue the passion for collecting Harvard professors. He enjoyed critical theory of varying kinds and denominations (literary as well as social and political), and he presided over what became a golden age of sophistry. The heir felt himself so blessed by fortune that nothing more was required of a theory (whether for a reordering of American education or a war in Asia) but that it conform to its own inner truth and beauty. The theorists borrowed the *raison d'être* of modern art, and in place of the notion of art for art's sake they substituted the notion of theory for theory's sake. Nothing was supposed to have unpleasant consequences, at least not for the artificers and scribes who never left Cambridge except to go to Washington and who could explain why their mistakes should be blamed on the trolls hidden in the forest of historical process. Even the riots at the universities constituted a form of conspicuous consumption. The students had sufficient money and leisure to demonstrate on behalf of theories they had never seen, and the professors looking down from their neo-Gothic windows could tell one another their ideas of Marxist revolution were something more substantial than *trompe l'oeil*.

The avant-garde disbanded and moved uptown with Andy Warhol, and the image of the politician was transformed from that of a portly assassin in a cheap suit (the standard portrait by Bertolt Brecht) to a hero in a tennis sweater (the standard portrait by Teddy White). The press announced that the alchemists of Camelot had discovered the secret of the philosopher's stone. Lead could be turned into gold, newspapers into collections of poems, social science into literature. The new reality superseded all previous realities and transformed a generation of caterpillars into butterflies. In every sector of the society, people acquired new shapes and forms. Young men whom I had known at Yale as fraternity drunks appeared as assistant secretaries of state; literary intellectuals formerly preoccupied with the imagery of Melville telephoned from the Pentagon to say that they were applying the canons of the new criticism to the analysis of weapons systems. Lawyers thought to be immured within the honeycombs of Wall Street emerged transcendent at the Department of Justice. All things were possible, and everybody was enraptured by the flux of things, by the sudden sense of movement (as of ice breaking up after a hard winter), by the glorious ascent into space and the moral awakening on the New Frontier. It became important to receive invitations to Washington;

whether to a dinner party or to a federal appointment didn't much
matter because in the minds of most people in New York the differences were so slight as to be barely discernible. The invitations
reserved a place on the prince's barge for the voyage down the
Potomac to the summer sea.

IF THE years between 1960 and 1968 established the thesis of the
1960s, the years from 1968 through the election of Jimmy Carter in
1976 developed the antithesis. The two periods present mirror images
of each other. Just as President Kennedy embodied the persona of the
American state as luminous romance, President Nixon embodied the
persona of the American state as grotesque melodrama. Prior to 1968
the world seemed more or less benevolent and ripe with opportunity.
It was enough to have been born American, presumably and by definition eternally young, beautiful, and rich. After 1968 these assumptions were no longer so easy. Even celebrities began to be found dead
in West Side hotel rooms, and the heirs to the American fortune began
to notice paradoxes. Social legislation embodying the hope of conscience apparently provoked race riots in New York, Los Angeles, and
Detroit. The multiple demands for freedom ended in the enslavements
of drugs and bureaucracy. The expectation of effortless victory resulted in the defeat in Southeast Asia. Nothing worked the way it was
supposed to work. Within a few months the stagehands in the intellectual theaters took down the brightly painted scenes of empire and
replaced them with the melancholy scenery of a nation betrayed. The
fashionable celebration of government became the equally fashionable abuse of government. The economics of expansion gave way to
the economics of retrenchment. The collective rapture of the Peace
Corps became the collective rapture of a march on Washington, and
the party of opposition moved from the new left to the new right. The
discovery of the obvious (that government costs money and that bul-

lets kill people) passed muster as sublime truth. Publishers offered huge rewards for the worst possible news about the United States, and the best-selling social critics searched diligently for enemies on whom to place the blame for the public unhappiness. Nobody becomes more obsessive on the subject of money than the rich man who has suffered financial constraint, and the opulent heirs of the early 1960s grew irritable and petulant. Observing that idealism is an expensive hobby, people went around muttering about exhaustion and debt, about the damage done to the environment and the lack of first-class accommodation on Spaceship Earth. The enthusiasts of the Kennedy era prided themselves on the earnestness of their concern for the commonwealth; by the end of the decade they were suffering the anxiety of the newly arrived, who, with their collections of pop art and their subscriptions to the zeitgeist, figured that it was about time that they devoted more of their attention to their swamis, their diets, and their jogging shoes.

Despite the reduced expectations of the 1970s, the heirs to the fortune apparently continue to believe that they possess unlimited resources (of grace and credit, if not of oil), and so they make little effort to replenish the family fortunes. For at least a generation the American democracy has been living on the capital (moral and intellectual as well as financial) accumulated by prior generations. The decline in the birth rate runs parallel to the loss of productivity in the economy; the lack of vitality in the arts coincides with the contraction of business enterprise.

LIKE JOHN Kennedy before him, the late Nelson Rockefeller embodied the spirit of the age of inheritance. Both in his life and in his death he provided an exemplary model of the behavior appropriate to the heir of a magnificent fortune. In many ways he resembled Tom Buchanan in *The Great Gatsby*. He had a fondness for collecting the objects of art and experience, and he conducted a lifelong and passionate love affair with himself. Like the other eulogists in *Time, Newsweek,* and the *New York Times,* Henry Kissinger, who delivered the eulogy at the funeral service in New York, had no choice but to talk about his patron's extravagant intentions. As Governor of New York, Mr. Rockefeller had accomplished so little and destroyed so much that the chronicle of his works and days couldn't bear close examination, much less praise. Thus, Mr. Kissinger cast his eulogy in language more becoming to a young man who had yet to fulfill his promise than to a man of seventy, borne down by the weight of years and civic honors. He spoke of Mr. Rockefeller's "gallant failure to win the nation's highest office" as if he were reciting an ode to an athlete dying young, and he observed, by way of a testimonial to Mr. Rockefeller's political wisdom, that "Nelson always had a marvelous time." That remark could as easily stand as a tribute to the exiled Shah of Iran. Both Mr. Rockefeller and the Shah inherited great wealth. They could buy mirrors in which to admire themselves, and they could make prodigious collections of things (paintings, houses, F-14s, Harvard professors, jewels, and women), but, much to their astonishment and regret, they discovered that they couldn't buy the future.

The wealth of the United States in comparison with other nations in the world makes the figure of the rich man representative not only of the country's gargantuan extravagance but also of what can be called the national habit of mind. Over a period of twenty-five years I have been writing about the character of the American rich kid in the age of inheritance, and all of the chapters in this book first appeared in either *The Saturday Evening Post* or *Harper's Magazine.* I have included only those essays and articles that sustain or illuminate the hypothesis, and I have revised or amended almost all of the texts in a way to make them consistent with the passage of time.

The Mandate of Heaven

AUGUST 1973

FOR THE time being the satisfactions of the Watergate scandal have interrupted the complaint about intimidations of the press. The Nixon Administration has been discovered in its iniquity, and the newspapers rejoice in daily proofs of anything that might contribute to the celebration of its public ruin. In part the press delights in the spectacle because it seems to demonstrate the truth of what much of the press has been saying for so long about Mr. Nixon's subversion of constitutional government. It is a pleasant thing to behold the coming to pass of a promised misery (even if that misery requires the pouring of slops on a man's own head), and so I cannot quarrel with the festival of gleeful self-congratulation.

Given the expense of adjectives, I expect that the euphoria of prize giving will be inflated into a delusion of moral grandeur. This is unfortunate, not only for the press but also for what remains of the freedom of expression. As a first sign of its impending folly the press already has been tempted to revive its requests for immunity and further privilege.*

This article unhappily proved to be prophetic. The press kept demanding further privileges and immunities, and by the end of the 1970s the media had come to be generally regarded as what one of the correspondents to Harper's Magazine described as "an army of occupation." The widespread antagonism resulted in Supreme Court decisions reflecting less generous interpretations of the First Amendment and the libel laws.

Those demands were presented to Congress last spring in the form of testimony advocating what has been described as a shield law. The press has a history of giving way to its temptations, and I expect it will use the Watergate investigation as a pretext to renew its passionate lament. Presumably the argument will take the following line: "If it were not for a vigorous press, then the Nixon Administration would have escaped its deserved punishments; what therefore is needed is an even more vigorous press, one that remains forever safe from the bullying of government." The editorialist will go on to construct a metaphor in which he portrays the press as knight errant rescuing the virginity of the Republic from the dark lust of H. R. Haldeman.

I can think of few things more injurious to the press than the passage of a shield law, whether in absolute or qualified form. When I read the declarations of journalists justifying the need for such a law I am reminded of convicts building the gallows from which they will hang. The law strikes me as foolish because the testimony advanced in its behalf depends on a romantic or mythological idea of the press. I take it as axiomatic that laws passed for reasons of mythology lead to effects confirming the worst fears of their most ardent proponents.

I have worked in various sectors of the press for sixteen years, and I have become skeptical of the local iconography and of the enthusiasts who talk about "the people's right to know." The slogans of the trade resound with the same hollowness as the slogans of any other profession (members of the New York Stock Exchange speak of "the people's capitalism"). The existence of any press, whether free or enslaved, also gives rise to a number of evils, among them a debasement of the language and the construction of a papier-mâché reality that becomes plausible only in times of national calamity. City editors give thanks for news of shipwreck and prominent suicide, and the press must always be said to welcome a declaration of war.

Even so, and despite all that can be said or proved about the ignorance of the press, a belligerent and unruly press raises the best defense against the abuses available to the present system of American government. My objection to the shield law is that its enactment would encourage the press in its most cowardly instincts and so disembowel it. The demand for such a law troubles me because I think that it proceeds from an inwardly admitted weakness rather than from a publicly proclaimed strength. I also think that a good many people in the press, far from being intimidated, seek a high-sounding excuse with which to relinquish a freedom that has become both too difficult and too expensive to sustain.

THE LAW now in question has to do with a reporter's right to protect the sources of his information. The advocates of an absolute shield law argue that reporters should not be required to divulge any source of any information (whether published or unpublished) to investigative agencies of any kind, whether grand juries, courts, executive commissions, or the Congress. The prevailing opinion holds that if the authorities can force reporters to disclose the sources of their information, then those sources will wither away like the flowers of the desert, and the public will be denied the information necessary to the conduct of a democracy. The argument assumes that the protected source of information works to the advantage of the press and so assists the free circulation of the news.

My own experience supports an exactly opposite conclusion. The protection of an informed source works to the advantage of the source, inhibiting the circulation of any news that does not advance the interest of the man circulating it. More often than not the reporter who agrees to deal in protected information transforms himself into a press agent. The contention that sources of news will wither away seems to me exaggerated. Few news stories of any consequence (to anybody other than reporters or the people entangled in the narrative) depend on an unknown source. James McCord decides to tell what he knows about Watergate, and his confession has an effect because he can be named. So also for the ship sinkings, the collapse of money markets, the onslaught of war, the loss of a World Series. If bureaucrats and politicians were deprived of the convenience of speaking off the record, they might learn to speak in plain words.

Contrary to fond expectations, the passage of a shield law would concede additional authority to those people whom the press chooses to identify as its enemies. Anybody who doubts this has only to consider the present reporting of the Watergate investigations. So many journalists have reported so many statements attributed to unspecified sources, most of whom must be assumed to be telling the story to fit their own ends, that the truth of the matter has been distorted into propaganda. The resulting confusion serves the purpose of the men hoping to excuse themselves from blame and criminal convictions.

The present debate about the First Amendment began to gather an audience about a year ago, when, in June of 1972, the Supreme Court arrived at what has come to be known as the Caldwell decision. Earl Caldwell, a reporter for the *New York Times,* had spent much of 1968 within the councils of the Black Panther organization. Eventually he published an account in which he mentioned having seen an arsenal of automatic weapons. This was understood to be an ominous sight, and the FBI asked Caldwell to disclose what else he knew about the Black Panthers. It will be remembered that 1968 was also the year of the Chicago riots and Robert Kennedy and Martin Luther King's assassinations, and even the most sensible people in the country had begun to stumble into the abyss of paranoia. (The mood of paranoia later assumed the dimensions of an epidemic, infecting not only the press, which came to imagine itself

suppressed by an illegal government, but also the Nixon Administration, which came to imagine itself surrounded by anarchists and
agents provocateurs.)

Caldwell subsequently refused to testify before a grand jury that
had been summoned to investigate the rumor of an attempt to assassinate President Nixon. Four years later the Supreme Court denied his
claim to protection under the First Amendment; in the same decision,
the Court also denied the claim of Paul Branzburg, a reporter for the
Louisville Courier Journal who had written a story about his two days
in a factory that refined hashish. Branzburg declined to name the people who had been manufacturing the drug, and the Court declined "to
seriously entertain the notion that the First Amendment protects a
newsman's right to conceal the criminal conduct of his sources."
Throughout the rest of 1972 other courts and jurisdictions attempted
to force information from unwilling reporters, a few of whom, refusing
to comply with the subpoenas, went briefly to jail.

BUT THE press grossly exaggerated the harassment, and for the most
part I think it was frightened by its own editorials. Even so mild-
mannered a man as Walter Cronkite was led to envision a government conspiracy. He subsequently regretted the vision, and several
months later, remembering his real rather than his illusory interests,
he repudiated it. The general outcry nevertheless brought forth
Congressional hearings on the First Amendment, and in the fall of
last year the emissaries of the press began traveling to Washington
to petition for a law granting them much the same kind of executive
privilege that they so forcibly condemned when it was claimed by
the operatives in Mr. Nixon's discredited White House. (Delusions
of moral grandeur can descend upon people of contrary political
beliefs, but usually they result in similar unhappiness.)

The first series of hearings took place in the House, before a subcommittee under the direction of Robert Kastenmeier (D-Wisc.), and then in the spring of this year the hearings were resumed in both Kastenmeier's subcommittee and in Senator Sam Ervin's Senate Judiciary Subcommittee on Constitutional Rights.

What was peculiar about the hearings was the unanimity of opinion expressed by so many people with divergent interests. A few journalists argued against the need for immunity of any kind, among them Clark Mollenhoff of the *Des Moines Register* and Benjamin Bradlee of the *Washington Post,* but the majority of witnesses testified in favor of an absolute shield law. They counted among their number not only William Farr and Peter Bridge (journalists who had been jailed for refusing to divulge information) but also the American Newspaper Publishers Association, Governor Nelson Rockefeller of New York, the managing editor of the *New York Times,* and the management of CBS. Publishers have little in common with reporters, and their appearance on the same side of the argument, particularly an argument addressed to a matter of conscience, should have encouraged somebody to ask a wretched question: How comes it that the self-proclaimed spokesmen for the oppressed find themselves aligned with the oppressors? Nobody asked the question because the answer to it requires the doing of violence to a precious illusion.

The romantic view of the press, much advertised at banquets and award ceremonies, favors the image of the reporter as the man against the system. The press as a whole supposedly stands as the watchdog of the Republic, tireless and ferocious in its pacing to and fro on the ramparts of freedom. The testimonial speeches then go on to explain how the press never slackens in its search for injustice, how it keeps the politicians honest and protects the poor from the cruel capriciousness of the rich. The speeches describe the mythological press.

The real press must be understood as an institution, no more or

less courageous than any other institution in the country. Most of the
news transmitted to the American public travels through the major
instruments of the media.* These are large corporations organized on
bureaucratic principles, and they do not suffer gladly the consequences of quixotic gesture. I grant that the American press is as free
as any press in the world, but it remains subject to the usual restrictions—the laws of libel, the economics of the advertising business,
the prejudices of its editors, and the interests of its owners.

The press discovers injustice largely by accident, often for reasons having to do with the news space available in an early edition.
Disgruntled politicians wander into newspaper offices with the evidence that will incriminate their enemies, or a systems analyst
believing himself to be the messiah appears with documents stolen
from the Department of Defense. The press seldom concerns itself
with the routine injustices committed by the people who own the
wealth of the country (for the logical reason that the same people
also own the press). If it must be compared to a watchdog, then the
watchdog should be imagined as one bred to recognize only the most
obvious kind of thief. The press pulls furiously at its chain when it
finds a politician stealing a few thousand dollars, but it dozes quiet-
ly in its corner when confronted with a pharmaceutical firm selling
medicines at a profit of 1,500 percent. The idea of injustice that
prevails in the press invariably assumes the ritual form of a morality

*As much as 90 percent of the news that reaches the American public arrives through
the channels of the two wire services (AP and UPI), the three networks (CBS, NBC,
and ABC), Time Inc. (Time, Fortune, Sports Illustrated, etc.), the Washington Post
Syndicate (which owns Newsweek), the New York Times Syndicate, and possibly the
Knight and Newhouse newspapers. The managers of these enterprises could sit quite
comfortably around a small table in a small room. The history of the newspaper business over the past few years has been one of monopolistic combinations. In 1970 the
ANPA succeeded in its Congressional lobbying for a limited exemption from the
antitrust laws.

play. A few stock characters (district attorneys, bank robbers, politicians, jewel thieves, detectives, etc.) perform variations on the Fall from Eden. The play insists on premeditated wrongdoing, and so it cannot accommodate itself to the ambiguities of business, medicine, diplomacy, literature, or science. Consider the indifference of the press toward poverty, hunger, the iniquities of the tax laws, or prisons on days when nobody riots.

ONLY ON rare occasions will the press publicly question the substance of an official statement. If the statement can be attributed to a man or organization with the appropriate credentials, then the press is content to publish even the most fraudulent nonsense. The mayor of New York, for instance, may issue a statement that he knows to be fantastic. The reporter recognizes it as fantasy (at best a plausible hope or remote possibility) and so does the editor, who expects eventual denials and more extreme fantasies. And yet the statement appears emblazoned on the front page of the next day's newspaper, dutifully transcribed according to the orthodoxy of "objective" journalism. The press falls into this habit not so much by choice as by necessity. It is too difficult and expensive to deny the statement by means of independent inquiry, and the press dislikes being made to look ridiculous.

Itself a bureaucracy, the press retains a conventional faith in bureaucratic paper. Much of the news therefore takes the form of official statements slightly revised to meet the expectations of the marketplace. Thus the grudging revision of press releases, press conferences, trial transcripts, sworn testimony, predictions from competent authorities, and, beyond all else, statements from government officials. The government and the press entertain inflated opinions of one another, and each flatters the other by exaggerating the importance of their mutual interests.

When arguing in favor of a shield law, the petitioners for immunity prefer to talk about justice and the police. They mention reporters who have found innocent men in prison or who have gathered evidence of municipal graft. But these stories account for an extremely small percentage of the news. The investigations conducted in twenty-six-point type seldom lead to convictions and almost never to substantive reform. Neither are they intended to do so. The press can accomplish its purpose when it commits itself to a prolonged assault (as it did with the Watergate affair), but for the most part it rests content with a headline and a two-day sensation. I can conceive of an instance in which a protected source of information might contribute something of value to the community (as distinct from something of value to the reporter), and I also can conceive of a need to protect such a man from an attempt on his life. But such occasions are rare.

THE VAST majority of sources whom the press seeks to protect have nothing to do with the administration of justice. Mostly they are government officials. By seeking to protect them, the press hopes to confer legitimacy on the practices that already supply it with the bulk of its news. The customary practice can best be illustrated by a gloss on the news from Washington. The aspiring correspondent finds himself asked to dinner in Georgetown by a Deputy Secretary of Defense.* They remark upon the weather and exchange complacent remarks about the provincialism of New York. Eventually the talk veers around to the affairs of state, and the undersecretary discourses at some length about a shift of policy in the Middle East.

---

*Not by an official in the Veterans Administration or the Department of Agriculture. Only a few government agencies possess the glamour necessary to command space in the paper (Defense, State, the White House, possibly the Treasury and Justice departments); the rest of the government happily goes about its business in obscurity.

The correspondent doesn't take notes. Having become accustomed
to small intrigues, he knows that the undersecretary expects him to
publish, without attribution, an abridged report of the conversation.
A few days later the story receives a prominent display in the correspondent's newspaper. The correspondent attributes his information
to a "high government source," and he knows enough to omit any
reference that might embarrass or identify the undersecretary.
Neither does he pursue, either in print or by further questions, all
the implications of the story. He wishes to retain the dubious confidence of his source, and for the time being he has accomplished his
purpose. Only in an indirect and subsidiary way does his purpose
have anything to do with "the people's right to know." The correspondent has been rewarded with his name in the paper, praise from
his editors, the envy of his peers, and the comfortable assurance
that he enjoys access to the wellsprings of political power.
Correspondents do not sell themselves for money. They come to
imagine that they have a distinctive voice in the affairs of state, and
I have known them to make grotesque sacrifices in order to preserve
that most seductive of illusions. They become so closely identified
with the offices to which they are assigned that they no longer
remember their own points of view.

The undersecretary also has advanced whatever stratagem he had
in mind. He may have leaked the story in order to conceal a sub-
terfuge of one kind or another, or to discredit a rival bureaucrat
within his own sphere of administrative influence, or possibly to dis-
arm an antagonist on Capitol Hill. He may have invented the entire
exegesis in order to assess public support for a possible line of
action. Sometimes the correspondent can guess the motives of his
source, and sometimes he can be utterly fooled. Both possibilities
implicate him in a deception.

This is the practice that the press now wants to sanctify with the

authority of the First Amendment. It thus confounds itself with paradox and contradiction. Ostensibly for the reason of reporting more
information, the press demands the privilege to remain silent. In the
name of the freedom of the press, it stands willing to abandon hon-
esty, rigorous inquiry, simplicity of language, the protection of the
Fifth and Sixth amendments, and the mechanism of law. Under the
guise of pursuing a secret to its deepest end, it condones a game of
intrigue and a government ruled by hints and whispers.

The protected source of information takes no risk, and neither
does the reporter who gives credence to his tale. If a man takes no
risk, then what is the worth of his opinions? What is to prevent the
source from distorting the news to conform to his own interest? What
is to prevent the reporter from disguising his own passionate opinion
as revealed truth? I understand why reporters want to engage in these
trades, and I am sympathetic to their need. The people who succeed
in the press do so because they have a talent for improvisation and
because they learn to play at politics with the deftness of courtiers.
They learn what constitutes news, what sells newspapers, what stories serve their ambition. It is a hazardous business, and the rewards
are extremely uncertain. Few people attain the eminence of James
Reston or Joseph Alsop, and the majority of lesser figures cannot
hope for either money or reputation. They leave nothing to posterity,
and it is the evanescence of their success that condemns them to an
almost constant state of credulous anxiety.

But the practices described in the foregoing paragraphs all work
to the advantage of the man distributing the information. The reporter
finds himself playing the government's game (at which the bureaucrat
always remains more of an adept than the reporter), and he comes to
depend on what might be called the "soft" virtues of journalism—
contacts, invitations to the right parties, an acquaintance with
celebrities. The source of information can always find a reporter

eager to come to dinner, but it isn't so easy the other way around. The more the secrecy, the more the balance of power shifts in favor of the bureaucrat. How can a reporter challenge a man he cannot name? The public, in whose interest the press supposedly asks for privileges, soon would find itself without the means to refute government testimony. Neither would Congress have access to an unknown cloud of witnesses. The substance of power would remain with the bureaucrat, the appearances of power with the press.

SO MUCH for my principal argument against the passage of a shield law. The argument seems to me to gain further coherence from two subsidiary effects that also imply a constriction rather than an enlargement of the news. The first of these has to do with the public attitude toward the press. That attitude is not amicable. I assume that the Watergate disclosures will inflame rather than quiet suspicion of a press that too gloatingly rejoices in the dismantling of the Nixon Administration.

To some extent the widespread antipathy toward the press arises from a misperception. The present generation of journalists cherishes social and intellectual affectations that would have provoked their forebears to mocking laughter. If a man has been graduated from Harvard, if he tries to keep up with the newest dances and the prettiest people, if he imagines himself conducting spacious discourse on the fateful issues of the day, then he doesn't like to be reminded of his resemblance to a hired footpad. The educated journalist unfortunately acquires the habit of self-doubt. His profession doesn't require the thorough knowledge of a specific discipline (as do the professions of law and medicine), and so the literate journalist feels uneasy with his pretensions to omniscience. He can disguise his uneasiness in one of two ways, either with a glib assurance that can be mistaken for arrogant disdain or by a fanciful prose style that conceals his lack of information. The latter technique obliges the author to write about his own perceptions of things rather than about the things themselves.

During the latter years of the 1960s the various anxieties of the press congealed into a pervasive righteousness. The loss of the Vietnam War brought forth obsessive excuses, and a number of journalists, together with an equivalent number of generals, came to imagine that they were better fitted to govern the nation than the men elected to political office. The press began to believe in the immaculate conception of its own virtue. The assumption of moral authority infected the reporting of other events, and the press gradually cast itself in the role of a secular clergy.

Most people might have been willing to accept this in good grace if the press had made the slightest show of giving heed to its own pieties. But it continued to sell indulgences, to shove microphones into the faces of dying men, to acquiesce to the advertising interests, to insist on its own privileges without conceding comparable privileges to anybody else, to consider itself beyond question or reproach. None of which is surprising or damnable, but it is ill-becoming in those who would anoint themselves with the oil of sanctimony. I find something unconvincing about journalists who have been persuaded to think of themselves as nightclub entertainers and who agree to set forth on the quest for truth only after they have received large promises of money.

The assumed hierarchy of the press led to embarrassing contradictions during this year's testimony (1973) before Congress. Almost everybody demanded immunity, but nobody could agree as to who qualifies as a bona fide agent of the press. Does immunity extend to anybody with a pencil and a rude question? To pornographers and the merchants of Tuesday sensations? Most witnesses answered such questions with shocked indignation, as if news reporting were an occupation that demanded exemplary ethics. They talked about "legitimate" practitioners of the trade, and the bias implicit in their testimony suggested that legitimacy adheres primarily to those employed by the larger and wealthier establishments.

The hierarchical longing within the press compounds the mistrust of people outside the press, and I expect that an immunity law would exacerbate both conditions. Too many people would consider an immunity law too patently unfair; it would violate their sense of the democratic rules, and so I assume that fewer people would consent to talk to reporters. The press would acquire a quasi-bureaucratic status, identified with the government and talking mostly to itself and to other bureaucrats. The more of a profession that it became, the more it would discourage the membership of rowdy amateurs. As with other professions, the custodians of success would encourage the promotion of people diligently second-rate.

A THIRD argument against the passage of a shield law has to do with the Congressional attitude toward the press. What the Congress grants, so also can the Congress take away. Whatever law the Congress passes certainly will be less forthright than the categorical simplicity of the First Amendment. The kind of thing that seems likely to happen, if not this year then two or three years hence, already has been hinted at by Senator Edward Gurney of Florida. As a member of the subcommittee listening to the testimony of the press, the Senator indicated a willingness to endorse an immunity law if it were granted on two conditions—i.e., that the present libel laws be changed in a way that absolves a public figure from the necessity of proving "actual malice," and that the Congress establish a "truth in news" commission with the authority to force the media to correct its errors. If either of these suggestions were to be embodied into law it could wreak far more havoc with the freedom of the press than any of the harassments now available to even the most zealous censors. Once the Congress arrogates to itself the right of interpreting the First Amendment, I can imagine it deciding to award licenses not only to newspapers and magazines but also to individual journalists. If the First Amendment becomes subject to legislative elaboration, then why not the rest of the Bill of Rights?

The more thoughtful people in the press surely must recognize the treacherous nature of the Congressional alliance; so also they must notice the resentment of the general public. They must suspect that both factions could combine to limit the freedom of the press, and yet they find themselves herded along by the majority of their colleagues, who cry out for an immunity law. It is a cry of alarmed mice. Having discovered economics and lost the valor of its ignorance, the press appears before Congress as suppliant and abashed truant. It has learned that full exercise of the First Amendment requires not only a great deal of work but also a great deal of money. Most reporters don't want to do the work, and few of the owners want to spend the money. It is this coincidence that explains the otherwise baffling presence of Peter Bridge and William Farr testifying on the same side of the argument as the American Newspaper Publishers Association and the management of CBS. The gathering of information can be a tedious process, but the relevant facts can be found if a man will search diligently enough among the available records, if he will talk to a sufficient number of people, and if he will work out the implications of his evidence. As early as 1962 the catastrophe of the Vietnam War had become apparent to journalists writing in *The Nation* and *The New Republic;* they had studied such uncongenial documents as the federal budget and the *Congressional Record,* and they had taken the trouble to infer the consequences of the national policy at a time when most agents of the major media still were rewriting the press releases published by the White House and the

Pentagon. The few notable exceptions involved themselves in bitter disputes with their editors. But that kind of arduous study confers neither money nor celebrity on a man ambitious to rise through the bureaucratic ranks of the *New York Times* or CBS News. It is much easier and far more profitable to acquire information from a few telephone conversations with a "highly placed administration source" or from notes taken over a leisurely lunch at the Federal City Club. People who spend too much time on any one subject incline to get lost in the labyrinth of their special information; they become obsessed, and their names seldom appear in the paper. They lose the easygoing triteness of phrase that marks the successful generalist, and what they have to say doesn't conform to the bland formulas of a Sunday newspaper column or a television talk show.

The hesitations of the media owners need little elaboration. Again, there are exceptions, but very few. Most owners know that their product is the audience delivered to the advertiser, and the larger audience repeatedly demonstrates its lack of interest in anything other than entertainment. Libel suits tend to be long and costly. Even if the plaintiff has no expectation of proving his case, he can still make an expensive nuisance of himself.

THE PRESS thus appeals to Congress for one of two reasons, both of them disappointing. Either the press secretly welcomes the prospect of government regulation or it makes the pathetic mistake of a movie actress who comes to believe her own publicity notices.

The first hypothesis depends on a recognition of the intensity with which the press desires the legitimacy of a social caste. It is this longing that I find implicit in the ceaseless comparing of journalists to doctors, lawyers, or priests. The analogies fail (unlike any of the others, the journalist retains the right to withhold information on no authority other than his own discretion), but they suggest the wish for definition as a spirituality. The longing becomes so desperate that the press offers to renounce its freedom in return for a secure pulpit and an established name. The hypothesis contains within it the tacit assumption that "the system" has emerged triumphant, that it has become impossible for even the most reckless politician to effect the miracle of social change. Thus the press remains content to preach, to pass noisy but futile judgment, to beg its living from its institutional benefactors.

The second hypothesis follows from an understanding of the romanticism of the press. The press earnestly wants to believe in the validity of its own images, to believe that the melodramatic world of its own invention bears some resemblance to the world of fact. It begins by wanting to believe that this is the best of all possible worlds, that love conquers all, that Presidents read the editorial page, and that yes, Virginia, there is an informed public opinion. When these images fall into disrepair, as in the decade of the 1960s, the press becomes as vengeful as a child among its broken toys. Once disillusioned, the press will believe anything, preferably the worst that can be said, of its former idols. The bitterness of its unrequited infatuation explains the more or less abrupt repudiation of the America advertised on postcards. Instead of the benign shepherd protecting a flock of innocents, America becomes the ravenous wolf of imperialism. Suddenly it is the worst of all possible worlds, love is for fools, and Santa Claus is found dead in a toilet. Having replaced one mythology with another one of equal banality, the press can still play at melodrama and so restore vivid light and shadow to a world of gray ambiguity.

The romanticism of the press reminds me of a dreaming woman enthralled by her reflection in a painted mirror. The mirror flatters her vanity and allows her to imagine herself more beautiful than Cleopatra or Snow White. Deceived by images, she fails to recognize herself and so misunderstands both her faults and her virtues. Like the princess in a fairy tale, the press waits to be rescued from its enemies instead of confronting them with its own strengths.

Anybody who has followed the argument this far will know that I think of the press as a necessary affliction rather than as a sublime good. But it is necessary precisely because it is an affliction, by reason of its ugliness rather than its imagined beauty. It is necessary for exactly those reasons that require of it little understanding and less compassion, no sense of aesthetics, and the gall of a coroner. Those are the attributes that give vitality and meaning to the press. Its courage resides in its plurality and in its resemblance to a mob in the street.

All this has been demonstrated by the Watergate news, and all of it will again be forgotten if the press uses Watergate as an excuse to plead for immunity. The press betrays itself when it tries to be "creative," when it attempts diplomacy, or when it seeks to imitate the decorous rhythms of Gregorian chant. Its pretensions leech the blood out of it and make it an easy prey for those who would gag its mouth with cinnamon and apples.

America's Guest

FEBRUARY 1975

For two days in November 1974, the late Nelson Rockefeller, former Governor of New York and man of all seasons and appetites, testified before the Senate Rules Committee on the magnitude of his fortune. He had been summoned to discuss his qualifications as Vice-President of the United States, an office to which he recently had been appointed by Gerald Ford, but the Senators couldn't get beyond the enormity of his wealth. So great is the American belief in the magic of money that when a man reveals his net worth even the skeptics feel moved to worship.

This is apparently what happened to the members of the Rules Committee and to the representatives of the national press. Covered with holy dread, none of the witnesses in the caucus room ventured to doubt the miracle of $218 million. The Senators asked questions that disclosed more about themselves than they did about Mr. Rockefeller, and the press reported the visitation with the solemnity that has become mandatory in any discussion of political affairs.

Few of them remarked on the humor of Mr. Rockefeller's greeting to former Supreme Court Justice Arthur Goldberg on the second day of the hearings. Mr. Rockefeller had caused a mean-spirited book to be written about Goldberg during the 1970 gubernatorial campaign in New York, and it might have been expected that Mr. Goldberg would come to Washington with a grievance. And yet, as Mr. Rockefeller surged out of the room on a tide of admirers, he paused to welcome Mr. Goldberg as if he had been a close friend. Grinning broadly and slapping Mr. Goldberg on the shoulder with a gesture of election-year enthusiasm, Mr. Rockefeller said: "Thanks for coming." The unconscious assumptions implicit in that remark might be stated as follows:

(1) Mr. Goldberg had come to Washington in response to Mr. Rockefeller's invitation, as if to a dinner party or a weekend at Pocantico Hills.

(2) The Senate caucus room somehow belonged to the Rockefeller family, either as an adjunct of his property on Foxhall Road or as an asset misplaced within one of several real-estate holdings.

(3) Mr. Goldberg had been granted time to reflect on Victor Lasky's book (sufficient time to realize that Mr. Rockefeller hadn't intended any harm), and so he had decided to put aside his grievance for the greater good of the nation (i.e., by recommending Mr. Rockefeller's confirmation as Vice-President).

At least two of these assumptions seemed to me plausible. Having had the chance to observe Mr. Rockefeller at varying distances over a period of at least fifteen years I didn't think that he intended anything cynical or disingenuous. His assumption that Mr. Goldberg would forgive him followed from his imperturbable faith in his own innocence. His misapprehension of the facts was characteristic of men who inherit great wealth. They cannot believe themselves capable of discreditable acts, and as a rule they know almost nothing about money or political reality. Like the State Department, they have no reason to learn.

The humor of the confirmation hearings thus depended upon Mr. Rockefeller's ignorance of his own character. With the self-dramatizations of an exuberant adolescent promising to behave himself, Mr. Rockefeller never understood what exactly it was that he was being asked to apologize for. Neither the members of the committee nor the representatives of the press could laugh at the joke because they were imprisoned within self-dramatizations of their own.

The Senators who asked questions about money, notably Senator Byrd, betrayed a touching naïveté about the way in which the Rockefeller family conducts its financial affairs. They kept trying to figure out who was paying whom, at what rate of exchange, and for what services rendered. They made sly suggestions about deals (with the Chase Manhattan Bank, Eastern Airlines, the Metropolitan Transportation Authority, et cetera), but they could find no evidence that confirmed their suspicions. Senator Byrd hoped to prove something criminal, as if he were investigating bribery in a West Virginia sewer district. It was difficult for him to believe that Laurance Rockefeller could invest $60,000 in the Goldberg book as a result of a brief conversation (so brief as to have been utterly forgotten) with an intermediary who knew nothing about politics or the publishing business. When it became clear that this was so, and that to the Rockefeller family the expenditure of $60,000 compared to another man's buying a lottery ticket, Senator Byrd retired in sullen confusion.

Other members of the committee beheld visions of Establishment conspiracies. Senator Cannon wanted very much to believe in the existence of men who knew what they were doing, men of Machiavellian ruthlessness who magnified their sinister influence through the unseen conduits of Eastern influence. Although popular both in the press and in the House Judiciary Committee, this romance proved to be as chimerical as Senator Byrd's. The Rockefeller advisers who testified before the committee revealed themselves to be dull-witted men who would have had trouble understanding the table of organization in even a small-time cabal.

But by the time they appeared as witnesses, the committee had succumbed to its own enchantments.

Still a third faction of Senators pursued what might be described as a religious line of questioning. Instead of assessing Mr. Rockefeller's value as a possible Vice-President, they chose to examine him on the conduct of his past life, on his record as a Christian man, and on the present state of his conscience. The American worship of money depends upon a paradox. The abstract conception of wealth is beautiful and holy (the Ford Foundation, say, or the perfect sum of $1 million), but when it makes itself flesh (whether in the hands of Sam Giancana or McGeorge Bundy), then it must be reviled. If Mr. Rockefeller had made his gifts to institutions, the Senators might have withheld even the timid scourging to which they subjected him. But Mr. Rockefeller had given money to his friends, and by so doing he had committed the sin of Pride. He had had the effrontery to distinguish between particular people, weighing them in a balance of his own invention and deciding that whereas MTA Chairman William Ronan was worth $625,000, innumerable other men (among them most of the Senators on the committee) were undeserving of recognition, even in so small an amount as a $50 campaign contribution. Such an arbitrary judgment makes light of the doctrine that all men are created equal, not only before the law (as set forth in the Declaration of Independence) but also in their innermost being (as guaranteed by the advertising business and politicians hoping for re-election). Mr. Rockefeller's pride might have seemed less objectionable if he had muffled it with the customary hypocrisy, but this he made no attempt to do. Even as he introduced his financial statements into the Senate record, thereby hoping to declare his meek intentions, Mr. Rockefeller made it quite clear that he liked to order people around, that he took pleasure in the cruelties of privilege, and that he didn't need to trouble himself with the pretense of humility. His unconscious assumption of grace both galled and frightened the members of the committee. Although several of them presumably believed Mr. Rockefeller to be lost beyond all hope of redemption, he had little trouble with the religious aspects of the interrogation. He offered responses he hoped were courteous, and presented the account books of his charity. When confronted with the cash equivalent of the candidate's virtue, the committee had little choice but to recommend his salvation.

The magical properties of Mr. Rockefeller's fortune also obscured the fear and resentment on the part of those Senators who thought they saw in Mr. Rockefeller a man who could do as he pleased. Most Senators enjoy the appearance rather than the substance of power, but they spend so much time concealing this (not only from their constituents but also from themselves) that they dislike anybody to whom they attribute omnipotence. Once elected as the free representatives of a free people, they find themselves dependent on other people's money (usually the money of rich men who demand a fair return on their investment), and so they learn to flatter the vanity of anybody who can buy them a vote. In the presence of a man who can buy his own votes (to the amount of $24 million over a period of seventeen years), they remember their humiliating afternoons waiting in the anterooms of money. The memory inclines them to enmity and suspicion. Senator Byrd thus seemed to identify Mr. Rockefeller with the coal operators of the West Virginia mountains. Senator Cannon confused him with the owners of Las Vegas gambling casinos, and Senator Pell, himself a rich man, probably thought of him as one of those pushy and unreliable rich boys about whom his father had warned him when he first went up to St. George's. If the resentments of the committee took different forms, so also did its fears. Several members must have asked themselves what they would do with an average annual income of $4.6 million, and I expect that they weren't comfortable with the answers. Unless they thought that Mr. Rockefeller somehow resembled a Mafia *capo* who could put in the incomparable fix, I can't understand why they should have spent so much time trying to establish a criminal motive in the matter of the Goldberg book. The evidence so clearly indicated carelessness, insensibility, and ignorance that even Mr. Rockefeller's press secretary admitted that "he [Mr. Rockefeller] just didn't pay attention to the details of the book's publication."

THROUGHOUT THE hearings the committee mistook Mr. Rockefeller's manner of self-assurance for firmness of political purpose, his command of the issues for proof of political vision. The misperception on the other side of the witness table seemed to me equally great. I doubt that Mr. Rockefeller understood what alarmed the committee any more than he had understood (in October, when the first rumors of his political loans glutted the newspapers) what it was that aroused the antagonism of so many people whom he had never met—all of them responsible citizens who surely would find him innocent if only they had a chance to examine "all the facts." He read a prepared statement about the separation of private wealth and public authority, but this did not quite answer the unasked questions. The habitual unawareness of men with inherited money (particularly if they have been schooled in a tradition of Christian piety) leads them to imagine themselves exempt from evil intent. They believe their own press notices—to the effect that they already have everything worth having—and so cannot imagine why they should bother to employ illegitimate means to acquire what belongs to them by right. If fault must be found, then it must have something to do with public misunderstanding rather than with an improper action.

Mr. Rockefeller never once conceded the possibility of moral blemish. Perhaps he had made mistakes, but they were technical miscalculations or temporary lapses of judgment; they never had anything to do with anger, egoism, ambition, or vanity. When asked for his motives he talked about "altruism," "a sense of duty," "service to my country," and something that he defined as "the challenge of tackling tough human problems." In his anxiety to make a good impression on the committee, he resembled a prep-school boy seeking to explain himself in the headmaster's study. Not only did he give the committee every record that it asked for but he agreed with almost every criticism the Senators cared to make. When Senator Pell suggested that he forbear giving money to government officials, Mr. Rockefeller responded with a dutiful pledge "to cut it out."

The portrait of Mr. Rockefeller that emerged from his own testimony was that of a man who, contrary to all rumor and expectation, perceived himself as a parvenu. He had acquired the manner and presence of an aristocrat, but he remained uncertain of his membership in the club. He had done everything he could to impress those whom he described as "the big people with whom you've got to be associated if you expect to do big things," but he wasn't sure if they took him seriously, if they entrusted him with their confidence and told him whatever it was that they told the other big people. He reminded me of the boy who belongs to the best fraternity on campus but feels himself ignored by the principal members.

Behind the facade of his obsessive affability, I had the impression of a man so constantly enraged that he had to constantly pretend that he wasn't angry. During one of the intervals in the hearings, Mr. Rockefeller took photographs of the reporters and committee members, and as he grinned at them across the witness table (turning the thing around, you see, showing himself to be a regular guy), it occurred to me that Mr. Rockefeller never had been a politician who enjoyed the confidence of the professionals. Among the amateurs (corporation presidents, journalists, bankers) he had seemed to represent the enlightened hope of the 1960s, but the professionals (people like Senator Hugh Scott and the county leaders in Omaha and Chicago) never trusted him. And so perhaps he was right about not being taken seriously by the big people, and maybe that's why he was so eager to do whatever anybody asked him to do in return for confirmation as Vice-President. Only one man stands higher in the national fraternity than the Vice-President, and if they don't tell the Vice-President the stuff they hide from the other fellas, then something must be very wrong with America.

MR. ROCKEFELLER'S willingness to please extended even to the point of exposing his family and friends to public scorn and ridicule. It couldn't be helped, of course, and Mr. Rockefeller no doubt was terribly sorry about it, but if the cause of justice was to be served by the publication of his financial statements, then he had no choice but to do the right thing. If he compromised the reputation of his brother Laurance, or if he reduced William Ronan in the general estimation to the rank of domestic servant, or if he subtracted from the sum of Emmet Hughes's credibility as a journalist, Mr. Rockefeller could say that he was complying with the law of the land. As a faithful servant of the Republic in whose name he had sent troops to quell the Attica prison riots, he was doing what he had been told to do. Although it may be unfair to suggest it, I doubt whether it occurred to him to put aside his ambition in favor of those people for whom he felt such "deep love, respect, and compassion." No more would it have occurred to John Ehrlichman or John Dean to subjugate their own ambitions to the requirements of the Constitution.

Nobody on the committee drew the parallel because nobody could imagine that anyone as rich or reputedly as powerful as Mr. Rockefeller could be intimidated. The superstition prevailed despite

Mr. Rockefeller's admission that he nearly always deferred to "the superior people with whom my father taught me to surround myself." It became apparent that Mr. Rockefeller retained a faith (analogous to Senator Byrd's faith in the magic of money, or Senator Cannon's belief in Establishment conspiracies) in committees of experts certified by established authority. He bought whatever was represented to him as the best advice and dutifully memorized the assigned lessons. Whether the lessons were right or wrong didn't much matter. Mr. Rockefeller's wealth allowed him to make mistakes, and if other people were hurt by those mistakes—his brother, Mr. Ronan, the citizens of New York—well, that was the meaning of free enterprise. Always innocent and habitually optimistic, Mr. Rockefeller could proceed to other projects in perfect confidence that, as he proudly informed the members of the committee, "I always tried to do my best."

The committee never troubled to inquire into the worth of Mr. Rockefeller's earnest effort. The members accepted the statement in the spirit in which it was offered (as proof of Mr. Rockefeller's benign intentions), and none of them had the temerity to observe that Mr. Rockefeller's "best" had been uniformly mediocre. His administration of the state of New York can be fairly described by the phrase once employed by Samuel Johnson to compare a woman's preaching to a dog's walking on its hind legs—"It is not done well," Dr. Johnson said, "but you are surprised to find it done at all." Even a cursory study of his record as Governor suggests a tradition of embarrassment and failure—the Albany Mall, the World Trade Center, the repressive and ineffective drug law of 1973, Attica, the increases in taxes and public expenditure, the degradation of the educational system, the general deterioration of housing and transportation, and the resignation of his office. No wonder the professional politicians distrusted him. Mr. Rockefeller and his family invested $12 million in three Presidential campaigns, none of which had a chance of success, and as a visionary prophet he went forth into the desert and constructed so banal a Utopia as the Commission on Critical Choices for Americans.

Given Mr. Rockefeller's admitted reliance on expensive advice, the shabbiness of his accomplishment must testify to the ability of the people who advised him. When he was Governor of New York his policy was formulated by whoever it was that was supposed to know about such things (by definition a coterie of hangers-on); at Attica Mr. Rockefeller did what the state police told him to do; in the matter of the Goldberg book he accepted the advice of a lawyer who had managed a losing political campaign. Contrary to Mr. Rockefeller's insistence upon the "brilliance" of his associates, those of his advisers who appeared before the committee left an impression of dullness. Consider the testimony of Mr. Ronan and Mr. Donal C. O'Brien, who identified himself as Mr. Rockefeller's chief family lawyer. Mr. Ronan had been given $625,000 for the express purpose of accumulating capital during the inflated bull market of the 1960s, and yet, against all trends over a period of ten years, Mr. Ronan succeeded in making little more than 50 percent on his money. He would have done as well if he had placed the money in a savings account. As for Mr. O'Brien, not even Senator Byrd could discover his field of knowledge or competence. In answer to a series of questions that became increasingly embarrassing, Mr. O'Brien said that he knew little about politics, taxes, or corporations. Among the many other people once associated with Mr. Rockefeller (all of them renowned for their "brilliance" and "integrity"), those who come most readily to mind do not reflect what Mr. Ronan blithely referred to as Mr. Rockefeller's "greatness." Emmet Hughes made his reputation as an author by exploiting the confidence of Dwight Eisenhower; David Young escaped indictment for his work as a White House Plumber by testifying on behalf of the prosecution; Judson Morhouse was convicted for bribery; Henry Kissinger has displayed a prodigious talent for subterfuge, prevarication, and the devious half-truth.

AS WITH the carelessness of Mr. Rockefeller's greeting to Mr. Goldberg, the question again became one of the candidate's assumptions. Mr. Rockefeller's self-delusion appeared to be sufficiently grandiose to allow him to think that he could bestow brilliance upon his associates by naming them brilliant, as if he were conferring fiefs and titles. The corollary delusion would hold that if a man chose to work for Mr. Rockefeller, then clearly he must possess the highest attributes, because these would lead him to find their expression on the highest levels of eminence, which, as everyone knows, brings him to the plateau occupied by the Rockefeller family. Variations on this delusion trouble almost all men who have inherited great wealth. When properly understood, it provides the answer to the question the committee kept asking about who was paying whom for what. Mr. Rockefeller was renting a mirror in which to find a flattering image of himself. Some men build monuments or endow museums; other men hire court painters or found universities. Mr. Rockefeller also could do such things (as could his forebears and his brothers), but he wanted to do something else: to play in the theater of politics and discover himself in the part of leader and statesman.

The vanity of wealth also explains why men like Mr. Rockefeller attract subordinates of questionable worth. Either they employ opportunists who take advantage of the prevailing delusion or they hire impressionable men who imagine themselves allied with omnipotence and so perpetuate the delusion. The men around Mr. Rockefeller continually told themselves that "the team" could work miracles. For the most part they were confirmed by the properly constituted authorities (the right schools, academia, old-line Wall Street banking firms, encomia in the *New York Times*), and if they insisted on the mythology of their own invention, that is because they came to believe it. Once having been rewarded with titles and estates, they must defend the legitimacy of the king.

The aura of unreality that thus attached itself to Mr. Rockefeller's enterprises often attained Wagnerian dimensions. During the Presidential primaries of 1968, I accompanied the Rockefeller campaign through twenty-three states, and I was astonished by the lack of sophistication or desire that pervaded the entire entourage. We were like children dressed up for a birthday party that nobody knew how to find. The campaign plane wandered back and forth across the country at expensive speeds, the Governor memorizing the issues and the advance men paying for airport bands, but none of it seemed to be going anywhere. Mr. Rockefeller understood that he didn't inspire the confidence of the Republican party, and so he hoped to demonstrate such overwhelming popular support that the party regulars couldn't afford to ignore him. To demonstrate that kind of support, he needed to improve his percentages in the public-opinion polls. Although invariably introduced as "a people-oriented man," Mr. Rockefeller spoke primarily to the machine of the national press; the crowds existed to be photographed, and the television cameras were assigned the best seats. We traveled in what seemed like a void, sending out messages and waiting two weeks (until the next poll) to find out if anybody heard or was convinced. The results were disappointing, partly because the candidate couldn't figure out what troubled people or what it was that they wanted.

Just as Mr. Rockefeller couldn't anticipate the possible trouble resulting from the publication of the Goldberg book, so also in the spring of 1968 he couldn't understand why all those people were rioting in the streets. He listened attentively to several explanations (Bobby Kennedy's recent assassination, the disillusionment with the war, a general feeling of malaise, et cetera, et cetera), but he was traveling at six hundred miles an hour at an altitude of forty-three thousand feet, and he couldn't comprehend the nature of the complaint. It didn't correspond to the upward curves on the graphs depicting the GNP; nor did it correspond to Mr. Rockefeller's experience of a world that seemed to have been conveniently formed in his own image.

MR. ROCKEFELLER spent his entire life at the metaphysical equivalent of forty-three thousand feet, suspended by the aerodynamics of money in a state of perpetual innocence. Nowhere was this more apparent at the Senate hearings than in his explanation of the loans he had made to his friends. He repeatedly returned to his prepared statement, in which he insisted that the money was "never designed to corrupt, or did corrupt, either the giver or the receiver." A man who can make such a statement obviously chooses to know only what it suits him to know about the world. He might possess a romantic image of it, but he sees no reason to distinguish between good and bad, between the flatterer and the sage. He might talk a great deal about the difference between good and evil, but that is a distinction that has little to do with those "tough human problems" that Mr. Rockefeller said he so much liked to deal with. His schedule didn't permit him the time to notice, much less to encounter, a tough human problem. Hurrying from place to place in order to avoid recognition of himself, he occupied himself instead with blue manila folders containing the data of political abstraction. Failing to feel the force of gravity that money imposes on people who don't inherit it, Mr. Rockefeller also seemed to be unaware of the ways in which the big people achieved their ambition. He had more money

than any of them, and yet he never managed to make it do all the
things that he wanted it to do. When he said to the committee, "I've
got to tell you . . . I don't wield economic power," I had the sense of
a man genuinely perplexed by the mechanics of Aladdin's lamp.

During the campaign of 1968 Mr. Rockefeller never carried
money on his person. If he had occasion to buy something, somebody else paid for it. I also remember a speech that he made to a
crowd of Puerto Rican steelworkers in a town near Cleveland, Ohio.
Exuding his familiar optimism, his arms raised in a gesture of broth-
erhood, Mr. Rockefeller addressed them in well-meaning Spanish,
promising that if he were elected President of the United States he
would do everything in his power to bring them justice, fiscal
responsibility, and a piece of the American pie. The crowd cheered
him with shouts of "*¡Arriba, Arriba!*" never knowing (as the candidate himself didn't know) that Mr. Rockefeller owned the steel mill.
He didn't own it outright, of course, in the way that a man owns a
house or a dog. Through a series of connections that I never quite
understood (perhaps because they were explained to me by one of
Mr. Rockefeller's political advisers), the Rockefeller family apparently owned the holding company that held a controlling interest in
the stock of the steel corporation.

In the statement that Mr. Rockefeller read to the committee, he
acknowledged the limitation that his money imposed upon him, and
he asked the rhetorical question that he thought fundamental to the
committee's decision. "Would my family background somehow limit
and blind me," he said, "so that I would not be able to see and serve
the general interest of all Americans?" He answered the question
confidently in the negative, explaining that he had "surmounted
privilege" and learned to see into the far, blue distances of national
policy. Although the committee voted unanimously in his favor, that
answer bespeaks a man who does not know himself.

The record suggests that Mr. Rockefeller seldom saw around the reflection in the expensive mirror held up to him by his company of admirers. As Governor of New York he recognized few interests that didn't further his formless ambition. If he had become President of the United States, he would have coveted some higher office, still wondering what the big people thought of him and why he hadn't yet received everything he assumed was owing to him. In pursuit of his desire to do "the right thing," I expect that he would have relied on the same kind of second-rate advice that prompted him to blame the mistake of the Goldberg book on his brother Laurance. In matters of civil discontent or foreign wars, he presumably would have done whatever the FBI or the Pentagon told him to do, convinced of the purity of his intent. Even now, more than a year after his death, I can imagine him walking jauntily through the bombed streets of Detroit or Washington, conferring on the survivors a handshake and a smile. To a man standing in the rubble of what was once a house, I can hear Mr. Rockefeller saying, "Thanks for coming."

Deadly Virtue

JANUARY 1978

*Remember to what a point your Puritanism has brought
you. In old days nobody pretended to be a bit better than
his neighbors. In fact, to be a bit better than one's neigh-
bor was considered excessively vulgar and middle-class.
Nowadays, with our modern mania for morality, everyone
has to pose as a paragon of purity, incorruptibility, and all
the other seven deadly virtues—and what is the result?
You all go over like ninepins—one after the other. Not a
year passes in England without somebody disappearing.*
— *Oscar Wilde*, An Ideal Husband

Sometime during the early autumn of 1977 the complaints about
President Carter's character and Administration began to
acquire a depressing uniformity. For the first several months of Mr.
Carter's first year in office, the criticism was diverse but familiar.
The usual people raised the usual objections against the foreign and
domestic politics of a newly arrived President. Advocates of specific
financial or ideological interests complained about the absence of
federal money or the damage done to articles of faith and doctrine.
None of this was in any way surprising. But in the second or third
week of October, sometime between the disappearance from

Washington of Mr. Bert Lance and the announcement of Mr. Carter's hope of a Palestinian state, it began to be said that Mr. Carter didn't know what he was doing and that perhaps he should resign his office in order to give more of his time to his Sunday-school teaching and his Bible studies. All of a sudden everybody seemed to be making the same observations, not only in the press but also in the exchange of confidences among those people whom the newspapers like to identify as oracles of informed opinion.

What was unusual about the complaint was its unanimity. Wherever I went in New York I met somebody who had just returned from Washington and who offered yet another proof of Mr. Carter's incompetence. People talked about the "parochial" attitude of the White House, about the "amateurish" way in which Mr. Carter approached the Soviet Union and the United States Congress, about the naïveté of "the Georgians," who had trouble remembering which countries belonged to which spheres of influence. Somebody mentioned Mr. Carter's inept betrayals of the traditionally Democratic constituencies (the unions, the minorities, the intellectuals, the poor); somebody else described the President as a profoundly ignorant man. One night I heard a lobbyist explain that Mr. Carter had decided against the deployment of the B-1 bomber because he had asked God about it, and God had told him that the bomber could do nothing but harm. Economists acquainted with the energy question pointed out that Mr. Carter's program was so poorly conceived that even if it passed the Congress it would accomplish none of its declared objectives. Other people preferred to talk about the incoherence of Mr. Carter's mumbling about human rights, about the foolishness of his welfare and tax reforms, about the falling off of the President's ratings in the public-opinion polls. No matter what the policy or issue under discussion, all the informants agreed that Mr. Carter relied on mediocre advisers (both at the staff and Cabinet

levels) and that he lacked the knowledge and experience to conduct
the business of government.

SO MANY people brought so much bad news that I found myself coming to Mr. Carter's defense. Although I had no doubt that most of the
reports bore a reasonable similarity to the truth, I didn't think that
Mr. Carter should be made to suffer so general and so self-serving
an indictment. Most of my informants were either journalists or
political job seekers, and I remembered them in the autumn of 1976
talking about Mr. Carter's moral virtue. What else could they have
expected of a man who presented himself as an "outsider" (a newspaper epithet temporarily confused with an existential state of
being) and who professed to know nothing of the perversity of
human nature? Mr. Carter was elected to redeem the country, not to
govern it. The press, as well as a majority of the electorate, chose to
believe that Mr. Carter's spiritualization of the issues conferred the
highest possible benefit upon the Republic. His supporters had persuaded themselves that they didn't want material results, that the
rituals of atonement (for Watergate, the Kennedy assassinations,
Vietnam, the CIA, and the environmental damage done to God's
green earth) took precedence over the more difficult business of providing people with jobs, housing, money, hope, and law.

During the spring and summer of 1976 Mr. Carter, like the
Wizard of Oz, contrived to remain invisible. For almost eleven
months he revolved like a mechanical toy in the bright ball of the
media, answering everyman's question and smiling into everyman's
camera; and yet, then as now, hardly anybody knew anything about
him. He had taken positions on both sides of every question that
could be identified as an issue, and in June, as in early February,
the public-opinion polls showed that liberals believed Mr. Carter to
be a liberal and that conservatives believed him to be a conserva-

tive. Not even his admirers seemed to know who he was, or what he stood for, or why he wanted to be President of the United States.

Several months before his election I listened to Mr. Carter make a speech at the Plaza Hotel in New York, and he left his audience in what later was to become the usual state of confusion. Most of those present were men of weight and probity, directors of companies and pillars of the community who each had paid $100 to attend a breakfast sponsored by such eminent Democrats as C. Douglas Dillon and Cyrus Vance. Mr. Dillon had been Secretary of the Treasury in the Kennedy Administration, and Mr. Vance, who already had been mentioned as a prospect for Secretary of State, had been Deputy Secretary of Defense in the Johnson Administration. Their endorsement of aspiring politicians conveyed an impression of respectable authority. Even so, the crowd was inclined to be skeptical. When Mr. Carter presented himself at the rostrum in the Grand Ballroom, smiling for as long as the television lights were on, the audience granted him a standing but halfhearted ovation. In the words of a dignified gentleman on my left, "I can't say that I trust a man who uses a boy's name, but if Doug Dillon vouches for the fellow, maybe there's something to him."

Mr. Carter chose to present himself in the persona of the innocent abroad, a latter-day Billy Budd, barefoot and without guile, wandering around the country in search of love and friends. A small and self-contained man, he gazed vaguely upward and was careful not to move his hands. Like a small boy reciting an inspirational poem he said all the dutiful things that a well-behaved child is supposed to say in the company of strangers. He told of how he never "evaded an issue," of how he was an "eager student" who was doing his best to learn all those complicated things that the folks talked about up there in Washington, D.C., of the many telephone calls he'd been getting from important politicians, of how it wasn't the American people who had decided to do all those "dreadful things" in Vietnam, Cambodia, Chile, the White House, and the CIA, of "the deep yearning for intimacy" he'd discovered out there "in this great country of ours," of how he had come to know "the people of this nation better than any other human being."

The effect of the speech was embarrassing. To men of considerable sophistication Mr. Carter had delivered a 4-H Club address, all of it very stale and very sweet, utterly devoid of feeling or thought. Over the last twenty years I have listened to a great many politicians make a great many speeches, but never before have I noticed such an absence of emotion among people who might have hoped to believe what they heard. The applause at the end was as small as Mr. Carter's voice. He had arrived punctually at 8:00 A.M., and when he left, exactly an hour later, it was as if nobody had been there.

Most people immediately began to talk of other things—the weather or the morning's business engagements, the cost of their property in Connecticut, or the best way to get to Maine in August. If they took the trouble to make even a passing mention of what they had paid $100 to see and hear, their remarks implied an attitude of condescension. They believed themselves capable of seeing through the paltry charade of American politics in a matter of a few minutes, and it amused them to look briefly at the new gorilla passing through town every four years on the way to its cage in Washington. Together with their counterparts elsewhere in the country, they constitute what might be called the party of the indifferent majority. Characteristic of their analysis was the following conversation, reproduced in its entirety, between two men hurrying toward the elevators.

FIRST MAN (Vaguely and without caring about the response): "Well, what did you think of it?"

SECOND MAN: "The usual small-time crook. Another liar."

FIRST MAN (Impatiently): "Yes, yes, of course, but so what? You can say the same thing about all of them. Think of Humphrey, of Jackson. My God—Jackson."

Among the few people who remained in the Grand Ballroom after Mr. Carter had left (to continue his portrayal of a little boy lost at a United Nations conference on nuclear war) the disagreement was comprehensive. There were as many opinions as there were small groups of people coming together to exchange theories and interpretations. Mr. Carter had come and gone in a magician's smoke, leaving his admirers with an empty canvas on which they could paint the images of their hearts' desire. The more devout thought that Mr. Carter was a saint. They told stories about his concern for the old and the sick, about the tears that once welled up in his eyes when he was told about a dying child. The candidate's critics denounced him as a swindling hypocrite. From their coat pockets they brought forth newspaper clippings on which they had marked passages of blatant contradiction. Other people spoke of the candidate as religious zealot or honest farmer, as effective administrator or protégé of the Ku Klux Klan. A man in a plaid suit described Mr. Carter as being "dirt mean," a poor boy from south Georgia who trusted nobody and would do his best, once elected President, to root out the evil that darkened the understanding of his enemies.

IF MR. Carter's presence inspired such little confidence among people willing to give him money, then his political triumph among the larger public must have depended on something other than the force of his mind or the largeness of his spirit. He wasn't an eloquent man, and his visions of America the Beautiful had the quality of the gilded figurines bought in penny arcades. But he was obviously intelligent, and he had been willing to work longer hours and take greater risks than any of the other politicians in the field. He also understood the magnitude of the national sense of defeat. He assumed, correctly, that the vast majority of the American people, like the two men hurrying away from breakfast in the Plaza Hotel, wanted to forget about politics. They were sick to death of politicians, tired of issues they didn't understand and that didn't admit of easy answers, disappointed by the chronicle of failure that seemed to delight the Eastern press. In Vietnam forty thousand Americans had been killed, apparently to no purpose. The Nixon Administration was a disgrace, and so was the goddamned Congress. Even when Mr. Nixon had been discovered as the Antichrist his absence didn't improve matters. Within a year of his departure the fine promises about a renewed code of official conduct began to sound as thin as Muzak. Multinational corporations continued to pay bribes to Congressmen as well as to foreign governments; judges were still going to jail; the Kennedys were no better than anybody else; and the FBI and the CIA apparently had been subverting the Bill of Rights ever since the Roosevelt Administration.

Given the general feeling of disgust, it was an easy thing for a great many people to imagine themselves betrayed. Mr. Carter brought them a focus for their discontent. Were they angry and resentful? Did they despise intellectuals and the Eastern Establishment? Were they sick of corruption and bad news? Well, so was Jimmy Carter. He hated all the vested interests that a poor boy is supposed to hate, and he meant to do something about it. To audiences consumed with impotent rage Mr. Carter used the language of Christian piety to convey a sense of the Lord's vengeance. Thus the paradox implicit in his success. He presented himself as the candidate of hope and new beginnings, but he floated to the surface of American politics on a tide of despair. In place of a vision of the future he offered an image of the nonexistent past, promising a safe return to an innocent Eden in which American power and morality might be restored to the condition of imaginary grace.

His witness was not much different from that of Billy Graham and Rev. Sun Myung Moon. He spoke to the unhappiness of people wishing for a world that never was. The popular suspicion of government is always well-founded. To a greater or lesser extent, all governments commit crimes against the common people. The law is usually unjust, the capitol always noisy with fools. No wonder that Mr. Carter found so many adherents for his crusade against the lords temporal and the kingdom of Caesar.

His success with the so-called governing class, with people who thought they recognized him as a demagogue, raises a more ominous question. Outside the walls of the citadel the suspicion of government can be taken for granted. Among people inside the walls the prevalence of an analogous feeling, expressed as self-disgust rather than as resentment, suggests the possibility of a civilization in decline. A surprising number of people who hold responsible office, in government as well as in the realms of law, finance, and the press, have acquired the habit of denouncing themselves as impostors. They distrust their own legitimacy, and they look for validation in drugs, sex, and Zen. Both in New York and official Washington I meet people who no longer believe themselves capable of directing the business of the state. When they try to envision the future they see nothing that doesn't look like a Saturday afternoon rerun of the past twenty years. The same slogans, the usual compromises, and the old lies—all of it miserably expensive and none of it made bearable by the romance of youth or the presence of the Kennedys. Their lack of imagination makes them sick of themselves.

AS LONG ago as 1965 Senator Eugene McCarthy had reached a similar conclusion. During important votes on the floor of the Senate it was his custom to remain in his office, ignoring repeated quorum calls while making ironic epigrams about the pointlessness of it all. A more perceptive man than most of his confederates, Senator McCarthy was, as always, in the vanguard of the fashionable sentiment. In 1965 his cynicism was regarded as a dangerous heresy; ten years later it had become the received wisdom.

Canvassing the mood of depression in Washington prior to the 1976 elections, *The Wall Street Journal* mentioned the large number of politicians who had decided to quit the government. No fewer than eight Senators and forty-six Congressmen, many of them younger men with safe seats, offered various reasons for refusing to stand for re-election. Politics, they said, was too hard or too degrading; the hours were too long, the issues too complex; too many people looked upon politicians with loathing; they had lost faith in the plausibility of representative government, and they chose to do something else with the rest of their lives.

An equivalent feeling of exhaustion prevented the Democratic party from ordering any resistance to Mr. Carter. Of the Democrats eligible to vote in the primary elections, only one in five bothered to show up at the polls. Despite the talk of denying Mr. Carter the nomination, nobody could find a moral or intellectual ground on which to make an argument. The party remained divided into factions, without any coherent objective beyond regaining access to the White House. Under the circumstances, what was the point of keeping up appearances? Mr. Carter had a new face; he had been winning primaries; the press accepted him at his word; and he would do just as well as any other candidate. If it was a question of money and jobs, and if the American people were foolish enough or apathetic enough to believe the sermons of a rapacious moralist, then why put obstacles in the road to Washington?

In New York Mr. Carter's supporters had a sheepish look about them, as if they were holding hats over their faces after being arrested in a police raid on a brothel. Instead of talking about the regenerative clarity of the candidate's political vision, they discussed their chances of a connection in Washington. The more squeamish among them already had begun to make excuses. They knew, or thought they knew, that Mr. Carter bore an embarrassing resemblance to Richard Nixon, and they didn't like to be reminded of their previous statements (some of them as recent as the early spring) about the necessity of restoring to the White House a man of principle. To anybody who would listen, but mostly to themselves, they said that Mr. Carter must be admired for his ruthlessness or his coldness of mind, for his having been "born again" in Christ or his successful campaign tactics—for anything and everything that might rescue them from a sense of their own uneasiness.

It stands to reason that Mr. Carter was not closely questioned about unemployment, taxes, foreign policy, social welfare, or the military budget. He wasn't asked the questions because not enough people cared if he knew the answers. Probably he didn't, but that was something that his supporters preferred not to know. They chose the condition of benumbed hope. If they looked too closely they might have found out that Mr. Carter was indeed the Wizard of Oz, which would have made it unpleasant to vote for him in November.

Nor did the press insist upon lines of questioning that might have proved inconvenient. Throughout the eight months of his advent, Mr. Carter was excused from anything but cursory examination. The rules of evidence in the national political debate prohibit the taking of testimony about a man's character, and so, until his nomination had been assured, the press obligingly confined itself to meaningless analysis of the candidate's shifting positions across a spectrum of abstract possibility. To do anything else would have been to suggest that the country was still in trouble, that the threat to the Republic had not ended with the resignation of Richard Nixon.

Given the evangelical context of Mr. Carter's election, I don't know how anybody could have expected him to do the work of government. Nor do I think that the press has much cause for complaint when it finds that instead of policies Mr. Carter has revelations.

All reports, both published and unpublished, suggest that Mr. Carter dwells peaceably within the fastness of himself, a more remote and walled-off presence than Richard Nixon. The newspapers give accounts of the long hours that Mr. Carter spends with official papers, seeking to penetrate to the essence of the last little bureaucratic secret. His obsession with detail apparently compels him to approve the lists of players who ask permission to use the White House tennis courts. The travelers from Washington make similar observations. An inward-looking man, they say, a complacently self-improving man who believes that, like St. Thomas Aquinas, he can comprehend all science, all art, all knowledge. I take it for granted that no President can be particularly well-informed, but Mr. Carter seems to place an extraordinary faith in his misinformation. It is said that he prizes his own ideas, and that he does not gladly suffer contradiction. His assistants, of sufficiently minor stature to hold the President in awe, do not engage him in debate. People take instructions, and so the White House remains a placid and oddly listless place, impervious to criticism and assured of its righteousness. The various narratives and accounts to which I have had access convey the impression of a man sitting in the study adjacent to the Oval Office, listening to opera (preferably *Tristan und Isolde*), working late into the night correcting the spelling mistakes on memoranda submitted by junior officials, struggling to reduce the storm of the world to an offstage noise in a puppet theater.

THE IMPRESSION of inwardness coincides with what I know of the Baptist habit of private meditation on the Word. The devotees apparently set great store on the vividness of personal experience and on the God-given capacity to choose and declare oneself. Salvation reveals itself as an inward feeling and a sudden recognition of inner truth. To those members of the congregation fortunate enough to have been "born again," Jesus appears as the savior who guarantees admission into a state of grace. If Mr. Carter believes himself rescued by Jesus (a figure somewhat comparable to a Southern banker who lends unlimited amounts of money without charging interest), then I can well imagine why he would find it difficult to take much of an interest in a world elsewhere. What other good news would Mr. Carter find it necessary or profitable to hear?

If he has revelations instead of policies, then it is equally possible that he identifies the temporal with the spiritual authority. I'm told that the Baptist tradition blurs the distinction between public liturgy and private devotion, and so it is possible that Mr. Carter imagines that he can apply the tidying up of systems analysis to the more complicated matters of war, death, fate, and human destiny.

No wonder his critics can make so little sense of the man. Having interpreted his moralizing as a clever political device, they now find it hard to believe that Mr. Carter means what he says, that he takes seriously his professions of piety. His self-righteousness and presumed innocence, perceived as useful attributes in a candidate, appear as bungling hypocrisy in the man who holds office. The newspaper columnists continue to write about "the enigma of Jimmy Carter" because they find it difficult to admit that the President might still think of himself as a prophet crying in the wilderness.

The people who talk about Mr. Carter's incompetence do him an injustice. They fail to understand that Mr. Carter considers it his business to bring visions from the desert or, as in promulgation of peace for the Egyptians and the Israelis, to the desert.

If the lost tribe chooses not to act on the news that Mr. Carter brings (at no small cost to himself and only after much labor in the desolate watches of the night), then the lost tribe has nobody to blame but itself. Mr. Carter has done his part, and if that is not enough, well, then, that is too bad, but it certainly isn't Mr. Carter's fault. Having already been absolved of sin, Mr. Carter obviously can do nothing wrong. He might express disappointment in people who still make the mistake of judging him as they would judge ordinary men (i.e., the increasing number of impious voices in the press less and less responsive to Mr. Carter's aura of grace); he might even go so far as to scold the people who persist in their wickedness (e.g., the greedy oil companies stealing all that money from the collection plate), but neither his disappointment nor his annoyance interferes with his good opinion of himself. Nor does he feel moved to do anything political that somehow might implicate his visions in the corruption of the world. He offered his energy proposals as a summons to repent and as an expiation for the massacre of the innocents in Southeast Asia and the destruction of the American wilderness. But if the congregation doesn't choose to repent, then there is nothing for it but that everybody will be made to suffer God's vengeance. Thus the complacence with which both Mr. Carter and Mr. James Schlesinger remind their audiences that if the Congress fails to pass the energy legislation the country will suffer the consequences of unemployment, worthless currency, depression, and riot. They remind me of Puritan schoolmasters ordering the nation to stand in the corner.

MR. CARTER'S interest in revelation also would explain why he can disregard the rumors of incompetence. In late October Mr. John Osborne of *The New Republic* paid a visit to the White House to inquire about the attitude of the staff toward the rising volume of criticism. To Mr. Osborne's surprise he found that nobody seemed much concerned. He was informed that it was not in Jimmy Carter's nature to do things any differently, and that if there was one thing that nobody presumed to question it was "Jimmy Carter's nature." What, after all, would it profit such a man to gain the whole world (or even so small a part of it as an energy or a tax bill) if he should lose his own soul?

A number of other visitors to the White House have remarked that the less Mr. Carter knows about any particular subject, the more stubbornly he insists on his command of it. When listening to such reports, I sometimes think Mr. Carter expects the world to be inhabited by hardly anybody over the age of twelve. He must recognize at least a few of his own lies and sleights of hand; he must remember that he didn't take a degree in nuclear engineering and that he has only a dim comprehension of American history. And yet he remains determined to present himself not only as a man for all seasons but also as master of all knowledge. Perhaps he believes that he is the only corrupt man in an innocent world. Perhaps it comes as a great shock to him to discover the world as being even more corrupt than himself.

Mr. Carter remains pure and inviolate to precisely the degree that he doesn't address himself to the contradictions of the empirical world; by so doing he preserves himself within a realm of abstraction in which it is enough to say the magical words and wish for something pleasant to happen. But this is a habit of mind that Mr. Carter unfortunately shares with many of his countrymen, and so it is surely fitting that he should have been elected President. His administration of virtue stands as a testimony to the vice of the times, which, as even schoolchildren know by now, is the preoccupation with self. In most sectors of American opinion the looking inward takes precedence over the looking outward. Feeling supersedes thought, complexity bows down before simplicity, science gives way to sorcery. Mr. Carter's self-contentment corresponds to the collective narcissism of what Tom Wolfe has characterized as "The Me Decade." His claptrap autobiography *Why Not the Best?* corresponds to the best-selling tracts of spiritual and physical self-improvement—*I'm O.K., You're O.K., The Joy of Sex,* et cetera, et cetera. If large numbers of people believe that they can learn to play the piano in ten easy lessons, then I don't think it surprising that Mr. Carter believes he can learn the art of diplomacy as easily as he can learn speed-reading.

If Mr. Carter was not elected to do the work of government, it is because the country as a whole has yet to be convinced that the work of government needs doing. The country prefers to look inward and brood upon the condition of its immortal soul rather than to take up the burdens of thought and study. The President's energy program stirred an enthusiastic response precisely because it was understood as a washing away of sin. So also his declaration of human rights was recognized as having nothing to do with the Second or Third worlds but as reflecting instead an uneasiness toward American blacks and the American South. Mr. Carter's idea of self-sufficiency corresponds to the popular belief that the country, like a successful individual who believes the lessons of Michael Korda's *Power: How to Get It, How to Use It,* must not be dependent on anybody for anything.

Of all the nonsense associated with the Carter Administration, this strikes me as both the most foolish and the most dangerous. Only madmen believe themselves existing in a vacuum. All living things depend on one another. This is the lesson taught by the environmentalists as well as by the practitioners of *Realpolitik,* by marriage counselors as well as by poets. How else can life be defined except as the vast play of interdependence among nations, molecules, sexes, species, cells—everything combining and recombining in the theater of light, space, and time? Most men tell lies to themselves and to other people, but the worst lies have to do with the hope of escape into the mirror.

The King's Pleasure

MARCH 1976

I read in the papers that I live in an age of disillusion. Almost every day yet another witness comes forward to announce that the society has become sick and jaded, that it grows cynical with the consumption of lurid spectacle. Nobody lacks the occasion for an impromptu sermon. The woman on my left talks about the beast of capitalism, about the CIA conspiring against the liberties of Peruvians and people dying every afternoon at the hands of incompetent surgeons, about federal judges indicted for conspiracy and multinational corporations paying bribes. The man on my right mentions the serpent of big government and draws dismal conclusions from reports of debutantes abandoning themselves to debauchery and professors of economics distorting their knowledge of the truth in exchange for government office. Intellectuals of both sexes and various political convictions remark on the decline of Western civilization and the debasement of art. Journalists of noble aspiration compete with one another to reach the largest possible audience with the worst possible news.

When confronted with rumors of so much wickedness in the world, I know that I am supposed to affect an attitude of regret. If I hope to make a favorable impression as a man of sensibility, I should also say that it is impossible to arouse the conscience of an indifferent public, that the people have lost their capacity for moral outrage, and that the United States resembles the Roman Empire under the reign of Caligula. I cannot say such things because I know them to be untrue. Most of the news advertised under the headings of sensational revelation falls into the category of routine human nature. To discover that the Lockheed Aircraft Corporation pays bribes to a foreign government, or that the New York banks speculate against the dollar in overseas currency markets, is to discover that clergymen drink distilled spirits.

Nor is it true that the American people have misplaced their capacity for moral outrage. Anybody who could count the profits of Billy Graham's evangelism would understand that we live in an age of belligerent innocence. Far from being disillusioned, a majority of the population appears to cling to their illusions as if they were teddy bears, insisting that their happiness depends upon rumor and opinion rather than fact. If they can pretend to be fifteen years old, and if they can perceive the world as the dreadful place they want it to be, then they can enjoy the pleasure of denouncing it.

So desperate is the wish for innocence that even the people who have succeeded in the world, who presumably know the difference between a press release and a private conversation, must pledge allegiance to a mythology that invalidates their experience and encourages the subversion of their real interests. I have listened to corporation presidents who proclaim their indifference to statements of profit and loss, to university professors who say they know nothing of departmental politics, to journalists who disavow their gratitude for catastrophe. They cannot afford to do otherwise. If they wish to maintain their reputations for seriousness they must pretend to a degree of naïveté that would embarrass a college sophomore. The man who defies the convention (who actually says, "What we need for the first edition is a really good plane crash") stands accused of heartlessness. In a society that insists upon the facade of innocence, this is heresy.

Even in New York, a city supposedly synonymous with atheist sophistication and shocking truths never before revealed, the rules of parliamentary procedure discourage the expression of any idea likely to offend the presiding sages.

THE NATIONAL preference for even the shabbiest of illusions— détente, peace in the Middle East, the romance of marriage, the courage of the press—results from the tendency to equate innocence with virtue. The man who knows nothing, who has not been tarnished by his passage through the world, supposedly retains the innocence of a child, still trailing, at age fifty-four, Wordsworth's clouds of glory. Such a superstition can only be supported by great wealth. Just as the rich man can afford to buy whatever mirrors protect him from the necessity of seeing other people, so also the United States still prefers to ignore the reality of interests inimical to its own. It is an expensive luxury, but a man with enough money to pay the musicians can listen to anything he wants to hear. He can do so because if he doesn't like the music, he can hire another band. The idea of marriage in the United States comes dressed in a trousseau of romantic nonsense precisely because a marriage can be so easily dissolved. Candidates for the Presidency can wear the costumes of circus clowns because most people continue to believe that it doesn't matter who gets elected President. The black man receives the benefit of civil-rights legislation because he is not considered an equal. In all instances the underlying assumption is the same. The affluence of the United States justifies its carelessness and permits the playing of charades. The rich man bestows his generosity on the little people. If the little people fail to appreciate the magnanimity of his gesture, if it turns out that they have interests of their own, quite apart from those in the script written for them by their benefactor, well then, there are always other little people, such as wives, minority groups, husbands, Presidential candidates, foreign countries, who will understand their proper place.

It is the backdrop of assumed innocence that makes the market in scandal. The discovery of crime or incompetence becomes news only if it can be presented as an exception to the rule. It is one thing to be told, in the words of a headline in the *New York Times,* that "thousands died because of faulty prescriptions," but is quite another thing to be told that thousands will continue to die for exactly the same reason, that all forms of energy are dangerous, that doctors are as incompetent as journalists, and that even a Senate subcommittee cannot restore the electorate to the Garden of Eden.

To the reader who doubts the national longing for innocence I can offer into evidence the official muffling of any discussion of the late John F. Kennedy's philandering. Even now, seventeen years after Mr. Kennedy's death, and with the towers of Camelot fallen, however temporarily, into ruin, hardly anybody wants to mention the President's sexual discontents. Whenever the subject threatens to float to the surface of the news, the custodians of responsible opinion do what they can to load it with weights and sink it into the swamp of rumor. Ordinarily they achieve their purpose without too much trouble, but the disclosures of Mrs. Judith Campbell Exner have proved to be awkwardly buoyant.

Not only did Mrs. Exner publicly admit to a sequence of encounters with President Kennedy, but she also admitted to a similar and contemporaneous acquaintance with prominent criminals. At a press conference in San Diego last December she announced that between the spring of 1961 and the spring of 1962 she met the President on several occasions in Washington, Los Angeles, and

Palm Beach. During the same year she kept company with the late Sam Giancana, a Chicago syndicate figure who, at more or less the same time, had been discussing with the CIA the possibility of murdering Fidel Castro. Obviously her story couldn't be confined to the pages of the *National Enquirer*. She had been questioned by Senator Frank Church's committee (than which no more virtuous tribunal presently sits in the United States), and so whatever she had to say, no matter how regrettable, intruded on the national interest. Giancana was himself murdered a few days before he was scheduled to testify in front of the committee, and it is possible that Mrs. Exner convened her press conference because she was in fear for her life.

The newspapers did what they had to do (even to the point of finding out that Mrs. Exner had been introduced to the President by Frank Sinatra), but they didn't seem happy with the story. The sober-minded papers abandoned it as soon as it was decently possible to do so. When *Time* magazine had the temerity to publish a few tentative paragraphs under the heading "Jack Kennedy's Other Women," the *New York Times*, in an article purporting to reflect a consensus of professional opinion, concluded that the more respectable sort of journalist thought that *Time* had smeared itself with mud. It was quite proper (so said the majority) to publish the news about Mrs. Exner (her connections to organized crime, to the CIA, to public policy, et cetera), but it was altogether improper to publish malicious gossip about President Kennedy's attachments to other women, among them Angie Dickinson and Marilyn Monroe. The approved line of argument held that the private conduct of public men should remain private unless it could be seen (as with Congressman Wilbur Mills on the stage of a Boston burlesque theater) to impair their capacity for the public business.

Such an argument represents an established taboo, and I undertake to comment on it only because it so often results in the election of inadequate and damaged politicians. For more than twenty years President Nixon's neurotic distrust was plainly visible in the public record. Whenever the occasion demanded it of him he broadcast his tearful aggressions on network television (cf. the Checkers speech and his last word to the press on losing the election for Governor of California), and yet none of these confessions could be admitted as evidence of Nixon's instability. The country had to wait for the Watergate havoc and for Nixon to provide the Congress with a transcript of his self-pitying evasions.

TO SPEAK of a man's private conduct is to speak of his character, which, despite the slightly musty sound of the word, affects the way in which he governs both himself and the state. This is something that unfortunately cannot be helped. If a man has abandoned himself to drink or voluptuous reverie, then it is useful to know that about him when trying to assess the texture of his thought and the meaning of his language. It isn't the ethical aspect of Kennedy's promiscuity that concerns me, and I have no wish to even approach what might be construed as a moralistic judgment. In theory at least, a man can collect as many women as he can afford without doing harm either to the country or to his talent for government. The legitimate question (still unasked and nowhere mentioned by the official historians of the period) has to do with the emotional weakness that apparently goaded Kennedy into seeking ceaseless proof of his omnipotence. Why would a man go to such extraordinary trouble to repeat the same empty charade? If he was talking to Mrs. Exner at least once a week for a year, and if, at the same time, he was making similar arrangements with several other women (each of whom required a modicum of time, thought, charm, explanation, apology, and logistical support), then how could he not have perceived the futility of the enterprise? What possible meaning could he derive from the perfunctory conquest of women whose names he probably couldn't remember and whose conversation presumably was as vacuous as the exchange of gossip between Hollywood celebrities? If it was in Kennedy's nature to make himself vulnerable to his sexual confusions, then perhaps he also made himself vulnerable to the more ominous seductions that glimmer around the brilliant light of the Presidency. He was surrounded by flatterers and camp followers; many of them were knowledgeable men who could speak in honeyed voices about the advantages of the occasional assassination in small and distant countries.

That President Kennedy pursued women with a remorseless obsession was a matter of common delight from the first days of his Administration. People spoke of his indiscretions with admiration and approval; their excited talk magnified his image as prince of the realm. It was as if Prince Hal had brought with him into the White House the bacchanalia of the Boar's Head Tavern. In New York during the thousand days, it was impossible to go to dinner among the forward elements of society (i.e., with journalists passing through town on their way from Washington to Hyannis Port, with White House advisers and Broadway directors) without listening to someone tell yet another amusing story about yet another actress who had discovered (much to her wonder and surprise) that politics wasn't always as boring as deficit spending or Berlin. Kennedy made politics fashionable, and by so doing he encouraged the fashionable world to look upon his Administration as an extended entertainment. Neither the press nor the people who traveled with the Presidential house party made much of a distinction between a weekend in Sun Valley for the skiing and an afternoon in Watts for the spectacle of black protest.

The atmosphere of revelry, of a clamorous progress through cheering peasants in a hospitable countryside, so thoroughly pervaded the Kennedy Administration that it was deceptively easy to think of it as frivolous. Even in the spring of 1962, when I was invited to one of the Kennedy entertainments in New York, I can remember being surprised by the squalid sycophancy of his courtiers. From a distance I had admired Kennedy's strength and youthfulness. In a room crowded with the people who then proclaimed themselves the city's *beau monde,* he seemed as absent as he was present, exhausted by the demands of his distracted appetite. It occurred to me that he might have aspired to a much nobler ideal of the Presidency, and I thought of a stag brought down by hounds. The romance of Kennedy's wealth drifted through the room like music. Who among his followers could have resisted the temptation to take everything that was offered?

IT WAS a common failing to admire the Kennedys for the wrong reasons, for the predatory ease with which they acquired virtue as well as property. They seemed to occupy both sides of all positions, to be idealists as well as realists, fierce patriots as well as pacifists, sexually uninhibited and yet the prototype of the happy American family. So many people were beguiled by Kennedy's charm that they neglected to remark on the grim rapacity of his desires. To rummage through women as if through a trunk of costumes cannot be a pleasant occupation. For at least ten years I have waited for somebody to interpret the character of the Kennedy Administration in the light of its specific softness and corruption. The excavations of Camelot suggest the possibility of sometimes criminal delusion, but I have read nothing that tries to deal with the political consequences of prolonged gluttony.

No doubt Kennedy was a gallant man, and I'm sure that he possessed both the wit and the courage that have been attributed to him. Although I do not know it for a fact, I suspect that his weakness followed from a belief in his own immortality. Like many people who have been born rich, Kennedy probably couldn't tell the difference between the people who loved him and the people who wanted to kill him. Except in an election year, what difference did it make? Who could possibly hurt him? Why not accept the flattery of a girl known to be sponsored by Sam Giancana? Why not undertake what Cardinal Cushing described as "Christ's war" in Vietnam or ride through Dallas in an open car? He must have felt embarrassed by the credulity of the less fortunate, who mistook his carelessness for what the newspapers celebrated as "the Kennedy style."

Nobody bothered to speculate about the divisions in Kennedy's mind because the prohibition against raising such questions (i.e., along the lines of a man's character) derives from a quasi-religious sanctification of the egalitarian ideal. Even now, despite the great number of people who attended the revels of the Kennedy Administration, the prohibition remains effectively in force. God forbid that anybody should make judgments that cannot be measured by statistics or by a summary of a man's votes on the standard political issues. Respectable opinion in the United States refuses to admit into evidence anything that borrows too heavily from art or psychology. The illuminations of history and literature count for nothing because they presuppose the seriousness of the imagination. The rules of democracy (at least as it is presently understood) tend to place the imagination in the category of special privilege. It cannot be accepted as valid currency because no one can know that it isn't counterfeit. What gives the historian (much less the journalist) the right to say such things? Why is his opinion better than anybody else's opinion? The same angry questions that diminish the quality of education in the country also force the participants in the national debate to confine their remarks to narrowly defined topics of public discussion. They talk about personages instead of people, about caricatures presumed innocent of complexity until they collapse under the weight of a burden they cannot bear.

As with most other superstitions, the fear of interpretation (particularly sexual interpretation) results in a self-induced blindness. The makers of the public record acquire the habit of telling only partial truths, and by so doing they collaborate in the invention of romances that nearly always end in disillusion. At the moment of appalling discovery (the release of the Nixon transcripts, the news of Kennedy's dalliance with women and assassins), the prior witnesses say that they didn't know, that somebody told them monstrous lies, that they were constrained by the rules of evidence or by a feeling of respect for the convention of privacy. The excuses are never convincing. They lead to bitterness and recrimination and thus to the construction of another romance, with Frank Church or Sam Ervin playing the part of the redeemer. The sequence works nicely on the stage, but in most other public places it gives rise to recurring cycles of violence and despair.

A Nation of Dreamers

SEPTEMBER 1976

The American preference for the invisible never ceases to aston-
ish me. Just when I begin to think that I live in a materialist
society, I find myself surrounded by people who choose to believe in
what isn't there.

This observation does not conform to the official portraits of the
American character. The American is said to be a practical man
who believes in what he can see and measure. The United States
supposedly inherited not only the earth but also the traditions of the
eighteenth-century mind—skeptical, inquiring, and given to experiment. This assumption receives the support of the many lobbyists
for the idea of American pragmatism, who, despite their political
and regional differences, agree on the triumph of reason and the scientific method. The artistic interests talk about the prevailing indifference to the ineffable; businessmen say that maybe they don't
know the difference between Beethoven and Molière but they sure
as hell know the difference between profit and loss; politicians mention "hard realities"; and the lost tribe of the counterculture speaks
of philistines squandering a third of the world's resources on the
manufacture of gaudy baubles. All the witnesses testify to the pre-
eminence of facts.

Would that it were so. The United States is a nation of dreamers, captivated by the power of metaphor. Whenever possible the American substitutes the symbol for whatever it is that the symbol represents. Social critics sometimes deplore the rapaciousness with which Americans consume the goods and services of a spendthrift economy. The critics fail to notice that the objects mean nothing in themselves, that the material acquisitions serve as tedious preliminaries to the desired immateriality.

THIS POINT was made plain on the Fourth of July, 1976, in New York Harbor, in the words of a sign propped against a fence at the southern end of Manhattan Island. Facing the sea and directed toward the largest flotilla of sailing ships assembled anywhere in the world in more than one hundred years, the sign read: "Welcome to Battery Park City." This was a fine sentiment but entirely abstract. Battery Park City is an empty lot, a barren mound of mud and sand.

The transcendental bias of the American mind can turn the whole world into metaphor. Entire vocabularies of symbolic jargon—academic, bureaucratic, scientific—describe entire kingdoms of nonexistent thought. Modern art depends on abstract theories that explain the absence of paint. American restaurants substitute the hyperbole of their menus for the taste of their food; so also do pornographic magazines publish literary essays that hardly anybody bothers to read. They appear as symbols of an imaginary conversation. The television image, which is itself a metaphor, goes forth to an invisible audience. Jimmy Carter succeeded as a political candidate because he presented the voters with an emptiness they could fill with images of their own.

Or consider the metaphor of New York City. By any material standard (comparison with Paris, say, or even with London) the city must be judged deficient. From a height or a distance it can be seen as beautiful, but the texture of the streets consists of fear, noise, ugliness, and anger. It is the metaphysical promise, the sense of the unseen but imminent possibility, that gives the city its character. Walking around beggars lying in the street, the citizens carry on fierce discussions of social injustice; they speculate about the interior dialogue of politicians whom they have never seen, about the chance of war in countries to which they have never traveled. The less they know about the subject in question, the more easily they can escape the coils of specific fact and float into the sphere of abstraction.

The unheard melodies of John Keats's Grecian urn fill out the implied harmonies in almost the whole of American literature. The writers remembered for their communion with the unknowable, among them Thoreau, Melville, Whitman, and Fitzgerald, lose themselves in what Irving Howe once described as "a sacred emptiness of space," in which each man becomes both performer and pioneer, inventing himself as he clears the wilderness of his mortality. The modern school of writing, much praised by the critics who teach theories of imagination, follows the tradition into the thin atmospheres of surrealism. In the novels of Robert Coover, Donald Barthelme, and Thomas Pynchon, the narrative exists only to be discarded. Like a first-stage rocket, it boosts the author's circus of ideas into the metaphor of space. Except in a figurative way, as representatives of abstraction, the people in the novels have neither meaning nor substance.

The eloquent theories of politicians and professors of sociology seldom withstand the judgment of practical result because, more often than not, they are meant to be appreciated as symbols. The politicians have no choice in this because they seldom see the things their laws describe. They talk about housing and federal health insurance, about poverty levels and public transportation, but they do not ride in subways or wait in lines for food stamps. Like the view of New York City from a helicopter, the idea of racial equality is beautiful as an abstraction. If somebody interprets it in a literal-minded way, mistaking the symbolic for the real, well, then, obviously the thing won't work. The race riots in Boston resulted from an error in translation. When Tom Wicker spoke encouragingly to the prisoners at Attica about the "inequities of the system," he offered them a metaphor instead of information. A number of them died because nobody told them that journalism is a form of fiction.

AN OBSESSION with metaphor also governs the conduct of American business. I have noticed that few highly placed executives understand money as a commodity. Perhaps this is because they almost never see it. The transfer of huge sums takes place as a sequence of abstractions projected on a screen. Making their way upward through the company hierarchy, once knowledgeable engineers learn to speak the ritual language of hierophants. On the highest tiers of organizations that resemble Babylonian ziggurats, the officials walk solemnly to and fro, bowing to one another in their circumambulations and making grave gestures of consensus. Every now and then they pause to examine the sky through the modern equivalents of the astrolabe—computer printouts, projections of oil reserves, summaries of the consumer-price index, et cetera. The technology furnishes them with metaphors.

Even the American approach to sex proceeds along the lines of religious pilgrimage. The confessional testimony, most of it in the form of best-selling disappointment, suggests that not many people (at least not those who write about it) find much pleasure in the act of love. Quite often they would rather be in Philadelphia, but they have been sent forth to find meaning and success. Like all the other toys in the department-store window, the sexual object must be acquired as proof of something else. Nobody knows quite what, but presumably (*vide* the manuals, clinics, advisories to the lovelorn) something beyond the merely human. Together with the Holy Grail, the ideal orgasm remains just over the horizon of their experience. Both men and women talk about their liaisons in the way that explorers used to write about their voyaging in unknown seas. By keeping logs and chronologies, they plot their positions in the world.

The tendency to think in symbols also accounts for the otherwise baffling American perception of time. It has often been demonstrated that Americans retain little more than a dim notion of the past. The universities continue to report a lack of interest in anything that took place as long ago as last week; a Gallup poll published in the Bicentennial year showed that only 50 percent of the respondents could remember what was the significance of the year 1776. People who cannot imagine the past cannot envision the future. The sense of time falls in upon itself, collapsing like an accordion into the evangelical present. The effect is greatly magnified by the symbolic nature of the television image, in which the visible part stands for the invisible whole. If three or four black men carrying signs can be made to represent the discontent of the Negro race, then they have been raised to the power of metaphor. The confinement in the present imposes a necessary preoccupation with what isn't there. Nothing can exist, because anything so foolish as to make itself visible must submit to the passage of time. To live always at the point of becoming makes it difficult to enjoy, much less to sustain, the sense of being.

I cannot imagine a state of mind less consistent with the orthodox definitions of materialism. If dissatisfaction becomes imbued with the significance of a religious quest, then the satisfied man stands condemned as a heretic. To admit being satisfied is to confess the squalor of one's aspirations. Which is why the traditional disappointment with success follows from the romanticism of youth. Having acquired the object of what he thought was his desire, the young man cannot feel the emotional correlative he had previously assigned to the grasping of that object. In the midst of his possessions he mourns the loss of innocence. Anybody who neglects to offer the convention-al denials risks alliance with the Evil One, i.e., with people who know or have what they want. God forbid that a man should enjoy the things of the world, that he should delight in its fruitfulness and sur-round himself with friends, works, and families.

In its courageous aspects, the longing for the invisible expresses the spirit of the American frontier. The *Mayflower* sails in search of the unknown Thomas Jefferson; Orville Wright imagines the flight of the unseen SST. But, at least for the time being, the dreaming American mind appears to have retreated into the caves of the supernatural. The crowds gathered in the tent shows of wandering evangelicals remind me of the crowds shuffling through the neon markets of sexual illusion. The preacher and the whore promise the transcendent moment of an escape from time. It is an escape that even Houdini found impossible to perform.

Talking to the White Rabbit

MAY 1968

The taxi reached Rishikesh an hour before sunset, and the driver pointed across the River Ganges to the religious settlement of Swarag Ashram, beyond which, hidden in the sheshum trees, the Maharishi Mahesh Yogi held court amidst the incessant squalling of crows. We had come eight hours and 128 miles north from Delhi, driving on dusty roads through market towns and herds of water buffalo. The last light glittered on painted temples decorated with gaudy sculpture and verses from the Song Celestial. From a monastery somewhere in the surrounding hills I could hear the tinkling of bells.

In the dry season at Rishikesh the Ganges is about 150 yards wide and still a greenish-blue color, the clarity of its origins not yet diluted by the mud and refuse of the plains. I crossed in a motor launch crowded with pilgrims, many of them laughing and asking if I was going to see the Beatles. On the far shore, squatting among a row of beggars, I encountered a man with a trident, whom I first mistook for a citizen of the town. Naked to the waist, his thin legs covered by a soiled white cloth, he seemed to be some sort of a religious figure. On his left arm was tattooed the Sanskrit character for the mystical "om"; on his right arm there appeared the motto

"Semper Fidelis." He rose slowly and greeted me with the languid indifference of a hipster who has made all the scenes.

"You're late, man," he said.

He identified himself as John O'Shea, formerly of Norwalk, Connecticut, and lately of Haight-Ashbury in San Francisco. The trident he explained as a symbol associated with the Lord Krishna.

It was true that I was late. The Maharishi already had recruited many adepts to the practice of his transcendental meditation. He had left India in the spring of 1959 and first appeared in the United States at the Masquers Club in Hollywood under the sobriquet of "The Beacon of Light of the Himalayas." Since then his movement had become profitable as well as fashionable; his disciples had established outposts in New York and Los Angeles, and at the University of California at Berkeley students were standing in long lines outside what once had been a sorority house, holding bouquets of flowers in their hands and waiting patiently to be initiated, at the cost of $35 a head, into the wisdom of the East. It was the winter of 1967; in the jungles of Vietnam less fortunate American students were being initiated into less obscure Asian mysteries, but for the happy few who could escape the draft and pay the going prices for God-consciousness, the Maharishi was all the rage.

Traveling from New York to India by way of California, I had been impressed by the desperate innocence of the Maharishi's followers and by their touching faith in the Maharishi's capacity to whisper a magic word that would grant them admission to "the kingdom of heaven within," or, as it was sometimes described, into the "state of unknowable bliss."

O'Shea apparently had gone even further into the interior of the world soul. He himself, he said, did not frequent the Maharishi's ashram, which he considered insufficiently serious for his purposes, but he offered to show me around. Walking along the stony shore of the river, O'Shea told of his own odyssey. For four months he'd been wandering in India, dressed as a sadhu and traveling on third-class trains.

"If you're a holy man," he said, "everything's free, and nobody bugs you about the hashish."

Together with several other Americans, he was living on an ashram in a farmyard, and from time to time they searched among the caves and temples for a guru of their own. In and around Rishikesh, he explained, there were hundreds of gurus, of every conceivable persuasion. Before coming to India he'd been in San Francisco, but Haight-Ashbury fell into the hands of the philistines, and besides, he'd been selling acid and felt the heat moving ominously toward him.

"I figured," he said, "that it was about time for the journey to the East."

About half a mile south of town, he left me at the lower end of a sandy path that led upward between a random series of low stone buildings. Across the path a banner strung between bamboo poles bore the single word WELCOME. Beyond, at the point where the path turned more steeply upward, a Hindu guard stood somberly in front of a wooden gate in a barbed-wire fence. The buildings at the higher elevations stood among sheshum and teak trees, but those below the gate straggled across open and stony ground. On a flat roof I noticed a monkey methodically breaking up a small, hard fruit the color of lemon.

Among the lesser outbuildings I found one marked ENQUIRY OFFICE, and therein I presented my credentials to a shy and smiling man named Suresh, the majordomo of the establishment. I had arrived at a difficult time, he said; they were having some trouble with the press, and he wasn't sure who was supposed to go where. He nevertheless gave me a blanket and assigned me a room in a stone house on the lower slope of the ashram.

The next morning it rained, and a heavy wind was blowing. At noon Suresh knocked on the door and said the Maharishi had consented to see me. Together we walked up the hill, past Hindu boys warming their hands over charcoal fires burning in braziers at the corners of the paths.

The Maharishi's house stood in an isolated grove of trees on the edge of a bluff that commanded a wide view of the Ganges. A modest but comfortable brick building, it was surrounded by narrow fountains and lawns. Suresh instructed me to leave my shoes on the veranda and wait in a small, dark room that appeared to be the Maharishi's bedroom.

A low bed covered with silk and an antelope skin stood against a wall sheathed in bamboo slatting; on the opposite wall hung a political map of the world, and above it, on a shelf decorated with Christmas tinsel, there was a painting of the Guru Dev identical to others I'd seen in New York and Los Angeles.

Twenty minutes later Suresh ushered me into the Maharishi's presence, but now when I try to reconstruct my first impression of the man I'd heard so much about and come so far to see, I can think of nothing startling or exceptional. No doubt I expected signs and wonders, and probably the expectation clouded my sight. I saw only a small, frail man, sitting cross-legged among cushions. His long hair, with streaks of gray in it, fell to his shoulders, and although he smiled and nodded at me, I noticed a vaguely troubled expression in his eyes. He had delicate hands and wore cheap wooden sandals.

Next to him, also cross-legged among cushions, sat Walter Koch, a physicist from Santa Barbara, and Mike Love, the lead singer of the Beach Boys. Koch had gathered a plaid blanket around his shoulders, and Love wore an astrakhan hat.

The Maharishi welcomed me as a representative of the United

States and said that if everybody in our two countries could be persuaded to meditate, then there would be peace in the world for one
thousand generations. His voice had a soft resonance in it, and he
ended his sentences on a rising inflection. Koch questioned me as to
my intentions, and when he had assured himself that they were honorable, he said to the Maharishi, "We'll hit 'em all at once,
Maharishi. TV . . . magazines . . . lectures . . . saturation."

"Groovy," said Mike Love.

We all laughed, for no apparent reason, and then, listening to the
wind, the Maharishi said, also for no apparent reason, "When Ringo
comes, the storm clears the passage . . . in the clear, Ringo comes."

Again he laughed, and his laughter contained within it a quality
of maniacal innocence. The conversation ended with the Maharishi
expressing the polite hope that I could stay for a few days.

Koch led me back down the hill in the rain, explaining that
things were somewhat unsettled at the moment and that I mustn't
misinterpret the Maharishi's courtesy. A naïve and worried man,
Koch clearly had appointed himself liaison officer between the
Maharishi and the great world. Paul McCartney and Ringo Starr
were expected that evening, and he hoped to avoid a repetition of
the events associated with the arrival of the other Beatles.

"It's supposed to be a secluded course," he said, "but it's getting
like Grand Central station around here."

That was Tuesday, and for the next three days I remained in a
state of ambiguous probation. Although denied admission to the
upper reaches of the ashram, I was allowed to stay in the stone
house below the gates. Suresh sent oranges and occasional messages, and every now and then Koch stopped by to make sure I
hadn't become dangerously cynical. He assured me that the
Maharishi knew about me and was considering my vibrations and
that pretty soon I'd be allowed up the hill.

"This is the hub of the universe," he said. "The world looks to Rishikesh."

Wednesday afternoon the Maharishi convened a press conference on the open ground below the gate. In the morning Hindu boys had set up his low dais and his antelope skin, and for the reporters they spread rugs on the ground. The reporters climbed the hill at noon, and as many as fifty of them had assembled when the Maharishi appeared an hour later.

Walking in a slow and stately way, followed by two Hindu monks in white robes, he descended the hill carrying a bouquet of marigolds. The taller monk held an umbrella over his head, shading him from the sun.

The reporters, speaking in English and obviously shocked by the size and luxury of his ashram, questioned him about the difference between his teaching and the traditional Vedic principle of renunciation. Answering with a distant calm and plucking the petals from his flowers, the Maharishi explained that Vedanta and Yoga had been grossly misinterpreted for many years.

Throughout the proceedings, which lasted over an hour, the taller monk continued to hold the umbrella aloft, raising and lowering it as the photographers stood up to take pictures. The smaller monk squatted at the Maharishi's feet, holding out the microphone of a tape recorder.

At the end a man who'd come from somewhere in southern India asked if he could read a poem of homage that had occurred to him on the train. He had not intended it, he said, but a spirit moved him. The Maharishi nodded and smiled encouragingly, and the man, who was close to tears, read in a lyrical voice in the Tamil language. When he finished, he kissed the Maharishi's foot, saying, in English, that he hoped to sit at the Maharishi's feet in heaven.

The Maharishi acknowledged the compliment with a modest gesture of benediction and then asked the company at large if any of them had seen the article about him in that week's issue of *Life* magazine. Nobody had seen it.

"Too bad," he said, ". . . huge picture."

With that he rose and walked back up the hill, followed by the monk with the umbrella, still carrying the remains of his flowers. Walter Koch stayed below, explaining to the reporters that none of them could go within the gate. The Beatles, who had arrived the previous night, insisted upon privacy, he said, and besides there was nothing to see except a lot of people meditating, which wasn't very interesting.

"This is not," he said, "a guru situation."

That evening I began to meet a number of the meditators, some of whom strayed down the hill for a subtle change of scene and others who came to consult with the tailor. The tailor lived in a tent opposite the Enquiry Office, and during the nine days that I was there, he never seemed to sleep. He made saris for the women and kurtas for the men; the demand was steady, and at night he sewed by the light of a kerosene lamp.

From the meditators I heard the gossip of the place and picked up miscellaneous bits of information. The Maharishi, for instance, disliked the color black. He preferred to see women in saris, most particularly gold and white ones. When he scratched, it meant he sensed negative vibrations in the atmosphere.

The Beatles appeared to be "straight kids," but so far they had kept pretty much to themselves. Mia Farrow had left after a week to go on a tiger hunt, but maybe she would be back. The menu consisted of rice and vegetables, all of it boiled for twenty minutes, and a lot of people were getting pretty sick of it.

The majority of those present were either British or American, but the Swedes were the best at the prolonged meditation, and one of them held the current record of twenty-one hours.

On the basis of the early returns, the meditators appeared to divide into the same factions I'd noticed in California. The older ones generally believed in reincarnation and assumed the Maharishi could work miracles if he so chose. The younger generation not only didn't accept the religious extensions of the meditation, but some of them had begun to entertain even more serious doubts. A television actor named Tom Simcox, a humorous and intelligent man with a blond beard, conceded that although the meditation still seemed useful and straightforward, some of the people on the ashram disturbed him. Too many of them, he thought, inclined to come on with alarming fantasies.

"You're sitting up there at lunch," he said, "and you think you're talking to a real person . . . then suddenly you know you're talking to the white rabbit."

On Friday I began to see what he meant. That morning Walter Koch granted me access to the whole of the ashram, and at noon I entered into a series of conversations I now remember as a single lunatic dialogue that lasted for six days.

The narrow dining table stood in a grove of trees a few hundred yards beyond the Maharishi's house and commanded the same fine view of the river. There everybody assembled between meditations, coming and going at random, changing places like the figures in a dance. Hindu boys served the same bland and tasteless meals at almost any hour of the day; in the lower branches of the trees the crows and monkeys watched for chances to grab off a turnip or a crust of toast.

At first sight the guests at the table seemed to resemble the company on a bizarre winter cruise. The women wore saris and shawls, and the men, many of whom had let their beards grow, sat with brightly colored blankets around their shoulders. Mike Love I noticed in a white coat, a blue satin tunic, and a pith helmet. At the table, which was covered in oilcloth, they passed one another things with careful politeness, and their talk, which had about it a feeling of tenuous speculation, veered off in oblique directions.

No sooner did I arrive than I heard two ladies arguing a subtle point in the doctrine of reincarnation. They both agreed that if a person's last thought happens to be of a cat, then the person must return as a cat. The discussion had to do with what kind of a cat. One of the ladies believed that if a person's spiritual attainment had been sufficiently high, then he would return as a happy and well-loved cat. The other lady dismissed this interpretation as being overly sentimental.

The Beatles appeared toward the end of lunch and the beginning of tea. Dressed in romantic combinations of mod and Indian costumes, they came as a group, accompanied by their wives, also in vivid and trailing silks. They moved slowly, their heavy gold chains and pendants swinging solemnly against their chests, and the girls, all of whom had long, blond hair, evoked images of maidens rescued from castles. Collectively they looked like characters from a strange and wonderful movie as yet unseen.

They sat in a row on one side of the table, and Paul McCartney said he'd had a dream. To Anneliese Braun, an elfin woman to whom everyone applied on such matters, he explained that in his dream he'd been trapped in a leaking submarine of indeterminate color. When all appeared lost, however, the submarine surfaced in a crowded London street.

Anneliese clapped her hands in the enthusiastic way she had, like a child seeing her first snowfall. How very nice, she said, wondering if McCartney understood. He smiled and said he didn't think he quite got all of it.

"Why," she said, ". . . it's the perfect meditation dream."

The voyage in the submarine she interpreted as the descent toward pure consciousness through the vehicle of the mantra; the leaks represented anxiety, and the emergence in the street indicated a return to normal life, which was the purpose of all good meditation.

The other people present applauded, and in the ensuing silence at the far end of the table, I heard somebody say, "I'm sure it's Wednesday, but they're trying to tell me it's Saturday."

ON THE heights of the Maharishi's academy in the Himalayas, the sweet, wayward discourse never ceased. The Beatles and the less celebrated guests appeared at stray moments between their meditations, wandering through the teak trees to the picnic table at the edge of the bluff. Sometimes holding flowers in their hands, sometimes throwing bits of toast to the monkeys, they talked of dysentery and cosmic consciousness, of poetry and their troubles with the tailor.

The same gentle wind blew steadily from the south, and the Ganges kept up its old and sacred progress to Benares and the Bay of Bengal. Vultures drifted high up in the pale sky, but they watched the other shore, and their affairs, like the affairs of the men and animals they watched, didn't concern the friends of the white rabbit.

Neither did the clamor at the gates. Every day the reporters from the Indian press assembled in increasing numbers on the lower slope of the ashram, waiting with cameras and tactless skepticism. They remained below the barbed-wire fence, and occasionally in the afternoons the Maharishi ventured among them to speak gently of "the ocean of happiness within" and the "dive toward truth and light." Behind him walked a bearded monk in a white robe, holding an umbrella aloft to shade him from the sun.

To the Beatles the Maharishi attributed the popular success of his spiritual regeneration movement, and he doted on them with the proud fondness of a singing teacher or football coach. Often he referred to them as "the blessed leaders of the world's youth," and in his happiest moments he described George Harrison as "a sublime soul for whom God and all the angels give thanks."

"We had all the material things," Harrison once said. "Fame and all that. But there was still something needed, you see. It can't be one hundred percent without the inner life, can it?"

He called the Maharishi "the big M," and I remember the intense earnestness in his face, conveying the impression of a man who'd been through a lot of changes, expecting each of them to be the last. Drugs, he said, had filled a gap and showed him many things, but death still remained what he called "a bit of a hang-up," which was where philosophy and religion began to get useful.

Ringo and McCartney didn't talk as much about the meditation. Yes, they'd had results with it, and no, it wasn't a put-on, but beyond that their attitude implied that it was George's thing, and if he wanted to go to India, okay, everybody went to India. Ringo and his wife, Maureen, admitted to a little trouble with meditations longer than a few hours, and McCartney regretted the extravagance of the Maharishi's praise and the grandiose nature of his metaphysics. Also he wished the Maharishi would avoid talking to them about subjects that he, McCartney, knew something about. In the mornings the Maharishi held private classes for them on the roof of his house, and occasionally he discussed aspects of modern life. McCartney found the Maharishi's support of the draft laws disillusioning, and his girlfriend, the British actress Jane Asher, wondered aloud from time to time what it would be like to see Bombay or the moon on the Taj Mahal.

The Maharishi's doting fondness for the Beatles disconcerted a number of the other meditators in residence, some of whom felt themselves too much reminded of headwaiters deferring to show-business personalities in Hollywood. Others, who had followed the

Maharishi so faithfully for so many years, at first resented the intrusion of usurpers. Jealousy being so obviously inappropriate to the circumstances, however, most of them managed to stifle it. They argued that the Beatles had attracted wide notice to their movement and had promised, after all, to build a meditation academy in London.

The extreme interpretation I remember hearing from Anneliese Braun, who, so it was said, could heal people by a laying on of hands. We were standing under a teak tree, looking at the river, Anneliese thoughtfully examining a dahlia she held in her hands. When she heard about the Beatles, she said, she'd assumed they were all wrong for the movement, big-time celebrities opening the Pandora's box of press agents and other evils. But on meeting them in Rishikesh she'd found them simple and good-hearted boys, uncorrupted by the temptations of the world. She looked at me in the sly way she had, her eyes glittering with the opaque brilliance of a cat's eyes.

"It wasn't for nothing that Christ's original disciples were simple men," she said. "Carpenters and fishermen, you know."

Through Anneliese I met Geoffrey, and it was he who showed me around and introduced me to many of the others. Like Virgil, he said, pointing out the sights to Dante. He enjoyed learned allusions, and on our walks together we talked of such things as the Punic Wars and the quality of the light in Rembrandt's last portraits. Yellow flags drooped from long bamboo poles set at random intervals along the paths; an occasional trellis marked the entrance to a vegetable or flower garden, and on the stone walls of the low bungalows, in letters reminiscent of military installations, appeared the designation: SILENCE ZONE.

Geoffrey was a painter and a teacher of painting in London. He wore a full beard, and his eyes, which were gray, seemed always to stare into the distance, as if he were estimating remote perspectives. He was anxious that I should know the other meditators as responsible citizens who wouldn't tilt at windmills or trudge after a piper playing a popular dance-hall tune. Thus, when introducing me, he would identify Gunther as the Lufthansa pilot, or Nancy as the wife of a television news analyst, or Tony as the blackjack dealer in a Las Vegas casino. All presumably practical people who knew the odds and were accustomed to hard, technological proofs.

Everybody would remain on the ashram for two months, he said, and then they would proceed, by chartered jet, to Kashmir. At Rishikesh they studied to become initiators in their native countries, and at Kashmir, where the Maharishi maintained a second establishment aboard a string of houseboats, they would take written and oral examinations.

In the evenings the Maharishi spoke to us in the lecture hall, a damp and hangarlike building with whitewashed walls and a floor of compressed cow dung. Little paper flags fluttered from the beams across the ceiling; near the wide doors charcoal fires burned in tin pots.

A display of ferns and palm fronds decorated the wooden stage at the far end of the hall. In the center of the stage, behind an array of microphones attached to tape recorders, stood a modest altar dressed with flowers, Christmas tinsel, and a painting of the Maharishi's master, the Guru Dev.

The Beatles and their wives occupied places in the front row of wood and wicker chairs; the rest of us sat scattered through the rows in back. Candles on the armrests of the chairs offered a dim and flickering light; the heavy scent of incense and coal smoke drifted on the night air.

The Maharishi invariably appeared at least an hour late, his hands folded in a pious gesture, nodding and murmuring praises to the Guru Dev as he walked softly down the center aisle. An almost coquettish smile straying across his face, he sat cross-legged on his antelope skin, often toying with a flower or a strand of beads. His voice remained gentle and soothing, as if he were speaking from someplace far away, where everything, somehow, was much simpler.

Always he began by asking how long everybody had managed to meditate since he'd last seen them, and I remember a night when a Swedish woman impatiently raised her hand. The Maharishi nodded to her with an encouraging smile.

"Yes?" he said. "How long, please?"

"Forty-two hours, Maharishi," she said.

She wore a dull-colored robe and spoke with the flat satisfaction of somebody announcing a record. The others turned to notice her, visibly impressed by her accomplishment. The Maharishi clapped his hands together and said, "What joy."

He inquired if the woman's meditation had been harmonious. Informed that it was, he asked if she remembered anything. The lady thought for an awkward few minutes, and then said, apologetically, "No, Maharishi."

He smiled with the same encouragement as before, assuring her that she had made no mistake, and then he asked if anybody could report forty-one hours. Nobody could. He inquired about forty and thirty-nine hours, and encountering no response then proceeded downward hour by hour. At thirty hours an Englishwoman raised her hand and admitted she hadn't managed it all at once, like the Swedish lady, but rather in ten-hour segments interrupted by fifteen-minute breaks for warm milk and honey sandwiches.

"And you felt what, please?" the Maharishi inquired.

In a precise, clinical voice the woman reported "the usual disassociation from my body" in the first segment, followed, in the second segment, by a sensation of intense and pleasurable warmth.

During the third segment she'd begun to sing old music-hall songs, the words to which she thought she'd forgotten.

The Maharishi nodded approvingly and continued his counting. At twenty-three hours Gunther, the Lufthansa pilot, announced that his friend, George, wanted to say something. George didn't understand English, and they whispered together for a moment. Gunther then said that George had experienced a feeling much like fainting, which depressed and alarmed him.

The Maharishi gave way to a fit of high and infectious laughter, in the midst of which he said, "In hospitals they call it fainting . . . We call it transcending."

For meditations of less than seven hours (periods that didn't warrant discussion), the Maharishi asked only for a show of hands. When he finished his review, he answered questions, most of which dealt with matters of considerable substance. People asked for a more exact distinction between "God-consciousness" and "supreme knowledge," or whether "rapturous joy" always accompanied the descent into "pure being."

The Maharishi considered carefully before giving his long and discursive answers, and in that pose, in that flickering light and aromatic haze, I could imagine him weighing the destiny of nations. (Geoffrey later explained that all the Maharishi's answers took place on at least two levels of meaning, corresponding to the levels of "gross or of subtle consciousness"; to make himself clearer, Geoffrey employed the metaphor of a tree, the profound levels of meaning being analogous to the sap, the superficial to the level of the leaf.)

When all the questions had been answered, the Maharishi rose and turned toward the altar. There, assisted by his monks, he performed a ceremony involving the burning of sandalwood, the chanting of a Vedic hymn, and the ringing of tiny bells. Although this constituted a simple offer of thanksgiving to the Guru Dev, many of those past the age of forty chose to endow it with a larger significance. They groped hesitantly with the unfamiliar words and rhythms of the hymn, and when they could, or when the ceremony seemed to call for it, they prostrated themselves at full length upon the cold floor.

EVERY NOW and then John O'Shea wandered up the hill from the town of Swarag Ashram, bringing the news and gossip of the Laksmi Café. The café I'd seen and remembered as a dingy bazaar on a mud street, into which cows often looked in search of sweets and vegetables. A sign on the wall advertised QUALITY FOOD AND TASTY SNACKS; slow fans hung from the ceiling, and the clientele drank tea at stone tables. It was, however, the only place in town, and O'Shea and his friends used to go there in the afternoons.

They were all of them very hip, having made the approved scenes in places like the Haight-Ashbury district, and they'd come to India, separately and by different roads, in search of their own guru. Swarag Ashram, on the banks of the Ganges, contained many gurus of various persuasions, and among them O'Shea's friends conducted their haphazard quest.

As yet, he said, they'd found no guru to teach them, but in the evenings they listened to Bob Dylan records and smoked hashish. They did it elaborately, he said, with a lot of Indians sitting around and the ceremonial blowing of a conch horn. This announced the religious significance of the proceeding and therefore exempted them from trouble with the civil authorities.

Lately, however, what with the publicity attracted by the Maharishi, they'd felt the tourists moving in on them. As an example of how bad things were getting, O'Shea mentioned an American friend of his who'd been in the Laksmi Café some days before when an Italian photographer showed up. The photographer mistook

O'Shea's friend for Steve McQueen, and the friend figured the photographer was George Harrison. Neither could speak the other's language (the friend thinking Harrison was putting him on with the nutty talk), and it took them an hour to straighten the thing out.

"What kind of scene is that, man?" O'Shea said. "I mean, where are we supposed to be?"

Sometimes O'Shea stayed long enough to attend one of the Maharishi's press conferences, but of these he remained critical. The Maharishi he thought too commercial, too often answering questions in an equivocal way, as if he had an interest to protect.

"Like a politician, you dig," he said. "A holy man has got to be set to be crucified, right?"

His opinion was shared by a clear majority of the Indian press. When the Maharishi came among them, they listened obediently to the radiant metaphysics, and then, at the end, asked the questions they'd come to ask, about the money and the Beatles and the airstrip the Maharishi was building in another part of the forest. The questions he found awkward the Maharishi answered with flights of charmingly evasive laughter.

The restrictions against reporters remained in force, and in the evenings they departed in bitterness to file stories about the congregation of "actors, divorcées, and reformed drug addicts." When the more sarcastic accounts reached the ashram, the monks took pains to hide them from the Maharishi.

For people with cameras, however, the restrictions sometimes could be waived. Permission to film within the ashram was given to Canadian and Italian television crews, also to a French photographer from *Vogue* magazine. The photographer stayed for several days, wearing a series of costumes designed by Pierre Cardin and explaining he'd been diverted from an assignment to take pictures of the milk-white tigers in the Delhi zoo.

The Maharishi posed for long hours, obviously delighting in cameras with the innocent enthusiasm of a child. He even considered himself something of a director, and this assumption was never more apparent than at the times he organized his group photographs.

First he supervised the building of a tier of bleachers, directing two monks where to place the flowers, the potted plants, and the painting of the Guru Dev. (His uncle, an old man who lived next to the Enquiry Office, did nothing but paint portraits of the Guru Dev and ranked as a leading authority on the subject.) Next the Maharishi drew a diagram indicating where everybody was to sit, and as the meditators appeared (in their best Indian clothes), he hurried them into their places.

While we waited for the last of the stragglers one morning, Tom Simcox explained about Mia Farrow. He had known her in California, he said, and they had come up to the ashram in the group with the others. But the Maharishi had made such a fuss over her, placing paper crowns on her head and insisting on so many photographs, that she had gone off after five days on a tiger hunt.

"Stuff like this," he said. "It reminded her of studio calls on the coast."

When everything had been arranged to the Maharishi's satisfaction, the Beatles next to him in the center of the set, he said to the photographer, "You must shout one, two, three before you snap . . . Any snap, you must shout."

The photographer, a man from Rishikesh who worked with an old-fashioned camera under a black cloth, planned an angle the Maharishi thought too low.

"Up higher," he said. "You don't get good scenes from there."

The photographer dragged his camera several feet up the hill, and the Maharishi, turning to the assembled meditators, smiled and said, "Now come on, cosmic smiles . . . and all into the lens."

More even than cameras, the Maharishi loved the helicopters. The morning they arrived, I waited for them on the shore of the Ganges with Nancy Jackson and Larry Kurland, who also loved the helicopters, but for different reasons.

A chic, blond woman in her forties, Nancy always dressed as if for a late lunch around one of her neighbors' pools in Beverly Hills. She had a brisk way of talking that suggested she was accustomed to managing things, and her conversation invariably contained references to the important people she knew. Larry conceived of himself as the archetypal hippie, a traveler returned from trips beyond any destinations dreamed of in John O'Shea's philosophy. He'd let his hair and his beard grow; he wore beads and sandals and Indian cloaks of many colors. He too had been through the drug scene and found it insufficient, and the Maharishi he recognized as "a cat right on top of the action." He'd heard of people who said the $500 for the course on the ashram amounted to a lot of money, but their objections he thought niggling.

"Where can you buy nirvana for less?" he said.

While we waited for the helicopters, Nancy made the kind of nervous talk characteristic of women filling in the silences between arrivals of the famous guests. The light had not yet reached across the river, and it was still cold. On the far shore I could see the smoke of cooking fires in a mud compound inhabited by mendicant monks.

She'd discovered the Maharishi several years before, Nancy said, on her way through Rishikesh to see the Dalai Lama. She didn't pay much attention to the Maharishi that year, but she remembered that when she and her companions got to Lhasa, the Dalai Lama peeked at them through a rhododendron bush, and she'd been uncertain about what to say.

There had been talk of the Abominable Snowman, in search of

which her friends had wanted to arrange an expedition. She called it "the *yeti*," introducing the term in a casual aside, and with a stick she drew the *yeti*'s footprint in the sand. The Dalai Lama hadn't granted them permission, she said, but had offered instead to loan them three miracle-working lamas. The idea was to take the lamas on tour in the United States, raising money for future expeditions. Among other wonders, the lamas could perform levitation and materialization, and they could drag the combined weight of seven deranged elephants.

"Fantastic," Larry said.

The conversation lapsed, and then, still in a nervous, gossipy way, Nancy said that if I really wanted to write about something interesting, I ought to get in touch with her husband, the television news analyst. Several years ago, she said, he'd been contacted by people from outer space, and a friend of theirs had gone off forever in a flying saucer.

"Wild," Larry said.

We were still in the midst of this conversation when two helicopters appeared, circling once over the river and then settling onto the beach in a loud swirl of sand. Out of the first of them stepped an obviously American couple, later identified as Fred and Susie Smithline from Scarsdale, New York. Susie wore white boots and a basic black dress; her husband, in dark glasses, a blue blazer, and tennis sneakers, got out of the plane already filming with his home-movie camera. Seeing Larry in his beads and taking him for a more authentic figure than either Nancy or myself, Susie said to him, "Hi, what time does the meditation start?" She said she had heard so much about the Maharish (she pronounced it to rhyme with hashish, omitting the final vowel), and her friends in Scarsdale had said, just before she left, kiddingly, that she ought to forget about the Taj or any of that and just go and see the Maharish, and well, here she was. On the path she looked suspiciously around her, as if fearful of snakes or dead things.

"Ten days in India and you're not supposed to be afraid of anything," she said.

In the Maharishi's house we sat on yellow cushions, and Nancy introduced the Smithlines and the helicopter pilots. The movement had bought the Maharishi a twin-engine Beechcraft, but he needed a place to land it.

"Nothing but the best, Maharishi," Nancy said.

The talk concerned itself entirely with arrangements for the Maharishi's flight that afternoon, first to see his ashram from the air and then to survey construction sites. The aviation gas to refuel the helicopters had not yet arrived from Delhi by truck, a delay for which the pilot apologized, and so Nancy suggested that the rest of us go up the hill to lunch.

The assembled meditators looked doubtfully at the Smithlines. Susie refused the food and asked only for a cup of boiled water, into which she emptied a package of powdered Sanka. Fred continued filming, walking around the table and asking people about the degrees of their God-consciousness.

Nobody said anything, and Nancy, conscious of the awkward silence, told an anecdote about a Tibetan friend of hers who'd sold his yak and left his native country a few years ago to marry an American girl. The girl had met him on a world tour, but when the Tibetan arrived at the Los Angeles airport, she thought he looked strange and so abandoned him.

"What's a Tibetan supposed to look like, for God's sake?" Nancy said. "Nobody looks more like a Tibetan than a Tibetan . . . if you know what I mean."

AFTER LUNCH, when the aviation gas had arrived, the Maharishi walked solemnly down the hill in front of a straggling procession of monks, Hindu porters, kitchen boys, meditators, and frightened animals. John Lennon took movies of the crowd of Indians on the beach, the Indians with box cameras took pictures of John Lennon, and Fred Smithline kept shooting great stuff of everybody.

The Maharishi gazed lovingly at the helicopter, like a child looking at an enormous, complicated toy. He absently clutched a bouquet of flowers, which, when the engines started, dissolved in shreds. He hardly noticed, still smiling and never turning away from the noise and the blowing sand. A monk placed his antelope skin on the co-pilot's seat, and somebody else handed him a single dahlia as he adjusted his seat belt. Nodding and smiling and waving in mild benediction with his flower, he cast his blessings from higher and higher up as the helicopter lifted into the clear air.

The racket of the helicopters circling overhead interrupted many meditations that afternoon, and more than the usual number of people showed up for early tea. The ensuing conversation veered off in the customary oblique directions.

Simcox and two or three of the other young Americans raised mild objections to the Maharishi's involvement with modern technology. Like O'Shea, they had expected romantic asceticism, of the kind they'd read about in books, and they'd been prepared to live on roots and berries. Their dissent was never harsh, reflecting instead a wistful disillusionment.

"In the beginning," Simcox said, "everybody was paranoid about expressing one little harmless doubt."

Since the first week, however, they'd gone back to smoking cigarettes and wondering if they would finish the course. The meditation they still thought helpful, but they found themselves spending less time alone in their rooms, and they talked more frequently of the salads and other pleasures they remembered in California. Mike Love, the lead singer of the Beach Boys, confessed that stray sexual images sometimes intruded upon his meditations.

"On a very gross level, man," he said.

Among the many others who came that afternoon for tea, Geoffrey reported a meditation the night before in which he'd seen landscapes such as those painted by Hieronymus Bosch, and Anneliese said she'd been without sleep for many nights, healing people with unaccountable pain. A hearty, blond Englishwoman named Edna, who'd been an opera singer in her youth, appeared in leopard pajamas, breathing deeply and swinging her arms in a bracing, athletic way. For some days she'd complained of her meditations as "a ghastly bore," but the new light in her face suggested sudden improvements.

"Two hours of perfection, darlings," she said to us. "Absolute perfection. And then you know all the rest is illusion, isn't it so, darlings?"

An Australian poet named Michael announced that he'd been lying in a hammock for several hours, and there, under his blankets, he'd understood the world and everything in it as aspects of "the cosmic joke." He preferred the shorter poetic forms, he said, on the order of Japanese haiku, and usually he began with a heavy sheaf of manuscript before he refined the thing down to its essence. His most recent poem he'd been writing for three months, and he thought he'd just about got it right. I asked him to recite it, and with a shy smile, looking off at the monkeys chasing one another through the trees, he did so.

"The Buddha sat," he said, "and would not say."

THE BEATLES arrived toward evening, and Harrison, who was sitting nearest to me at the table, remarked that if he could turn everybody on to transcendental meditation and Indian music, then he could go. Somebody asked him what he meant exactly, and he said, "You know . . . out . . . like on a road tour when you leave for the next town."

Somebody else asked him about his own meditations, and he said his mantra was an English word. This caused considerable surprise because it was assumed that into most people's ears the Maharishi or one of his deputies had whispered unintelligible Sanskrit syllables. Nobody, of course, ever told anyone else his mantra, because to do so would damage them, but that was the common understanding. Harrison further astounded everybody by saying he assumed the Beatles all had the same mantra. He didn't know for sure, but his appeared in Lennon's song "I Am the Walrus."

The night balloons appeared in the lecture hall, Geoffrey mistook them for decorations in honor of the god Shiva's marriage to the goddess Parvati. The musicians seated on the stage, among them a Sikh wearing slippers that curled at the toes, seemed to support his assumption.

"How nice," he said. "Shiva day."

We talked of Shiva's many tricks and disguises, which so pleased Geoffrey that he didn't mind when it turned out he was wrong about the balloons. Like the musicians, they had to do with George Harrison's birthday.

The Maharishi brought the Beatles onto the stage with him, and they sat on cushions to one side of his platform while a pundit from Rishikesh, himself a wise man of wide reputation, began a lyrical Hindu chant. Other monks made their way about the stage on their knees, dabbing yellowish smudges of ocher mixed with saffron on the foreheads of the Beatles and their wives.

"To cool the nervous system," Geoffrey said.

The chant lasted for what seemed like a long time. Every now and then the Maharishi affectionately stroked Harrison's head, and Edna, in her leopard pajamas, moved discreetly through the audience, handing each of us a garland of wet, fresh marigolds.

"To give to George," she said.

When the chanting ceased, we all walked up to the stage and placed our garlands around Harrison's neck, until in the end, embarrassed and smiling sheepishly, he looked like a man in a life jacket. The Maharishi then spoke to us in a long and dreaming soliloquy, his head tilted to the side like a bird's and his voice more musical than I'd ever heard it, as if he were conjuring benign spirits from the incense-heavy air.

There was a good time coming, he said, and a great new hope abroad in the world. Ever since he'd seen George Harrison and his blessed friends, the Beatles, he knew his movement must succeed and that men would no longer suffer.

At the end we all sang "Happy Birthday" to George, to whom the Maharishi presented a cake with two candles and a plastic globe that he offered upside down, saying, "This is the world. It needs to be corrected."

The laughter and applause subsided, and then the Maharishi led everyone into a meditation, the long silence at last being softly broken by a single note plucked on a stringed instrument. That note I remember as indescribably lovely, holding within it a glimpse of infinite possibility, as if it had arrived from someplace as far off as the calm height from which the Maharishi spoke to us. Slowly the melody took shape, faintly supported by the rhythm of a drum.

Donovan arrived on the evening of the following day, walking up the sandy path to the gate with his guitar over his shoulder and a cigarette drooping from the corner of his mouth. His friend, Gypsy Dave, carried their few belongings in a knapsack. From a distance I saw them confer with the Hindu guards, who at first didn't recognize them, and then a monk came and conducted them up the hill past the charcoal fires burning at the corners of the paths.

Instead of a lecture that night we heard the pundit from Rishikesh in another chant (this time, to Geoffrey's delight, celebrating Shiva's marriage to Parvati), and afterward Donovan and George Harrison discussed the music.

They sat across from each other at the table under the trees, the other meditators listening as if for momentous announcements. (As always, when present at conversations between high-ranking celebrities, the others assumed the characteristics of townspeople watching from doorways as the sheriff walked out to meet the man named Slade.) Donovan had light eyes and an almost childish face, and both he and Harrison, conscious of the attendant interest, delayed their opening remarks.

The candles flickered on the table, and across the river we could see the lights of the antibiotics factory built with Soviet foreign aid. At last Donovan said, "It built."

Harrison nodded approvingly.

"It's rock," he said. "That's what it is."

Everybody smiled, and there followed a general agreement that the chant had been a groove. Harrison briefly mentioned his idea about ear plugs replacing record players (so that people could hear the music better) and also his conception of the academy the Beatles hoped to build in London. The Maharishi had great hopes for the academy, and Harrison assumed the group could raise enough money to build it by giving a single concert. "Figuring the tax deductions for that sort of thing," he said. He envisioned a large and colorful place where the kids could dance, and I sadly remembered the proposals of some of the older meditators, who had spoken to me of remote sanitariums surrounded by neat lawns.

The Beatles seldom stayed late at the table, preferring to retire to their bungalows and the comforts they had brought from London. They had tapes of their own and other people's music, also a large supply of canned goods. They even had their road manager with them, a man named Malcolm Evans who obligingly practiced the meditation; and if they ran out of anything, Evans sent for more.

Before leaving for the night, Harrison and the others filled their hot water bottles from the pots in the primitive kitchen. The nights were still cold at that time of year, and Donovan, who stayed to drink another cup of tea, borrowed an extra blanket.

Donovan seemed as sweet and vulnerable as the others, speaking in an almost inaudible voice and talking about the terrible time last summer at the D.A.R. auditorium in Washington. He'd found the place unsympathetic, and there had been police in the back of the hall, waiting for the riot that never occurred. Meditation calmed him before his concerts, he said, and the kids in the United States he thought very beautiful, in search of spiritual peace instead of a cheap sensation in the pit of their stomachs. Gypsy Dave, a big, shambling man with long sideburns, smiled and poured the tea and didn't say much of anything.

The next morning it rained, and Mia came back. Simcox confessed his amazement, and people who'd seen her going to the Maharishi's house reported that she looked much better than when she'd left, less harassed, they said, and with a clearer light in her eyes.

She appeared at lunch, wearing white cotton pajamas and gold-rimmed glasses. In conversation with John Lennon she said she'd been to Goa, and there, with her brother, she'd bought a stove for a few rupees and lived on the beach for a week.

"You've got to do it right, to be with the people and never mind the rotten conditions," she said. "Otherwise you miss the magic of this magical land."

Her voice had a lost but intelligent quality to it, and with Lennon she could talk as if to somebody who understood. They'd traveled across the same high plateau of fame, where the air is different than in other places, and they had "all of it" at a young age. They mentioned the "boxed-in" generation, the people older than they who lived with silly, artificial rules and insisted on "putting everything in bags."

Later that afternoon, watching the rain squalls on the river, she talked about her own pilgrimage to the ashram. A romp, she called it, like being a kid again.

"I'm flying from flower to flower," she said, "looking for a place where people will let me be."

She said nothing about the tiger hunt or about quitting the place a few weeks before; the Maharishi had been glad to see her and had restored her to her place in the front row, together with Donovan and the Beatles and Mike Love. There was "great wisdom lying around," she said, but most people missed it because they got hung up with television sets and cars and their names in the paper.

"Oh, wow," she said. "They think bliss consciousness is when you get those things. But when you make it, when you have it all, what then?"

ON MY last morning there the storm passed over, leaving behind it one of those freakish spring days that shift between sudden clouds and bright sun. At breakfast a porter brought a note from a man at the gate who, he said, wore a jewel in his turban. The note read: "We have shot a tiger. Anyone interested is welcome to come and see it."

We'd heard rumors of tigers in the surrounding hills, likewise of elephants, but none of us had ever seen them. Ringo, who also was leaving that day, figured the note to be a photographer's trick.

"A mile down the road," he said, "and twenty of 'em pop out of the trees."

He and Maureen missed their children, he said, and the long meditations he thought he could practice just as successfully at home. Also the flies bothered him. With the approach of the hot weather, the flies had begun to settle on the food, and Maureen liked the flies even less than he did. They had consulted the Maharishi on the subject, but the Maharishi told them that to people lost in their meditations, the flies no longer mattered very much.

"But," said Ringo, "that doesn't zap the flies, does it?"

I left him arranging with his road manager about a car and went to say good-bye to the Maharishi. He received me in the small porch of his bedroom, and through the windows I could look out on the familiar view of the Ganges.

We talked mostly of metaphysical things, about his movement and the revival of a religious spirit in the West. He wanted to make sure, however, that I understood about the drugs. Rumors had reached him that certain people on his ashram openly discussed marijuana and LSD, but he hoped I knew they no longer used such things. I said I did, and he smiled in a kindly and satisfied way.

"Meditation brings the satisfaction in the mind which students seek in drugs," he said.

We talked also about war, which he described as "a nuisance," and about the American mind, which he thought "so very precious" for the world. The power of the tree, he said, comparing the other peoples of the earth to the bark and branches.

Like the Indian reporters, I asked him about the money invested in his organization, but he only laughed and said he had no idea about budgets.

"Somebody must know," he said. "It's only unknown to me. I keep saying, 'Do this, do that.' How they do it is their headache."

Neither would he answer questions about himself. From an assistant I'd learned that as a young man, before seeing the Guru Dev in a religious procession, he'd studied physics at the university in Allahabad. Beyond that he told me nothing, explaining that he didn't think much about himself and that the personality of a man was but a passing and not very important thing. At the end he presented me with a rose.

"Mention my love for my master," he said. "I consider myself only a loudspeaker."

Walking through the vegetable garden, I encountered Mia Farrow playing with a flower and smiling at her own secrets. She thought she'd heard the scream of a wild peacock in the woods, she said, and George Harrison had promised to teach her the guitar. Unhappily, she had to go to London next week to do a movie with Elizabeth Taylor, but she knew she would come back to India, and maybe she would buy a place near Bombay.

Geoffrey and Anneliese I met on the sandy path leading down to the river. They gave me marigolds and oranges, and Geoffrey said something about the color of the sky. It reminded him of El Greco, and he wondered if I quite appreciated the subtle textures at the edge of the horizon.

I still remembered them smiling at me as I turned away toward the ferry and the passage across the Ganges. From the opposite shore, I saw them all again, at a distance and for the last time. By a trick of the weather on that sudden, shifting day, it was raining on my side of the river, but they remained in the clear sunlight. I saw them as small bright figures, sitting in a circle on the stony beach against a background of immense trees. I thought I could see the light reflecting from the Maharishi's white robe, and I knew they had gathered to listen to Donovan sing.

Lost Horizon

FEBRUARY 1979

In the late autumn of 1978 I found myself besieged by people asking bewildered and angry questions about San Francisco. Those of them who knew that I had been born in that city assumed that I had access to confidential information, presumably at the highest level of psychic consciousness. Their questions were indistinguishable from accusations, as if they were demanding a statement about the poisoning of the reservoirs. Who were those people that the Reverend Jim Jones murdered in Guyana, and how did they get there? Why should anybody follow such a madman into the wilderness, and how did the Reverend Jones come by those letters from Vice-President Mondale and Mrs. Rosalynn Carter? Why did the fireman kill the mayor of San Francisco and the homosexual city official? What has gone wrong in California, and who brought evil into paradise? Fortunately I don't know the answers to these questions; if I knew them, I would be bound to proclaim myself a god and return to San Francisco in search of followers, a mandala, and a storefront shrine. Anybody who would understand the enigma of San Francisco must first know something about the dreaming narcissism of the city, and rather than try to explain this in so many words, I offer into evidence the story of my last assignment for the *San Francisco Examiner.*

I had been employed on the paper for two years when, on a
Saturday morning in December of 1959, I reported for work to find
the editors talking to one another in the hushed and self-important
way that usually means that at least fifty people have been killed. I
assumed that a ship had sunk or that a building had collapsed. The
editors were not in the habit of taking me into their confidence, and
I didn't expect to learn the terms of the calamity until I had a
chance to read the AP wire. Much to my surprise, the city editor
motioned impatiently in my direction, indicating that I should join
the circle of people standing around his desk and turning slowly
through the pages of the pictorial supplement that the paper was
obliged to publish the next day. Aghast at what they saw, unable to
stifle small cries of anguished disbelief, they were examining twelve
pages of text and photographs arranged under the heading LOS ANGE-
LES—THE ATHENS OF THE WEST. To readers unfamiliar with the ethos
of San Francisco, I'm not sure I can convey the full and terrible
effect of this headline. Not only was it wrong, it was monstrous
heresy. The residents of San Francisco dote on a romantic image of
the city, and they imagine themselves living at a height of civilization accessible only to Erasmus or a nineteenth-century British
peer. They flatter themselves on their sophistication, their exquisite
sensibility, their devotion to the arts. Los Angeles represents the
antithesis of these graces; it is the land of the Philistines, lying
somewhere to the south in the midst of housing developments that
stand as the embodiment of ugliness, vulgarity, and corruptions of
the spirit.

Pity, then, the poor editors in San Francisco. In those days there
was also a *Los Angeles Examiner,* and the same printing plants supplied supplements to both papers. The text and photographs intended for a Los Angeles audience had been printed in the Sunday pictorial bearing the imprimatur of the *San Francisco Examiner.* It was

impossible to correct the mistake, and so the editors in San Francisco had no choice but to publish and give credence to despised anathema.

This so distressed them that they resolved to print a denial. The city editor, knowing that my grandfather had been mayor of San Francisco and that I had been raised in the city, assumed that he could count on my dedication to the parochial truth. He also knew that I had studied at Yale and Cambridge universities, and although on most days he made jokes about the futility of a literary education, on this particular occasion he saw a use for it. What was the point of reading all those books if they didn't impart the skills of a sophist? He handed me the damnable pages and said that I had until five o'clock in the afternoon to refute them as false doctrine. The story was marked for page one and an eight-column headline. I was to spare no expense of adjectives.

The task was hopeless. Los Angeles at the time could claim the residence of Igor Stravinsky, Aldous Huxley, and Christopher Isherwood. Admittedly they had done their best work before coming west to ripen in the sun, but their names and photographs, together with those of a few well-known painters and a number of established authors temporarily engaged in the writing of screenplays, make for an impressive display in a newspaper. Even before I put through my first telephone call, to a poet in North Beach experimenting with random verse, I knew that cultural enterprise in San Francisco could not sustain the pretension of a comparison to New York or Chicago, much less to Periclean Athens.

Ernest Bloch had died, and Darius Milhaud taught at Mills College only during the odd years; Henry Miller lived 140 miles to the south at Big Sur, which placed him outside the city's penumbra of light. The Beat Generation had disbanded. Allen Ginsberg still could be seen brooding in the cellar of the City Lights Bookshop, but Kerouac had

left town, and the tourists were occupying the best tables at
Cassandra's, asking the waiters about psychedelic drugs and for connections to the Buddhist underground. Although I admired the work
of Evan Connell and Lawrence Ferlinghetti, I doubted that they would
say the kinds of things that the city editor wanted to hear. The San
Francisco school of painting consisted of watercolor views of Sausalito
and Fisherman's Wharf; there was no theater, and the opera was a
means of setting wealth to music. The lack of art or energy in the city
reflected the lassitude of a citizenry content to believe its own press
notices. The circumference of the local interest extended no more
than 150 miles in three directions—as far as Sonoma County and
Bolinas in the north, to Woodside and Monterey in the south, and to
Yosemite and Tahoe in the east. In a westerly direction the civic imagination didn't reach beyond the Golden Gate Bridge. Within this narrow arc the inhabitants of San Francisco entertained themselves with
a passionate exchange of gossip.

At about three o'clock in the afternoon I gave up hope of writing a
believable story. Queasy with embarrassment and apology, I
informed the city editor that the thing couldn't be done, that if there
was such a place as an Athens of the West—which was doubtful—
then it probably was to be found on the back lot of a movie studio in
Los Angeles. San Francisco might compare to a Greek colony on the
coast of Asia Minor in the fourth century B.C., but that was the
extent of it. The city editor heard me out, and then, after an awful
and incredulous silence, he rose from behind his desk and
denounced me as a fool and an apostate. I had betrayed the city of
my birth and the imperatives of the first edition. Never could I hope
to succeed in the newspaper business. Perhaps I might find work in
a drugstore chain, preferably somewhere east of St. Louis, but even
then he would find himself hard-pressed to recommend me as anything but a liar and an assassin. He assigned the story to an older

and wiser reporter, who relied on the local authorities (Herb Caen, Barnaby Conrad, the presidents of department stores, the director of the film festival), and who found it easy enough to persuade them to say that San Francisco should be more appropriately compared to Mount Olympus.

I LEFT San Francisco within a matter of weeks, depressed by the dreamlike torpor of the city. Although in the past eighteen years I often have thought of the city with feelings of sadness, as if in mourning for the beauty of the hills and the clarity of the light in September when the wind blows from the north, I have no wish to return. The atmosphere of unreality seems to me more palpable and oppressive in San Francisco than it does in New York.

Apparently this has always been so. Few of the writers associated with the city stayed longer than a few seasons. Twain broke camp and moved on; so did Bierce and Bret Harte. In his novel *The Octopus,* Frank Norris describes the way in which the Southern Pacific Railroad in the 1890s forced the farmers of the San Joaquin Valley to become its serfs. The protagonist of the novel, hoping to stir the farmers to revolt and to an idea of liberty, looks for political allies among the high-minded citizens of San Francisco. He might as well have been looking for the civic conscience in a bordello. A character modeled after Colis Huntington, the most epicurean of the local robber barons, explains to him that San Francisco cannot conceive of such a thing as social justice. The conversation takes place in the bar at the Bohemian Club, and the financier gently says to Norris's hero that "San Francisco is not a city . . . it is a midway plaisance."

The same thing can be said for San Francisco almost a hundred years later, except that in the modern idiom people talk about the city as "carnival." The somnambulism of the past has been joined with the androgynous frenzy of the present, and in the ensuing confusion who knows what's true and not true, or who's doing what to whom and for what reason? The wandering bedouin of the American desert traditionally migrate to California in the hope of satisfying their hearts' desire under the palm trees of the national oasis. They seek to set themselves free, to rid themselves of all restraint, to find the Eden or the fountain of eternal youth withheld or concealed from them by the authorities (nurses, teachers, parents, caliphs) in the walled towns of the East. They desire simply to be, and they think of freedom as a banquet. Thus their unhappiness and despair when their journey proves to have been in vain. The miracle fails to take place and things remain pretty much as they were in Buffalo or Indianapolis. Perhaps this explains the high rate of divorce, alcoholism, and suicide. The *San Francisco Examiner* kept a record of the people who jumped off the Golden Gate Bridge, and the headline always specified the number of the most recent victim, as if adding up the expense of the sacrifice to the stone-faced gods of happiness.

GIVEN THEIR suspicion of civilization, the wandering tribes have little patience with institutional or artistic forms, which they identify with conspiracy. Who dares to speak to them of rules, of discovering form and order in the chaos of feeling? Like the detectives in the stories by Dashiell Hammett and Raymond Chandler, the California protagonist belongs to no Establishment. He comes and goes as effortlessly as the wind, remarking on the sleaziness and impermanence of things, mocking the shabby masquerades (of governments and dictionaries) by which the prominent citizens in town cheat the innocent children of their primal inheritance. No matter how grandiose the facade, every door opens into an empty room. Without rules the bedouin's art and politics are as insubstantial as tissue paper or interior decoration, and in the extremities of their sorrow they have nothing to hold on to except the magical charms and amulets sold by

mendicant prophets in the bazaars. Sometimes the prophets recommend extended vacations at transcendental dude ranches.

Maybe this is why the conversation in California is both so desperate and so timid. What passes for serious talk, at the Center for the
Study of Democratic Institutions as well as in the cabanas around the
pool at the Beverly Hills Hotel, has the earnest texture of undergraduate confession. Everybody is in the midst of discovering the obvious. Middle-aged producers, well-known for their greed and cunning,
breathlessly announce that politics is corrupt, that blacks don't much
like whites, and that the wrong people get killed in the wrong wars.
Women in sunglasses enter from stage left saying that they have just
found out about Freud; somebody's literary agent astonishes the company with a brief summary of the French Revolution. Nobody wants
to ask too many questions because usually it is preferable not to
know the answers. More often than not the person to whom one happens to be speaking turns out to be playing a part in his own movie.
Given the high levels of disappointment in California, people retire
to the screening rooms of their private fantasy. The phantasmagoria
that they project on the walls seldom bears much resemblance to
what an uninitiated bystander might describe as reality. Thus if a
man says that he is a writer, it is possible that he writes notes to his
dog, in green ink on a certain kind of yellow paper that he buys in
Paris. If a woman says she's an actress, it is possible that she once
stood next to Marlon Brando in an airport and that he looked at her
in such a way that she knew he thought she was under contract to
Paramount. To ask such people many further questions, or to have
the bad manners to remember what they were saying last week or last
year, constitutes an act of social aggression.

CALIFORNIA IS like summer or the Christmas holidays. The unhappy
children think that they are supposed to be having a good time, and

they imagine that everybody else is having a better time. Thus the pervasive mood of envy and the feeling, common especially among celebrities, that somehow they have been excluded from something, that their names have been left off the guest list. In New York nobody wants to be David Rockefeller. They might want his money or his house in Maine, but they don't want to change places with the fellow, to actually wear his clothes and preside over the annual meeting of the Chase Manhattan Bank. But in California people literally want to be Warren Beatty, or Teddy Kennedy, or Cher Bono. If only they could be Teddy or Warren or Cher, even for a few hours in a car traveling at high speed on Sunset Boulevard, then they would know true happiness and learn the secret of the universe.

In California so many people are newly arrived (in almost all declensions of that phrase) that their anxieties, like those of the parvenus in Molière's plays, provide employment for a legion of dancing masters (i.e., swamis, lawn specialists, hairdressers, spiritual therapists, swimming-pool consultants, gossip columnists, tennis professionals, et cetera, et cetera) who smile and bow and hold up gilded mirrors as false and flattering as the grandiose facades with which their patrons adorn the houses built to resemble a baroque chateau or a Spanish hacienda. The athletic coaches of the human-potential movements take the place of liveried servants in the employ of the minor nobility. Every season since the Gold Rush, California has blossomed with new money—first in gold, then in land, cattle, railroads, agriculture, film images, shipbuilding, aerospace, electronics, television, and commercial religions. The ease with which the happy few become suddenly rich lends credence to the belief in magical transformation. People tell each other fabulous tales of El Dorado. They talk about scrawny girls found in drugstores and changed overnight into princesses, about second-rate actors made into statesmen, about Proposition 13 initiator Howard

Jarvis revealed as a savior of his people. Everybody is always in the process of becoming somebody else. If the transformations can take place in the temporal spheres of influence, then why can't they also take place in the spiritual sectors?

Perhaps this is why California is so densely populated with converts of one kind or another. A young man sets out on the road to Ventura, but somewhere on the Los Angeles Freeway he has a vision. God speaks to him through the voice of a disc jockey broadcasting over Radio Free Orange County, and he understands that he has lived his life in vain. He throws away his credit cards and commits himself to Rolfing and salad. Thus Jane Fonda discovers feminism and Tom Hayden declares his faith in "the system"; Eldridge Cleaver renounces the stony paths of radical politics and embraces the luxury of capitalism; Richard Nixon goes through as many conversions as he finds expedient; and Ronald Reagan begins as an ADA Democrat and ends as the conscience of the Republican rear guard. As with the prophets who gather the faithful in the compounds of pure truth, so the politicians conceive of politics not as a matter of practical compromise but as a dream of power and a fantasy of omnipotent wish.

THROUGHOUT THE decade of the 1960s I kept reading in the newspapers about the revolutions coming out of California, about the free-speech movement at the University of California at Berkeley, about the so-called sexual revolution, about the counterculture and the "revolutionary life-styles" portrayed in the pages of *Vogue*. As recently as last year, people were talking about "the taxpayers' revolt," as if, once again, California were leading the nation forward into the future. Sometimes when reading these communiqués from the front I am reminded of Lenny Bruce and the bitter jokes with which he used to entertain the crowd at the hungry i in San

Francisco. California sponsors no revolution and only one revolt. This is the revolt against time. In no matter what costumes the self-proclaimed revolutionaries dress themselves up, they shout the manifesto of Peter Pan. They demand that time be brought to a stop. They declare time to be circular, and they say that nothing ever changes in their perpetual summer, that they remain forever suspended in the enchantment of their innocent garden. History is a fairy tale, in which maybe they will consent to believe on the condition that the scripts have happy endings. The media advertise California as the image of the future, but to me the state is the mirror of the past—not the recent, historical past but the ancient and primitive past of ninety thousand years ago, with the light of paleolithic fires flickering in the windows of the stores on Rodeo Drive.

Even the people who go to California to die hope to find a connection to another world. Maybe they will be initiated into the mysteries of reincarnation, or perhaps they will meet the pilot of a UFO. But most of the people who make the trek across the mountains expect that they will remain forever young. I remember once going to see Mae West in her shuttered house on the beach at Santa Monica. On a brilliantly blue afternoon the house was as dark as a nightclub. Miss West received me in a circle of candlelight and white satin, and although she was in her late seventies she affected the dress and mannerisms of a coquette. The effect was grotesque but only slightly more exaggerated than the disguises worn by people trying to look anywhere from ten to thirty years younger than their age. In California nobody is middle-aged. For as long as they can afford the cosmetics and the surgery, people pretend that they are still thirty-five; then one day all the systems fail and somebody else vanishes into the gulag of the anonymous old. I'm sure that the desire to obliterate time also has something to do with the weather. The absence of clearly defined seasons helps to sustain the illusion of the evangelical present. Perhaps this is also why people make such a solemn business of sport in California. Among people determined merely to be, and who therefore conceive of the world as a stadium, leisure acquires an importance equivalent to that of work. People get very serious about tennis because from the point of view of a child at play in the fields of the Lord, tennis is as serious as politics or blocks.

I left California because I didn't have the moral fortitude to contend with the polymorphousness of the place. It was too easy to lose myself behind a mask, and I had the feeling that I was wandering in a void, feeding on hallucinatory blooms of the lotus flower. The emptiness frightened me, and so did the absence of culture, of politics in the conventional sense, of art and conversation, of the social contrivances that make it possible to talk to other people about something else besides the degree of their God-consciousness, of all the makeshift laws and patched-together institutions with which men rescue themselves from their loneliness, their megalomania, and the seductions of self-annihilation. Had I been blessed with great genius, like Robinson Jeffers perched upon his rock in Carmel, I might have been able to make something out of nothing. But in San Francisco, as in Los Angeles, I woke up every morning thinking that I had to invent the wheel and discover the uses of fire. I needed the company of other men who had roused themselves from sleep and who had set forth on the adventure of civilization.

City Lights

JUNE 1976

A lthough I have listened to a great many people talk about the catastrophe in New York, I have heard little said about the principal reason for it. The usual authorities offer the usual graphs and statistics, making reference to the indices of crime, poverty, ignorance, and municipal debt, but none of them says anything about the national hatred for the freedom of a great city. Nobody likes to introduce the question of prejudice into a conversation supposedly about something else, and I can well understand the general reluctance to admit to so base a sentiment. But without taking into account the metaphysics of the city's distress, the political and economic explanations make little sense.

More than anything else, it is the idea of a city that is in trouble. If a sufficient number of people come to look upon a city as a godforsaken heath, then it is obvious that the city will reflect the majority opinion. Like the streets and the schools, the concept of civilization falls into disrepair because that is what most people want and expect. The proof of worldly ruin gives credence to their theories of transcendental grace.

Much of this is traditional. The idea of a great city never has occupied a comfortable place in the American mind. In both the lit-

erary and political history of the country the city stands as a
metaphor for evil—the port of entry for things foreign and obnoxious
that threaten to pollute the pure streams of American innocence.
Virtue proverbially resides in villages and small towns. For at least
one hundred years the rhetoric of political reform has borrowed its
symbolism from the Bible and the visionary poets. Under the open
sky (or a reasonable facsimile thereof) the faithful gather by the fire-
light to denounce the Wall Street interests and the big-city political
machines.

So also the dominant voice in American literature. The writers of
genius wander off into the wilderness of self, there to seek their own
salvation rather than to discover an image that might explain their
age. Thoreau beside his pond and Melville in the vastness of southern oceans contended with apparitions of their own devising. Their
contemporary followers do likewise, going on pilgrimages to Las
Vegas or sending back cryptic accounts of their meetings with
Mexican shamans.

THE SUPERSTITIONS associated with the fear of cities enjoyed a
renaissance during the decade of the 1960s. In a period that gave
rise to a frenzy of purification, both moral and environmental, the
location of the ideal good moved further inland on the gypsy wagons
of the counterculture. The religious and political movements of the
decade (often so similar as to be mistaken one for the other)
promised the fulfillment of self and an end to ambivalence. Eugene
McCarthy campaigned for President on a platform not much different from those supporting Bob Dylan, Eldridge Cleaver, Charles
Reich, Billy Graham, Abbie Hoffman, Timothy Leary, and the Sierra
Club. Most of these people declared themselves prophets of one
kind or another, crying in the wastelands of injustice. They professed a common aversion for the virtues applicable in cities, for

anything that suggested the ambiguity of irony, tolerance, civility, or restraint. Who had time for the civic virtues when Mephistopheles loomed on every horizon? All institutions large enough to employ more than twenty people came under suspicion merely because they represented complexity. Every scientific advance was seen as an omen of death, every Asian peasant a Communist in embryo, every democratic compromise an offense against the single-mindedness of the heart's desire.

The media exaggerated the claims of righteousness because they were so easy to render into dramatic form. Subtlety presents insoluble problems to the producers of television news. As a result of the technical limitations the prevailing fashion moved from anonymity to celebrity and from the uncertainty of freedom toward the guarantees of redemption.

Throughout the whole of the 1960s a vast multitude left New York for the islands of the blessed—writers going off to Nantucket to write the Great American Novel, college students and middle-aged women climbing the foothills of the Himalayas in search of the peace which passeth all understanding, corporation lawyers buying farms on which to grow organic vegetables in Nova Scotia. The writers seemed the most misguided of the pilgrims. More than most people, writers draw their strength from the diversity of the city. In a city nothing is quite what it appears, and so the writer who would understand the nature of mankind must constantly revise his own definitions. Certainly no dramatist could prosper in a village, and I can think of few novelists who, lacking an acquaintance with cities, wrote anything but pious nonsense. The peace of the country is the peace of a deserted battlefield, its silence the silence of an empty room.

The excitement of a city is its sense of infinite possibility, of its ceaselessly becoming something else. It attracts librarians as well as actors, stockbrokers as well as lawyers, police detectives as well as

jazz musicians. In the city they can follow whatever beast they have
in view with a minimum of interference from the authorities. Nobody
asks them to constantly explain their purpose. The city offers them a
blank canvas on which to draw whatever image they have the
courage to conceive. They remain free to join the minority of their
own choosing. Among people whom they regard as their equals, who
share the same obsession for Baroque music or Edwardian licen-
tiousness, they can come and go in whatever direction their spirit
beckons. The freedom of the city is the freedom of mind and the
freedom of expression.

So precious is this freedom that the inhabitants of the city pay an
excessively high price to obtain it. What provincial opinion regards
as unmitigated evil—bad air, noise, crowds, tenements, dirt, heavy
taxes, corrupt government, and crime—the resident of the city
regards as the cost of liberty. It is in the nature of great cities to be
filthy, loud, and dangerous (cf. Elizabethan London and the Paris of
the Enlightenment), but the freedom of mind allows the inhabitants
to ignore or make light of their circumstances. They take for granted
the pervasiveness of corruption, recognizing it as the leaf mold of
civilizations. All markets trade in ideas, and the city's squalor is
judged a fair price for its promise.

The swarming exuberance of a city encourages the rise of such a
thing as civilization precisely because the numbers of different people, so many of them unlike oneself and so many of them armed
(either with weapons or dangerous thoughts), impose an appreciation of tolerance and restraint.

Without those virtues the entire structure falls apart. The multiplicity of forms demands the evolution of a perspective that can deal
not only with contradiction but also with declared hostility. The
police department statistics tell a false story. Where else but in a
city does so much potential violence resolve itself into relative tran-

quillity? Where else is it so easy to publicly revile the law while enjoying the protection of the police? Anybody who has seen civil disobedience in New York and rural Georgia would much prefer the risk of urban indifference to the risk represented by a county sheriff. Better to read one's manifesto in town.

THE COMPLEXITY of life in the city engenders an equivalent complexity of thought and expression, a tone of mind that can make a joke of paradox. It is the ironic sense of humor that allows the dweller in cities to welcome the diversity that so terrifies the dweller in suburbs. Together with so much else about the city (its hypocrisy and sophistication, its emphasis on survival rather than apotheosis) it is the habit of irony that offends the village seer. Prophets see their visions in the primary colors of the desert, preferably at high noon and without benefit of laughter.

Not content with the idea of the city as merely corrupt, the purifying spirit of the 1960s insisted on a more extreme image. In a reversal of meaning reminiscent of George Orwell's bleakest satire, the locus of civilization became synonymous with the abyss. The movies and television serials delighted in showing the city as a killing ground. Predators of all species (pimps, whores, real-estate speculators, detectives, assassins, drug addicts, lawyers) roamed through the streets of New York as if they were beasts wandering across the Serengeti Plain. The successful protagonists learned to rely on their animal instincts. If they chose to remain human and to rely on a belief in reason, they inevitably found themselves dying a brutal death.

The same imagery of despair haunts the newsmagazines and the television announcements. What is curious about the image is its manufacture by people who live, or at least work, in the city. Presumably they come to New York to escape the boredom of the country, and yet they choose to believe that they inhabit an urban wilderness. The fashionable truth takes precedence over anything in their own experience that might bring about a lessening of what I take to be their pleasurable fear. If they live in the suburbs, they know most of the city through the windows of commuter trains. The perspective distorts their sense of the streets. It is their failure of imagination, a failure to believe in other people's passions, motives, and aspirations, that puts them at the mercy of the cliché.

Either that or the fear of cities has to do with the spirit of the age. In a time of general pessimism the necessity of choice presents itself as a burden instead of an opportunity. Freedom itself comes to be seen as perilous. Because the city offers an abundance of choice, people turn and rage against it when they seek to escape the moral dilemmas implied in the making of choices. They can buy anything they want to buy, do anything they want to do; they can steal from unsuspecting orphans and perform nameless acts in the sexual darkness that gives life to the city's infinite transformations. So many whispered promises frighten people. They fear the loss of their Sunday rectitude, of the rules by which they judge and condemn. Far better the quietness of the country, in which few choices confuse the local market and where nobody comes to disturb the villagers with news from Byzantium.

Whenever I read in the papers that yet another corporation has decided to quit New York and move its offices to Poughkeepsie, I think of the United States descending that much further into barbarism. In order to place the effect of the departure in its clearest light, I like to imagine the company vice-president who commutes to an office in the Pan Am Building, proceeding directly to his office on the forty-fifth floor without having to pass through the wickedness of the streets. Even so cautious a vice-president gains something from his brief passage through the city. The jostling of the crowd in the station must give him reason for occasional doubt. So also the view from his high window, southward across the rooftops of the Lower East Side, beyond the shipping in the river, receding into the haze over Brooklyn. Perhaps he might be struck by the diversity of the city, by the huge industry of his fellow citizens, by the immensity of their collective enterprise. Nothing of this will remain to him in the time capsule of the suburbs. Already isolated by the paper world in which the nature of reality comes to resemble a map or a table of organization, my imaginary vice-president will become even more fearful of blacks, Puerto Ricans, rats, pestilence, and crime. His hatred of the city might even aspire to the condition of loathing common among Presidential candidates.

This is unfortunate because the more people who perceive the city as a violent and desolate wilderness, the more useful their disillusion becomes to those who would destroy the idea of the city. As has been said, Americans prefer to live outside the city limits, and both Washington and Hollywood represent the prejudice of small towns. The weight of federal legislation already lies heavily upon the intellectual and financial markets in New York, and the righteous assumptions underlying most government regulations, particularly those pertaining to the environment, favor the rural at the expense of the urban. The same bias animates the technicians who dream of planned economies and the professors of urban science who blandly announce, usually at the behest of the Ford Foundation, that the United States no longer has need of large cities. From the point of view of civil servants and Baptist ministers this is perhaps so, but not from the point of view of anybody still interested in freedom.

Thus my suspicion whenever I listen to politicians talking about what they invariably describe as "the crisis of the cities." The more well-intentioned their avowed intentions, the more I distrust their motives. They come forth with programs and sociological theory, but behind the screens of their statistics I imagine them well pleased with the destruction of an ancient enemy. The prejudice against cities is a prejudice against liberty. To say, as so many people do, that New York is a dark and terrible inferno is to say that they hate and fear the multiplicity of both the human imagination and the human face.

The American Bedouin

JUNE 1978

As has been noticed by numerous columnists and real-estate brokers, the Arab ascendancy confirms the superstitious belief, widely held within the moneyed oligarchies of New York and the feudal bureaucracies in Washington, that the power of money corresponds to the will of God. Americans at all times have been peculiarly subject to this superstition, but they lose what little remains of their skepticism when they see the coming to pass of their most extravagant fantasies. They cannot help but be amazed by the miracle of the Arab triumph. They admire it because it is entirely unearned, because El Dorado rises in the desert as if by magic and thus offers another proof of the divine intervention that also conferred upon the faithful the Florida land boom and the market in computer stocks.

Until the 1920s few people in Saudi Arabia had seen the wheel. The nomadic tribes inhabited a desolate waste, barely managing to sustain the meager levels of subsistence. Within the memory of living men they found themselves enriched beyond the dreams of Tamerlane. The transformation required nothing of the Arabs but their passive acquiescence to the will of Allah and the foreign oil consortiums. They inherited their wealth from people elsewhere in the world who had accumulated it over a period of centuries. The Western societies first had to conceive of political constitutions and the rule of law, to wage civil and world wars, to put down strikes, organize labor unions, impose taxes, and suffer all the other ills to which the modern industrial state owes both its discontent and its existence. The cost of this enterprise in blood, labor, and sacrifice cannot be counted. But to the Arab the cost is as little worth as smoke drifting in the wind.

MUCH THE same light-mindedness has become habitual among those classes within American society that regard themselves as patrician. The number of people belonging to these classes has multiplied since World War II at a rate commensurate with their expectations of privilege. Having come of age during an era of extraordinary prosperity, they assume as their rightful inheritance not only the refinements of Western thought but also an economy of such supernatural power that it renews itself in the same way that the grass comes north with the spring. This superstition excuses them from the bourgeois preoccupation with trade. The fathers and grandfathers might have been merchants and farmers, but the sons and grandsons disdain the work of cultivation. They have taken up the professions that confer an aura of dignity and that allow them to deal with platonic forms rather than with the uncertain shadows in Plato's cave. Whenever possible they have become lawyers and foundation officials, diplomatists, professors, journalists, government functionaries, critics, and critics of critics—people who decide what lesser people will do, who supervise the manufacture of memoranda rather than goods. They have inherited the stewardship of the principal American institutions without knowing what constitutes the burden of their authority, or whence it came, or what it cost their forefathers.

Only the inheritors of fairy gold can afford to live in the magical present, to rest content with fantasy and rumor. If the chronicle of

the Arab wanderings reduces itself to the tale of a man and his
camel, the history of the American mandarinate over the past thirty
years reduces itself to the tale of a man and his trust fund. In many
ways it is the same story, demonstrating the parallel pathologies in
the primitive and decadent modes of barbarism.

The man who makes things—whether families, cities, ideas, or
works of art—learns to look around or behind the mirror of self. He
comes to understand the obduracy of the soil or the stone, and he
measures his victories (usually Pyrrhic) over periods of time longer
than those sold on television. If he depends for his livelihood on the
value of his work in a market, then he also learns something about
other people—what they want, hope for, feel, and believe.

Not so the bedouin. The nomad regards himself as an aristocratic
predator and looks with contempt on the work of cultivators. He
swears fealty only to the sovereignty of the moment and justifies his
narcissism as being a preliminary condition to the search for morality, consciousness, and truth. Dwelling within the texts of the human-
potential movements, he cannot bear to foreclose what he calls his
"options," or to limit the availability of infinite choice. He avoids
"commitments" and finds it demeaning to bind himself to any specific loyalty. Believing the line of succession ends with his claiming
of the inheritance, he feels no obligation to provide for the next generation. Other people play the piano and bear children. The patrician counts it his duty to encourage and admire, to pass vaguely
through the room while displaying the purity of his intentions and
the delicacy of his sensibility. He defines himself as a "generalist,"
a man who knows about rather than knows, a constitutional monarch
who congratulates himself for his appreciation of the rituals of
democracy. This is the aristocratic habit of mind, as characteristic of
Nelson or David Rockefeller as it is of the countless lawyers and
academics who, briefly transformed into federal bureaucrats but

remembering very little about the geography of Alaska or the mechanics of the energy industries, nevertheless take it upon themselves to formulate public policy.

By travelers returning from the Persian Gulf I have been told that few princes can concentrate their interest on anything other than themselves for longer than fifteen seconds. The same brief span of attention distinguishes the American equestrian class. Knowing nothing of history and expecting nothing of the future, they cannot escape the fearful isolation of the present. In their sadness they join together in a melancholy herd. They want so much more than the world offers, and so, like children, they clutch at everything but hold nothing fast. Their desires must be promptly and easily satisfied, or else they become listless and despondent. They build houses but sell them before they have lived in them; they take up and abandon professions as if they were trying on masks, and their lives become a sequence of failed attempts to find their way out of the interior desert of alienation.

No matter that all life, all science, all art depend on organization. To the bedouin, organization implies stasis and death. He associates it with authority, with dying, sickness, and cities. This attitude of mind is currently very much in vogue in the United States. By way of illustration I would offer lists of characteristics affiliated with the nomad and the citizen, and I would invite the reader to decide which list more accurately portrays contemporary American society. As follows:

NOMAD	CITIZEN
wander	build
innocence	experience
power	authority
pleasure	happiness
journalism	literature

polymorphous	heterosexual
barbarism	civilization
wish	will
passion as truth	truth as passion
war	peace
celebrity	achievement
magic	science
certainty	doubt
pornography	drama
legend	history
violence	argument
whore	wife
dream	art
banditry	agriculture
prophecy	politics

Obviously both sets of characteristics can be found within any society, as well as within any individual, at any and all moments of time. Throughout most of its history, the United States has been fortunate in that it could employ the vagrant impulse in the service of the national interest. The United States is a nation of immigrants, and American history is the chronicle of their wanderings: first as discoverers and pioneers, later as frontiersmen and fur traders, bargemen, cowboys, prospectors, bandits, vagabonds, robber barons, steamboatmen, and bounty hunters—all of them traversing a vast and fertile wilderness, drifting down the great rivers and westward across the Great Plains. Who else is the American hero if not the man who goes forth on a ceaseless quest? Melville sends Ahab voyaging through the oceans of the world, and Thoreau sets out on a journey into the wilderness of self. Between them they mark out the trail of American literature. Mark Twain sails down the Mississippi, and Huck Finn lights out for the Territory; Hemingway outfits hunting expeditions and goes in search of the perfect phrase, the perfect truth, the perfect kill—which, in the end, requires the killing of oneself. The popular entertainments, whether mounted as political fable or as violent melodrama, present the wandering hero in the caricature of the gunfighter, the private detective, or the investigative journalist. The archetypal man on horseback (sometimes known as John Wayne or Humphrey Bogart, at other times taking the alias of Gary Cooper, Clint Eastwood, Norman Mailer, or Woodward and Bernstein) rides into the dusty, wooden town (i.e., Abilene or Washington, D.C.) and discovers evil in even the most rudimentary attempts at civilization. The villains invariably belong to "the system," which, as every herdsman knows, represents authority and the loss of innocence. The hero appears as if he were a god come to punish the sin of pride and to scourge the wicked with a terrible vengeance. After the requisite number of killings, the hero departs, leaving to mortal men (i.e., shopkeepers and fellaheen) the tedious business of burial, marriage, and settlement.

Like other politicians before him, Jimmy Carter borrowed what he could of this persona in his campaign for the Presidency. The political candidate traveling thousands of miles in pursuit of public office appears as a romantic figure somehow comparable to the knight errant. The immense labor of the campaign endows the office with a temporary meaning that, once attained, it ceases to possess. The traveling excites sympathetic interest, but the administration of the public trust (unless discovered to be criminal, and therefore allied with banditry) inspires boredom.

MUCH TO everybody's disappointment, the old American frontier closed down its whorehouses and faro games in the early years of the twentieth century. The succeeding generations could make do for a while with the Roaring Twenties, the Depression, and World Wars I and II. But after 1945 the horizon no longer receded into a blue distance. Too many people had become too prosperous, too weighted down with possessions. They had been brought up to believe that they should go on pilgrimage or crusade, but they couldn't figure out where to go. Obviously Vietnam was the wrong place, and at Woodstock it rained. The present generation of nomads, largely urban and affluent, contents itself with the pursuit of pleasure and the excursions made possible by alcohol, pornography, and drugs. What else is the consumer society if not a devouring horde, grazing off the available grass, transforming an oasis into a desolation, and then moving off to next year's greening of America? The so-called gay movements stand in line of succession to the hoboes of the 1930s and the strolling minstrels of the 1960s. The bedouin is always in flight, if not from the railroad police or the narcotics agents then from his own loneliness and anxiety; he finds solace in any fugitive encounter that will relieve his fear of the void.

Most Americans believe that movement, in and of itself, means something, and they confuse the freedom to come and go with the freedom to think and act. About one family in every five moves its household every year. Unknown numbers of people reside in trailers or vans. The poor come north on the rumor of employment or government money; the rich go south on the rumor of tax reductions and eternal youth. Farm children drift into the cities dreaming of wealth and celebrity; city children trek into the countryside with the vague idea of talking to bears. The American bedouin conceives of democracy as a pastoral existence. If not the abundance of nature, then surely the abundance of government will provide the people of the caravan with limitless pasture and privilege.

The prosperous nomad imagines himself blessed by fortune and destined, by right of his innate sweetness, to a heroic journey only slightly less eventful than the wanderings of Odysseus. More often than not he travels at somebody else's expense. Consider the troupe of actors and marabouts who transport their babbling prophecies from talk show to talk show, of camp followers going to Washington to root around for patronage and spoils, of university graduates traveling on trust funds, and business executives feeding on the fat of corporations. The gaudiest of the tribes, sometimes known as "the jet set," shifts its tents from New York to Hollywood to Palm Springs, always with the hope of discovery in next week's love affair or tomorrow's repetition of a conversation between Jackie Onassis and Truman Capote. Much magnified by the gossip-mongering of the media, the gilded figures of celebrity bear witness to the magnificence of Allah's favor.

IF THE nomadic melancholy were confined to the equestrian classes, then it might be dismissed as simply another variation on the truism that unearned wealth brings unhappiness to the people who possess it. Unfortunately the same melancholy and the same sense of magical inheritance pervade the whole of American society.

Business corporations provide their executives not only with munificent salaries but also with privileges worthy of the eighteenth-century French nobility—with yachts, limousines, bodyguards, luxurious food, first-class travel, memberships in golf and shooting clubs. The members of Congress pay themselves $57,500 a year and vote themselves equivalent tokens of self-esteem. The labor unions have become notorious for the practice of demanding payment for work that nobody performs. Professional and amateur criminals, more obviously predatory in their nomadism, carry out their raids against society in the routine manner of commuters going to an office. The unreported income assumed to be taken each year by organized crime, gambling, and prostitution amounts to as much as $100 billion. Just as a rich man sustained by a trust fund feels himself entitled to his sinecure by virtue of his innate dignity, so the man receiving transfer payments feels himself entitled to a benefice by reason of his misfortune.

The general unhappiness communicates itself to the lower reaches of society and helps to make the market exploited by travel agents and the peddlers of sexual illusion. The advertisements in the windows of the media offer plans of escape—from anxiety, boredom, old age, children, time, and the prison around the self. High-powered automobiles hold out, as do divorce and religious conversion, the promise of freedom. On freeways all over the country people defy the speed limit as if they were defying the laws of gravity, imagining that maybe somewhere west of Toledo at one hundred miles per hour they might attain liftoff from the sphere of their sorrow. The airlines hold out promises of romance in the Bahamas or Honolulu, where, after many years in the sand, the weary bedouin might rest himself beside the fountains of a Muslim paradise. Like the primitive nomad or the devotee of movies, the tourist trusts nothing so much as his visual perception. Often he understands little or nothing of what he sees, but he expects to be constantly astonished, to return from his travels with the assurance that the mere fact of having made the passage or seen the movie confers great honor upon his camel.

In the metaphysical regions, the American bedouin wanders in search of the soul's oasis. The holy city of absolute truth shines in the eternal sunlight beyond the next range of abstractions. In New York or Los Angeles, as well as in Houston or Cheyenne, men exchange travelers' tales about their journeys into Freud or Zen. They confuse metaphysics with geography, and they speak of their newfound philosophies as if they were places on a map. Like the twice-born President, they assume that because once they were foolish they therefore have become wise.

The man who spends his life taking postgraduate courses exists in the endless summer of adolescence. Ceaselessly declaring the inadequacy of self, he cannot renounce the self, and so he remains forever dissatisfied—with towns, landscapes, women, and political theories. Instead of asking, Who are they? or, What is this? he asks, over and over and through a thousand novels of confession, Who am I? This question accounts for the strident and self-indulgent character of what passes for American literature (cf. the work of Carlos Castaneda, Erica Jong, et alia), as well as for the waywardness of American foreign policy and the fondness for electing politicians who offer themselves as prophets in the wilderness. The desperate need for celebrity attests to the misfortune of a people who have lost the knowledge of time past and time future. They inhabit the isolation of the present. Who can verify the worth of their presence except the companions traveling with them on the same journey? Of what use is the judgment of posterity?

During the last generation, the nomadic spirit of the consumer markets has weakened the institutional structures of American intelligence and government. Almost indistinguishable from the holy men of the television talk shows, the makers of public policy wend their way back and forth across the country to attend ceremonial councils in the multi-colored tents of the Ford Foundation and the Aspen Institute. They bring news of what they have seen in the desert, and because somebody noticed a strange light in the sky the sheikhs decide that the caravan will travel by a different track. The energy crisis succeeds the water crisis, which succeeded the missile crisis, which succeeded the environmental crisis, which succeeded the racial crisis. The idea of a victorious nation gives way within the space of a few seasons to the idea of a nation betrayed. Abundance becomes scarcity, conservative becomes liberal, big becomes small. One year the Soviet Union appears in the dowdy costume of an old bureaucracy; the next year it presents a "new look" of fierce, totalitarian chic. The best and most forward-thinking people revise the laws of the United States as if they were shifting around the tissue paper in the background of a fashion photograph. They do so without thinking that perhaps they might damage the machinery of government, and their light-mindedness has an unsettling effect on the other nations of the world. Who can be sure that the policy of the United States, like the worth of its currency and the presence of its army in Vietnam, will not vanish like so many nomads in the desert? What can be expected of a society that ignores or abandons the old, the young, the poor, and the sick? How else can this be explained except as the attitude of the bedouin toward the people who cannot keep up with the caravan?

To THE degree that the society cannot relinquish the pleasures of barbarism, the society remains suspended in Paleolithic time. The conquering tribes traditionally have come out of the desert, because in an emptiness that corresponds to their own inner desolation the bedouin can be persuaded to behold visions. Exhorted by fantastic prophecy and believing themselves immortal, the tribes make war to repudiate death and to give the lie to their own feeling of insignificance. Surely this was the story of the 1960s in the United States. Stopping up their loneliness with frenzied professions of faith (in the environment, black power, civil rights, feminism, peace in Asia, Consciousness III, et cetera), the bedouin proclaimed a *jihad* against the institutions that provided them with their patrimony. Throughout the 1960s I kept meeting self-professed revolutionaries, usually at a cocktail party given by George Plimpton, and I was invariably reminded of the French aristocrats in the late eighteenth century who so sympathetically discussed the books and pamphlets that supplied the social theory for the guillotine.

But instead of goats and automatic rifles, the American bedouin possess nuclear submarines and F-15s. Although Mr. Carter explained the arms sale as being conducive to peace, I suspect that it had more to do with the restlessness of a rich nation that couldn't bear to deal itself out of a market or a war. Like the journalist and the desert nomad, the American bedouin has only a weak and unstable sense of self. Isolated in the magical present and lacking the habit of thought, in many ways the rich man can be said to barely exist. How else can he assert his presence except by the use of his money? How else can the United States demonstrate its importance except by providing the wherewithal for the most spectacular of the performing arts?

This debasement of the American mind has sinister results, not only for the United States but also for people elsewhere in the world who look to the United States as the sheltering force for stability, order, and freedom. The democratic idea presupposes the worth of human effort and reason; it implies a continuing process working forward in time, and it presumes that man, if not in this generation then maybe in the next, might learn to rid himself, at least in some small part, of fear, poverty, and injustice. The strength of the idea, which is the strength of the commonwealth as well as of the individual aspirations that make up the commonwealth, rests on the corollary idea of the citizen. The balance of self-government falls apart unless a sufficient number of people subordinate the sovereignty of their immediate desire to the task of making laws, gardens, and families.

Certainly the imams of the media, like the lawyers and muftis who advise the government and the corporations, have no interest in disturbing the dreams of the wandering horde. They rely for their profit on the weakness of the national memory. Cities rise on the foundations of imagination and morality, but imagination and morality need to be cultivated over sustained periods of time. Who or what can restore the American vision of the future and prevent the American desire to build from being contravened by the whoring after Arab money?

The world waits for the United States to rouse itself from the seductions of barbarism. The world waits and grows anxious because if the United States cannot put aside the things of a child, then who can prevent the desert from engulfing the city of Western civilization? The American bedouin sometimes remind me of children in a theater, suspended in the excitement of an endless overture, waiting for the curtain to go up on what they imagine will be the musical comedy of their lives. But life, as Francis Bacon long ago observed, is a theater with no audience.

The Assassin as Celebrity

NOVEMBER 1975

Less than an hour after he had been menaced with assassination in Sacramento President Ford spoke to the California State Legislature about the troubling rise in crime in the United States. Under the circumstances it was a disappointing speech. The little of it that was quoted in the newspapers suggested that the President contented himself with platitudes. "Peace on Tenth Street in Sacramento," he said, ". . . is as important as peace in the Sinai Desert"; "a man or woman or child becomes just as dead from a switchblade slash as from a nuclear missile blast"; "the billions of dollars spent at all levels of government since 1960 have not done the job," et cetera.

The President had looked into the barrel of a heavy-caliber pistol and seen the nearness of his own death (a witness reported that his face "turned completely white"), but he apparently failed to understand that he also had seen a magical transformation. With a single gesture a deranged girl named Lynette Fromme, age twenty-six and dressed in the red robe of an imaginary religious order, had become a national celebrity. Within a matter of hours it became necessary to know about her early sorrow and unhappy childhood, about her belief in "the people's court of retribution," about her squeaky voice and her devotion to the person and murderous fantasy of Charles Manson. By nightfall she had acquired a publicity value temporarily equivalent to that of Henry Kissinger or Barbra Streisand. On the following Tuesday *Time* and *Newsweek* printed her photograph on the covers of 8 million magazines, *Time* taking the trouble to buy space in the New York papers announcing "exclusive photos and passages from Squeaky Fromme's unpublished memoirs . . . the world of the social misfit and psychological cripple . . . fascinating, penetrating reading in this week's *Time.*" I doubt whether Nathanael West, even when drunk and trying for savage irony, could have invented so grotesque a billing.

Unhappily for Mr. Ford's expensive efforts to reduce the national crime rate, the transformation accomplished by Squeaky Fromme (comparable in its simplicity to hitting the jackpot number in the $1 million lottery or being discovered by Russ Meyer in Schwab's drugstore) constitutes a debased but popular interpretation of the American dream. As yet only a few people (among them Arthur Bremer) have been willing to pay quite so high a price for the first five minutes of the six o'clock news, but if the rewards continue to get bigger (book contracts, major motion-picture deals, product endorsements, talk-show appearances) I see no reason why their number should not increase.

I would have felt more hopeful about the President's speech if he had said something to the effect that he presides over a country in which crime so often leads not to poverty, death, or disgrace but to record box-office attendance and high public office. The society that guarantees the profit of criminal enterprise (whether in the form of a Mafia gambling casino or a corporation's theft of its own common stock) can expect to find a great many people wandering through the streets with guns in their hands. This is an awkward thing to say, and I can well understand Mr. Ford's reluctance to do so, but unless he begins with the facts of the matter, I don't know how he can expect to do anything useful. The pretense of virtue obliges the government to spend additional billions of dollars to prove a false premise. The parallel is with Vietnam or with King Canute commanding the ocean. I do not mean to suggest that the United States has descended into anarchy or that most of its citizens do not obey the law. For the most part they do, but for reasons that can be ascribed to common sense rather than to the exemplary conduct of people who hold positions of trust and authority.

EVEN A cursory reading of the newspapers during the past few years would incline a fair-minded man to confuse certain kinds of crimes with national policy and standard business procedure. The CIA employs Mafia assassins to arrange the killing of Fidel Castro; the United States Air Force carries forward a secret bombing of Cambodia. In Vietnam the U.S. Army encourages a tactic of indiscriminate murder and finds, after a prolonged investigation, that the entire burden of guilt rests with Second Lieutenant William Calley. Mr. Ford's predecessor in the White House forswears his oath of office and then retires on a government pension and sells his memoirs (both as a book and a television special) for $6 million. A dismal procession of business corporations (among them Gulf Oil, American Airlines, United Brands, Braniff International, Goodyear Tire and Rubber, Lockheed, Northrop, and Ashland Oil) admit to various charges of bribery and illegal campaign contributions, but in most instances the responsible officials receive a sympathetic vote of confidence from their boards of directors. New York City bankrupts itself because a succession of municipal administrations endorses fraudulent accounting practices; in the same city the United Federation of Teachers follows a policy of extortion (if you don't give us what we want, we will close the schools), and the Board of Education discovers that it can do nothing but pay the ransom. In the less public-spirited quarters of society the drug trades and gambling rackets return an immense profit (possibly as much as $100 billion a year); and the funerals of police officers become more or less commonplace events. In New York the odds on being convicted of a crime stand at one in five, and a conviction for felony murder results in an average jail term of ten years.

If Mr. Ford has any further doubts about the amusements of the crowds with which he so eagerly shakes hands, he might consult the best-seller lists or the Nielsen ratings. His fellow citizens take a romantic view of crime and hold the successful criminal in high regard. More often than not the big money properties require the presence of a heroic predator—the Godfather, Joe Kennedy, Xaviera Hollander, James Bond, John D. Rockefeller, Aristotle Onassis, Meyer Lansky, a great white shark—anybody or anything that takes what it wants and shows an appropriate contempt for something so chickenhearted as the due process of law. A similar ruthlessness is an admired characteristic of the government prosecutor who abuses the rules of evidence in order to obtain a just conviction.

The belief that the ends (always noble) justify the means (sometimes treacherous) corresponds to the idea that anything worth having can be bought for money. To the extent that this is true (i.e., that high government office sells at prices asked for houses in the Bahamas) the extremely rich man becomes equivalent to the idealist commissioned to serve the higher law. Both kinds of men induce in their followers the euphoria of omnipotence. It is the same feeling that surrounds a known killer or a victorious politician on election night. For the time being the people within his sphere of influence believe themselves safe from death, pain, taxes, and disease.

A few months before he was shot to death in Umberto's Clam House, Joey Gallo, the well-known Mafia figure and bon vivant, enjoyed a brief vogue in New York as a fun sort of person to have around. He occasionally appeared at a restaurant frequented by people employed in the manufacture of national images (journalists, movie directors, fashion photographers, et cetera), and his arrival inevitably caused the talk in the room to drop away into abrupt stillness. Over a period of years I had seen a procession of celebrities walk in and out of the same restaurant, but the cognoscenti always managed to preserve an attitude of disdain, pretending to continue their conversations as if they had noticed nothing out of the ordinary. Gallo never failed to impress them, and they could not prevent themselves from offering him the homage of silence. The presence of a man so closely associated with violence and notorious crime carried with it the same kind of giddy excitement that accompanies the first news of a political assassination.

The present admiration of the criminal (both the act and person who commits the act) no doubt arises from what the sociologists would describe as a condition of alienation. As the law becomes a game for lawyers, so also does it lose its meaning for anybody who can't afford the balls and the court and the racquets. If the state can be perceived as hostile abstraction (far away in Washington, where the politicians are always lying), and if too many people have no memory of family or cannot conceive of a nation held together by a common idea of justice, then we must make do with the primitive loyalties of the Mafia. The collective glamorization of organized crime seems to me analogous not only to the psychotic fantasies of the Manson family but also to the wistful longings of those intellectuals who wish that the world could be restored to the spiritual purity of the late Middle Ages. I can understand the desire for simplification, but the celebration of the criminal is a confession of defeat. The predatory mode of doing business depends upon the equation of something for nothing: draw the three of diamonds and live happily ever after; steal another man's invention and sell it into the mass market; borrow from the government and let the next generation pay the debt; fake the soundtrack and try to fix the critics.

All well and good, and maybe even successful, but to what purpose? If I think of the thieves, whores, and confidence men whom I have met, I remember the boredom in their eyes and their lack of interest in anything beyond the next day's scam. Contrary to popular report, the criminal mind is remarkably dull. The grand predators come and go like so many lizards in the desert, killing and feeding and leaving nothing to their heirs except a tape-recorded conversation with David Frost.

No doubt it is unfair to expect President Ford to think of such things at the moment when Squeaky Fromme pointed a gun at his stomach. One virtue of the politician is his willingness to learn slowly, changing his opinion to conform with the opinions held by a majority of his constituents, but unless Mr. Ford learns to recognize his enemies in all their personae (as corrupt judge as well as demented girl), he must bear the constant risk of assassination. Some people might say that a President accepts such a risk with his office, that he is a brave man for doing so, that he should be congratulated for the risk that he also imposes on everybody else in the country. Possibly true, but it is the courage of lost causes and inevitable defeats, the courage of the man who prefers to die with his stupidity rather than try to find a way out of the desert. The newspapers gave the distance between the President and Manson's "main lady" as two feet, but the distance in time was much greater. It was the distance between the Neolithic hunt and the articles of the American Constitution, between the ritual sacrifice of the Aztecs and the science of celestial navigation. The distance is worth preserving, but it is a difficult thing to do in a society that makes celebrities of the people who would destroy it.

Fear of Heights

DECEMBER 1976

O n the same day that Earl Butz was resigning his office as
Secretary of Agriculture I received a letter from a physician in
Minnesota who had reached the conclusion that at least half the
people who died of cancer in the United States probably were com-
mitting what he described as "a form of suicide." Over a period of
thirty years he had become convinced that many of his patients contrived their own illness and early death. Although he presented statistics about the incidence of cancer, he thought that much the same
thing probably could be said about people dying of heart disease,
diabetes, cirrhosis of the liver, accidents, and emphysema. His letter encouraged me to wonder about the human capacity for self-
destruction, and the spectacle of Mr. Butz in tears led me to begin
the inquiry in the realm of politics.

So many politicians have gone out of their way to fall off the public stage in recent years that I wonder if they might be suffering the
effects of vertigo. No matter how they explain it to themselves, or
what they say to the reporters assembled for the solemnities of the
farewell press conference, I cannot help but think that somewhere
in the corners of their minds they know what they're doing. Perhaps
they wish to escape the glare of the television lights; perhaps they

become sick and desperate with feelings of remorse. Surely Mr. Butz must have appreciated the risk of saying anything, much less attempting a joke, in the presence of John Dean. Dean's reputation rests on his talent for betraying confidences, and I'm told by responsible authorities in Washington and California that prudent men make it a point to avoid being seen in his company.

Mr. Butz presumably knew this, and yet he found himself compelled to arm Mr. Dean with the equivalent of a deadly weapon. He might just as well have followed Arkansas Representative Wilbur Mills into the Potomac River or across the stage of a Boston burlesque theater. I cannot hope to guess at these men's reasons for wanting to retire from government. Nor can I hope to guess why President Nixon made recordings of his conversations in the White House, or why Senator Edward Kennedy went off the bridge at Chappaquiddick, or why Representative Wayne Hays persisted in his dalliance with Elizabeth Ray.

Their misfortunes remind me of a story that I read in a newspaper last spring about Grant Keehn, aged seventy-six and formerly the president of the Equitable Life Assurance Society, who was granted a separation from his second wife on grounds of cruel and inhuman treatment. The judge issuing the papers felt moved to write a twenty-four-page decision in which she characterized Mr. Keehn's wife as "a grimly determined, evil-tempered woman who sought to turn an active and successful businessman into a useless and indolent creature, old before his time." The judge said that Mrs. Keehn, a Hungarian woman of romantic provenience, sought to achieve her purpose by "hysteria, screaming tantrums and . . . vicious physical violence practiced on a man thirty-one years older than she and ill-equipped for fistfights with a shrieking woman." Mrs. Keehn never rose before noon, and on most weekends she never rose at all, insisting that her husband "(a) take her shopping and traveling, and (b)

stay in bed with her, catering to her emotional and sexual needs."
Mr. Keehn often arrived at his office with "massive bruises all over
his body and multiple nail and teeth marks"; one morning he
appeared with both his ears bitten and split; on another occasion his
eye was hemorrhaging so badly that his doctors feared blindness.

THE WILL toward self-annihilation is a familiar human characteristic.
The plays of Shakespeare and Sophocles, the history of the Roman
Empire, and the civil wars in Ireland and Lebanon attest to man's
fondness for murdering himself. Even so, and without meaning to
belittle the accomplishment of other nations in other times and
places, I think it fair to say that something in the modern American
spirit reveals a peculiar genius or affinity for the self-inflicted
wound. What other country in the world could make a folk hero out
of Evel Knievel? Or proclaim Chris Burden an artist because he had
the wit to crucify himself on a Volkswagen? Or afflict itself with a
Presidential campaign between two incompetent candidates, each of
them relying on the other's eagerness to discredit himself?

The genius for self-destruction shows up in so many other ways
that I sometimes think that the United States, despite the well-
known rhetoric to the contrary, bears a grudge against the very idea
of a future. I tend to make connections between random or miscellaneous events, and so when I read about the infant mortality rate in
Chicago or New York, I think about violence at the movies. When I
read about the poisonous chemicals flowing into the James River or
pass by slag heaps or wrecked automobiles, I think of 8 million people unable to find work or the enormous numbers of schoolchildren
who cannot expect to receive an education. The waste of people corresponds to the waste of every other known resource. I find further
correspondences between the national levels of drug addiction and
the murderous self-delusion of the Vietnam War, between fifty thou-

sand people killed every year in traffic accidents and the American investment in the international arms trade (roughly $32 billion between 1965 and 1974), between the number of suicides among citizens aged fifteen to twenty-four (up by about 250 percent in the past generation) and the richness of the market in pornographic fantasy. In the realm of social and political ideas I notice that the current fashion in pessimism is appropriate to a literary tradition that celebrates the doomed voyager. The fervent apologists for "The End of Affluence," "The Death of Progress," or "The End of the American Future" remind me of mad Ahab embarked on his hunt for the white whale. When talking to investigative reporters about the villains they have discovered in public office I think of the shiftless private detectives played by Humphrey Bogart, all of them rejoicing in their abandonment to the pleasures of gin and disillusion. The Watergate investigations, recriminations, and confessions of the last four years have come to constitute a subdivision of the entertainment industry. Almost all the principal figures in the conspiracy have published best-selling variants of the canonical text; they continue to wander through the countryside giving lectures and showing slides of their stigmata. Their publishers rely on the all but nonexistent memory of the general public, which also bespeaks a kind of self-destruction. Celebrities come and go like summer moths. With smiles of anxious self-congratulation they pass through the lighted ballrooms of the national media, clutching their proofs of prior existence in the forlorn hope that these might prove to be somehow more useful than passports to oblivion.

Among people determined to do violence to themselves the weight of anxiety takes palpable form. It is a look in the eyes that I associate with three o'clock in the morning. I have seen it in the faces of people who talk about their prospective ruin as if they were children going to a birthday party. They mention a divorce or the loss of their children; they say that they mean to leave town, that they don't care what anybody thinks, that the weather in Stockton isn't as bad as everybody says. Something in their voices suggests that they cannot be persuaded to delay the excitement of immediate departure. Several years ago I had such a conversation with a man who had hoped to become a painter. He had had no success with his painting, and he had decided, at the age of thirty-four, to write television serials. Much to his disgust, he had a talent for melodrama.

"Don't talk to me about it," he said. "I need the money, and for a year I figure I can afford to hate myself."

I wish I had known what to say to him. Early last summer I heard that he had died of stomach cancer. I resist drawing any conclusions about the prior causes of his death, but I cannot forget the expression in his eyes. I'm reminded of it when I read in the papers that a prominent tax lawyer has fallen out of a window or that a child has been devoured by a dog.

In *Civilization and Its Discontents* Sigmund Freud speaks of the ceaseless struggle, both within the individual and within the society at large, between the instinct toward life and the instinct toward death. He goes on to say: "This struggle is what all life essentially consists of, and the evolution of civilization may therefore be simply described as the struggle for the life of the human species. And it is this battle of the giants that our nursemaids try to appease with their lullaby about Heaven."

In the United States the lullaby has a sentimental sound. I think of wistful country boys dragging their guitars through the honky-tonk bars of Southern river towns. They sing of lost love and the world's indifference. The peculiarly American forms of self-destruction follow from the national presumption of innocence. No other hypothesis takes account of so many otherwise contradictory phenomena. I have noticed, for example, that among people newly arrived on the heights of celebrity or authority the well-known fear of failure is surpassed only by the fear of success. Their freedom terrifies them, and the intensity of their excitement exposes them to attacks of conscience. Having been taught to deny the existence of their own aggressions, they sometimes find it impossible to acknowledge the satisfactions to be found in the unleashing of those aggressions. If they discover that they enjoy doing harm to their friends, children, wives, subordinates, husbands, and constituents, then how can they answer the inquisition of their Sunday school teachers? To prove that they still despise the world and all its wickedness, that they have retained, in spite of everything and against heavy odds, the imaginary saintliness of their youth, they often find it necessary to cast themselves into the nearest pit.

In the realm of private affairs this results in the injuries sustained by Mr. Keehn, or in the casualties reported among gamblers and stock-market speculators. The same impulses can produce even more fearful effects in the realm of public affairs. The American experiment has proved so successful in the past two hundred years that I can well understand the fear of divine retribution. Not only did the American people have the courage to raise up a government on the volatile principle of freedom but they also had the temerity to explode an atomic bomb and thereby make nonsense of the Day of Judgment. If the American mind can defy the laws of both God and Newton, then how great must be the temptation to inflict punishment on itself and return to the pantomime of childhood.

At any given moment in history, relatively few people want to protect both the idea and the fact of freedom. A great many people say that they want to do these things, but when confronted with awkward choices it usually turns out that they have been talking about property or the continuance of their customary privileges. Freedom is a troublesome thing to live with or sustain. The condition presupposes a constant struggling with the tyranny on the right and the anarchy on the left. I make the parliamentary division along more or less straight Freudian lines, associating the right-wing position with, among other things, the established religions, King George III, CBS News, the Lockheed Aircraft Corporation, and the harsher judgments of the superego. The left-wing position I associate with the religions of the self, Nixon's conspiracy, the pornographic press, the bomb squads of the IRA, and the perversities of the id. Most people find it extremely difficult to resist the temptation, always and everywhere present, of aligning themselves with either or both of these factions.

Although I can easily appreciate the giddy excitements of giving way to those temptations, I think that they might lose some of their appeal if they could be separated from their corollary assumptions of innocence. I notice that the statisticians report an abrupt increase in the incidence of suicide and child abuse in the week before Christmas every year. Mr. Nixon and Mr. Kissinger no doubt had their reasons for bombing North Vietnam, but it occurs to me to wonder why they ordered the raid on Christmas Eve. In a country possessed of a thermonuclear arsenal, it is a mistake to believe in fairy tales. The citizens of that country can conquer their aggressions, perhaps transforming them into music or architecture, but they do themselves great harm if they pretend that the aggressions don't exist.

Hostages to Fortune

APRIL 1978

Before I had children of my own I used to think that America was the land of the fortunate child. For as long as I could remember, I had heard what seemed like a continuous announcement about the "child-oriented" nature of the society, about the "appalling sacrifices" made on "the children's behalf," about the sacred grove of childhood and the patriotic obligation to defend it against cynics who believed in neither Freud nor Santa Claus. What else was America about if it wasn't about being a child? What else was the American dream if not a dream about children growing up in the shade of green trees, nurtured by camp counselors and football coaches, initiated into the mysteries of the junior prom and the Little League, led safely through the labyrinths of the schools and so out onto the spacious lawns of the successful middle class? Events sometimes might inhibit the fulfillment of the dream, but surely it was true, as the Christmas charities so often and so complacently observed, that Americans loved their children more than life itself.

Until I became a father I had no reason to doubt the truth of this proposition, but about the time my first child reached his second birthday I began to suspect that American society bears a grudge against the future. At first I attributed this impression to the circumstance of my residence in New York City. I live on the East Side of Manhattan, in a part of town not known for its devotion to children. The inhabitants concentrate their attention on their pleasure and ambition, and they prefer to subordinate whatever they can (feeling, thought, virtue, et cetera) to the whims of their all-consuming egoisms. Their belief in the restorative power of money persuades them that they can remain forever young, and to this end they go on crusade through the department stores and the sequences of fashionable amusement, searching for the enchanted mirror in which, at long last and after much travail, they might see themselves reflected in the transfiguring light of immortality. Children obviously make a shambles of this enterprise. They remind their parents of too much that is unpleasant—of death, time, loss, and failure—and so they come to be seen as unwelcome messengers bringing bad news to the prince.

As reprisal for their existence as *memento mori,* children in New York bear the weight of a resentment that sometimes can be mistaken for hatred. The city government assigns a low value to children and spends as little money as possible on their well-being, their safety, and their education. The ruin of the public schools testifies to the extent of the local ill will. Except in a few schools in a few neighborhoods, hardly anybody expects the students to do much more than learn to read the signs in the subway and stay out of jail. The prevailing attitude toward children suggests that they constitute a threatening minority, somewhat comparable to the peasants of the Third World. Either they must be bought off (with presents and federal money instead of with grain shipments and expensive weapons systems) or they must be suppressed. The welfare laws encourage families to abandon their children to a bureaucracy. As with American foreign policy, this practice flatters the vanity of the people who make the laws, but it means that the children brought up under the care of a sullen and ignorant authority have little hope of escaping the nets of violence, crime, and drug addiction.

Just as the antagonism toward children reveals itself in the politics and landscape of the city, so also does it lend force to the social conventions under which the great cause of self-advancement demands domestic sacrifices. In New York much of the supposedly important business takes place in the evening. It is assumed that people will stay late in the office or studio, that they will find time to go to dinner parties with their patrons or clients, that they will attend the lectures, conferences, screenings, and miscellaneous cultural events that constitute their reward for enduring the privations of the city. These arrangements, invariably justified as proofs of high seriousness or an artistic sensibility, have the effect of denying children the company of their parents and parents the company of their children. (In Washington the long hours worked by prominent officials in various departments of government accomplish the same purpose, but the explanations usually have to do with the safety of the Free World.)

Because my children are still very young, both of them under the age of seven, I seldom go out in the evening, and so I miss innumerable occasions to meet the season's novelist or marvel at the gossip of celebrities. People in my own profession regard my absence from these *levées* as a mark of irrational and self-destructive behavior. Well-meaning friends invite me to lunch to explain that I do myself irreparable damage, that I cannot hope to catch the tide of opportunity. How is it possible, they say, that I should choose to read stories to my children when I might have the chance to see Norman Mailer throw a drink at Gore Vidal? If I say that I cannot find a baby-sitter to whom I would entrust my children, they point out that this is an unacceptable excuse. Given the social necessity to neglect one's children, the people who would do so with a reasonable degree of equanimity have no choice but to believe that anybody can take care of a child. To believe otherwise would force them to consider the extraordinary susceptibility of a child's mind, and this would impose upon them a terrifying burden. I can think of nothing more difficult than the rearing of a child. It is a task that requires constant thought, patience, and imagination, and it demands the continual rooting out of one's own childish egoism.

WHEN I first began to think about the antagonism toward children in New York, I assumed that it was a parochial attitude that could be ascribed to the wonders of metropolitan sophistication. But then I began to take notice of reports about the brutalization and neglect of children elsewhere in the country. In Los Angeles the police department estimated that thirty thousand children, many of them under the age of five, were used as objects of pornography. Those who weren't sold by their parents could be bought for the price of a milk shake and a sandwich. In Washington the Department of Labor reported that child-care specialists were paid the same wages as dog-pound and parking-lot attendants. It also occurred to me that among the people in New York who warned me about the tyranny of children many happened to be employed in the manufacture of the images distributed by the national media. This coincidence prompted me to notice the absence of children from the center ring in the circus of the American press. Children were displayed in the sideshows (the women's magazines, *Sesame Street*, three or four columns in the *New York Times* on Wednesdays and Thursdays), and there they were kept unless they could be exploited for a commercial or symbolic purpose. Unless they had been implicated in a sensational or hideous crime (Patricia Hearst, the Vietnamese girl in flames, any child who had been murdered or raped), or unless they could be presented as advertisements for the American way of life (i.e., the children eating cereal in the television commercials), they remained invisible. Even more unwelcome than the Victorian children, who at least were expected to be seen if not heard, American children in the late twentieth century never intrude upon the front pages of the national discourse. Again, as with the fashionable milieu of New York, the resentment of the media could be ascribed to jealousy. Journalists pride themselves on their alliance with momentous change, but in fact they hate and fear anything that threatens to destroy the perpetuity of the moment. Thus they distrust children because children cannot help but embody the movement into the diverse and unknown future. In the mind of a child tomorrow is truly another day, not a rerun of last year's situation comedy or political analysis, and this alarms people who seek to reassure their audience that only the appearances change and that the Old Order, of which they are part, continues to hold its serene dominion.

MUCH THE same thing can be said about most politicians. During election years they make the customary gestures in the direction of "generations yet unborn," but once in office their policies have a way of serving the forces of reaction and justifying the corruptions of the *ancien régime*. They speak of the future in abstractions, as if it were something on the order of Disneyland or the World's Fair of 1939. The vacuity of the present quarreling about the environment and President Carter's energy policy testifies, on all sides of the argument, to the lack of a coherent vision of the future. Hardly anybody knows quite what to say because hardly anybody can conceive of the future as something other than the past. The apologists for both the environmental and the industrial interests cannot see much farther than next week, and so they stare into the mirrors of ideology, in which they discover what they believe to have been true forty years ago. The same unwillingness to visualize the shape of the future accounts for the customary failure of even the most well-intentioned efforts at political reform. Despite the efforts of the past ten or fifteen years, the women's movement has yet to relieve many of the burdens that traditionally fall on women and children. Despite the declining birthrate and the large sums of money invested in government subsidies, the community of impoverished children still constitutes the poorest minority in the United States, and the one that has made the least progress toward the hope of a decent life. The United States sustains a rate of infant mortality higher than that in sixteen other countries, and at least 17 million American children continue to live in hopeless poverty.

The nation spends $150 billion a year under the rubric of education, but of this sum only a small part pays for the teaching of children. As with the numerous poverty programs, the bulk of the money finds its way into the hands of people lucky enough to have something to do with the disposition of the funds. In New York I have heard it said by textbook publishers that without the guarantee of federal price supports they couldn't make a decent profit. It doesn't matter if the students never learn to read or write. In the same way that the Vietnam War provided a market for the makers of munitions, so also do the schools, no matter how degraded, provide a market for inept translations from the French.

By assigning the management of its schools to a bureaucracy, the society achieves in the realm of public policy what parents achieve in the realm of private decision by assigning the management of their children to the medical, educational, and psychiatric establishments. In all instances the authorities can be counted upon to discourage the movement toward radical change. The indoctrination begins at birth.

The hospitals insist that the newborn child be taken away from the mother and placed in a nursery, under strong lights and on a feeding schedule that may or may not accord with its needs. Like most other things prescribed by hospitals, this is done for reasons of institutional convenience. Pediatricians offer advice that conforms to codes of preferred behavior rather than to the development of a particular child. In New York it is common for pediatricians to insist upon the early toilet training of children, even to the point of recommending that a child be locked in a dark room and allowed to cry itself sick. The discipline suits the convenience of the parent, and it is the parent who pays the fees. The legion of child psychologists that arises in every generation, publishing its revolutionary discoveries in the women's magazines, depends for its success on the willingness of parents to remain in a state of perpetual ignorance. It is a difficult thing to observe and to imagine the perceptions of a child; it is much easier to believe in magic and to become enthusiastic about the fashionable theories of the moment.

Children thus serve as objects of experiment, and the psychologists recommend whatever the parents require to relieve their feelings of fear and inadequacy. If the age demands a belief in self-expression, then a generation of schoolchildren must go through the rituals of progressive education. If the values of social justice come to weigh more heavily in the scale of conscience than the values of art or scholarship, then another generation of schoolchildren must suffer the effects of reduced standards and expectations. Whatever will make the parents feel happier with themselves, that is the price that their children must pay.

WITHIN THE wealthier quarters of society the hatred of children often presents itself in the disguise of high-minded moralism. The rich believe themselves entitled to whatever it occurs to them to want, and they resent having to compete with their own children for the available toys and attention. The generation that came of age after World War II assumed that it would inherit the earth, that it could afford everything, that everybody who went to Harvard could be a famous poet or a renowned statesman, and that the stock market, like Aladdin's wonderful lamp, would grant an unlimited number of wishes. When the illusion vanished, parents suddenly recognized their children as rivals or burdensome possessions. Unlike municipal bonds, children couldn't be discounted or sold. The next best thing was that they should be made to appreciate the cost of their maintenance.

During the wilting of flowers in the last days of the Woodstock revolution I can remember parents taking quiet satisfaction in the punishments and retributions visited upon their own children. In particular, I remember a senior partner in a Wall Street investment bank who described, with barely concealed pleasure, his son's arrest in Mexico on a drug charge. A few months in a Mexican jail, said the banker, would teach the boy a lesson. He would learn things that Groton had failed to teach him, and the experience might purify his spirit. He might learn to appreciate the true values in life, among them a proper respect for one's parents.

Variations of the same doctrine appear in the press and commencement addresses. The children had gone too far, taken too many liberties, interpreted too literally the benevolent injunctions to do their own thing. Sermons of a similar nature now accompany the prophecies about the limits of growth and the exhortations to protect the ecological sanctity of Greenwich, Connecticut, and Marin County, California. Seen in a psychological perspective, the politics of environmentalism appear as a part of the first act in the Oedipal drama. The parental and institutional classes play the part of King Laius. They have been to the oracle (in this instance, the fabricators of the zero-growth philosophy), and the oracle has persuaded them their son means to kill them. The son (i.e., the poor or anybody too young to understand the value of property) thus becomes the sacred representation of evil. By striking at the son, the fathers hope to postpone, perhaps indefinitely, the day of their own deaths.

Perhaps this is why so many people, parents as well as pediatricians and bureaucrats, find it convenient to believe that children cannot feel or think. To the extent that children can be conceived of as objects, they can be exploited as a market for junk food, worthless toys, and the newest experiments in education. Considered as an abstraction, the legend of childhood remains comforting to the society as a metaphor for perfect happiness. But in order for the metaphor to sustain itself, the child must not turn into a monstrous Galatea and assert an identity of his own. In the few years that I have been a father I often have heard children being told that their pain doesn't really hurt, that they didn't see what they thought they saw, that they didn't hear what was being said. It becomes necessary to belittle a child's comprehension precisely because the child might understand all too well what is being said and done; if this capacity were allowed to go unchecked, who knows what havoc might be let loose in the streets.

By denying the reality of its children, the society expresses its rage against change. During periods of extraordinary and baffling social flux, the denial undoubtedly takes more embittered forms than it does during periods of relative stability. All well and good, and probably a phenomenon that can be plotted on a sociologist's graph. But if the nation loses its capacity to visualize the progress of the generations into time future, then it also rebels against its hope of renewal.

Confusion Worse Confounded

APRIL 1977

On a Friday afternoon in February I received a telephone call from a gentleman who identified himself as an editor of *Hustler* magazine and who said that he was enlisting volunteers for a defense of the First Amendment. His publisher, Larry Flynt, had been sent to jail in Cincinnati on charges of pandering obscenity, and so the editor had drafted a statement that likened Mr. Flynt's sufferings to those of Alexander Solzhenitsyn. The statement was to appear as an advertisement in the *New York Times,* and the editor was looking for interested parties, most of them in the publishing business, to set their names to it. If Mr. Flynt could be persecuted for the courage of his convictions, then nothing was safe.

Ordinarily it wouldn't have occurred to me to sign any manifesto, no matter what the cause in question. I have an aversion to polemics, partly because I think of them as futile gestures taking place in an empty hall and partly because I am accustomed to seeing them in the hands of overly excited celebrities who have trouble remembering which social justice it is that they have been asked to sponsor on which television show.

But from what I could tell by reading the papers it appeared that Mr. Flynt had been badly used by the courts. Having been convicted of pandering obscenity, a misdemeanor, he had been sentenced to between seven and twenty-five years in prison on a charge of "engaging in organized crime." It wasn't clear what the court meant by this, or why the statute obtained only in Cincinnati. Nor was it clear why Mr. Flynt had been denied bail or why the jury had not seen fit merely to prevent the local sale of his magazine.

The summary judgment reminded me that an angry suspicion of the press has been making itself increasingly manifest during the past two or three years. In New York last spring a federal judge awarded $250,000 to a restaurant because its premises had been invaded by a camera crew from CBS News. During the Congressional hearings into the matter of CBS reporter Daniel Schorr, the more belligerent members of the subcommittee kept asking witnesses to define the press, to tell them of what it consisted and by what divine right, as they chose to put it, did the press set itself above the duly elected representatives of the people. Elsewhere in the country small-town judges had relapsed into the habit of sending reporters to jail.

Within my own sphere of interest I had noticed that I was being accosted, more frequently than in years past, by people who wanted to make fairly long speeches about the vanity, ignorance, and hypocrisy of the press. I found it impossible to disagree with them, but I found it equally impossible to make them understand that it was in the nature of the press to be vain, ignorant, and hypocritical. What, in God's name, did they expect? Did they imagine that it was possible to write *Faust* on an afternoon deadline? Had they not found proof of vanity, ignorance, and hypocrisy in themselves, or in any other institution about which they knew slightly more than what they read in the papers? Their unhappiness always proceeded from mistaken assumptions, as if they expected the press to conform to the idealizations given credence by the Watergate news. They objected to the lackluster but accurate definition of the press as that which gets printed, sold, bought, and read. Their disappointment suggested that they were looking for God revealed as a headwaiter, flatteringly subservient but sufficiently omniscient to answer all their questions and so excuse them from the tedious business of having to think for themselves.

All of which prompted me to take seriously the imprisonment of Mr. Flynt. Not having seen his magazine, I assumed that I could make the conventional argument in support of the so-called free press. The argument relies on the paradox that the freest press is also, by definition, the most licentious press. If it is possible to assert, with Jefferson, that a free press constitutes the hope of man's enlightenment, so must it also be possible, with Balzac and Orwell, to define the press as a compendium of gossip and lies. As an abstract principle the argument has the advantage of symmetry. I think I may have said as much to Mr. Flynt's editor. That was on Friday afternoon.

ON SATURDAY I made the mistake of buying Mr. Flynt's magazine. This complicated the question. Mr. Flynt doesn't make it easy to quote passages from Milton's *Areopagitica*. The juxtaposition would be as ludicrous as the juxtaposition of Larry Flynt and Alexander Solzhenitsyn. Except as a matter of arbitrary impression I never have been able to distinguish between the categories of obscenity, pornography, and erotic art. The words mean different things to different people. One man's good time is another man's sermon. But what was I to say to Mr. Flynt? Looking through the pages of his magazine, I couldn't place him in any category but that of nihilist. He presented me with an object, with a product I conceivably could defend in an argument before the Federal Trade Commission, on more or less the same grounds that I might defend the sale and manufacture of cigarettes or automatic weapons. But what did this have to do with the First Amendment? The First Amendment states that Congress shall make no law abridging the freedom of speech or of the press. But unless I made nonsense of the language, I couldn't see how Mr. Flynt's magazine qualified under the meaning of the word *speech*. Mr. Flynt achieved his effects with the subliminal suggestions of cannibalism, sadism, narcissism, and homicide. I grant that each of these occupations has its pleasures, but what have they to do with speech? How is it possible to construe the degradation of human beings as a constitutional right? Probably I put the proposition in too subjective a form, but I do not know how else to phrase it. In Mr. Flynt's magazine I found myself confronted by the negation of the meaning embodied not only in the First Amendment but also in the idea of civilization. Why should I protect the man who seeks to destroy what so many others worked to build? If I found somebody passing out leaflets that demanded my assassination, would I argue for his right to free expression?

I have no answers to these questions. Neither, apparently, do the courts. In 1973 the Supreme Court failed to define obscenity, choosing instead to assign the task to local jurisdictions. Each community sets its own standards and takes whatever course of action it deems necessary for the protection of the public morals. In theory I can agree with this approach to the difficulty, but what happens when the local jury extends its authority beyond the local newsstand? Obviously the law remains obscure, and I expect that it will be brought back to the Supreme Court for further clarification. But I can see no reason for the press to make loud protestations about the First Amendment. Given the shabbiness of its present circumstances, the press does itself a disservice by choosing to defend its elevated principles on such doubtful and muddy ground as that offered by Mr. Flynt in Cincinnati.

On Monday I called Mr. Flynt's editor and asked that my name be removed from his advertisement. I thought no more about the subject until later in the afternoon when a reporter from the *New York Post* called to ask if it was true that I had abandoned the faith of her forefathers. She went on to say that all the best people in New York literary society (among them John Dean) had subscribed to the declaration. Her line of questioning suggested that the defense of Larry Flynt, eminent pornographer, had become as much of a *cause célèbre* as the Dreyfus affair.

NO WONDER the press has fallen so low in the public esteem. If the leading exponents of what passes for thoughtful opinion make such careless distinctions between their real and their illusory interests, then what can be the worth of the rest of their scribbling? What is the use of listening to people who chase after slogans as if they were butterflies, and by so doing allow themselves to be exploited in no less grotesque a manner than the men and women who pose for the photographs in Mr. Flynt's magazine? The people who plead the First Amendment in Mr. Flynt's behalf no doubt will say (as many of them already have said, although queasy with embarrassment) that if the constitutional guarantee can be breached in this one, admittedly distasteful, instance, then who knows what will happen next? What other trespasses will the state commit? Concede so much as a fraction of the principle, so runs the speech to the freshman class, and the enemies of freedom will descend like ravening crows.

But this is mostly let's pretend, the argument of rich children who can afford to play at being poor. In Czechoslovakia or Chile it would be seen as an absurd joke. In New York, among people who have not the opportunity to make the acquaintance of a totalitarian state, the argument costs less than a ticket to the movies. By pretending to descry fascism on the horizon, the people who would uphold the the-

ory in defiance of the practice ignore the fascism implicit in the
most vicious levels of pornography. Sooner or later the dehumanized
vision of man leads to the raising of pornographic theaters at
Dachau and Auschwitz.

Certainly I couldn't prove such an assertion in a court of law, and
I doubt that I could even carry the point in a conversation with people who insisted on statistical tabulations. The best I could do would
be to offer the historical record and to quote, exhaustively if necessary, from the works of wiser and more eloquent writers. Even this
becomes difficult in an age when the meanings of words can be so
easily shifted to balance the weight of money. Take for example the
dictum, which happens to be Tocqueville's, that usually accompanies the loftier arguments about the paradoxes necessary to the freedom of the press.

> In this question, therefore, there is no medium between servitude
> and license; in order to enjoy the inestimable benefits that the
> liberty of the press ensures, it is necessary to submit to the
> inevitable evils that it creates.

But what does he mean by "license," and what constitutes an
"inevitable evil"? He was writing in an age of political pamphlets,
many of them seditious, and I suspect that he referred to the profligacy and ignorance characteristic of even the most well-intentioned
newspaper. But if the press no longer accepts this somewhat unflat-
tering view of things, choosing instead to imagine itself courageous,
truthful, and omnipotent, then where must it look for its supposed
weaknesses except in the images purveyed by Mr. Flynt? By refusing to acknowledge its own inevitable corruptions, the press has no
choice but to wrap itself in the sorcerer's robe of inhuman villainy.
This is a foolish and wasteful deception.

The raucous confusion of the press is not nihilism. If as many people as possible can publish whatever information they can find (much of it wrong), or as many opinions as possible (most of them misleading), then somebody with a purpose in mind might come across something useful in the rubble. In this respect the press resembles a gigantic midden heap from which, over varying periods of time, some of the innumerable but miscellaneous particles of truth can be fitted together into the shape of invention or a new idea. Like the profligacy of biological combination, the profligacy of the press nourishes the gradual awakening of an infinite number of human possibilities. The process, which is also the process of life, reaches forward into the future. The nihilist impulse slouches backward in time toward barbarism, magic, and death.

In the latter years of the eighteenth century people like Jefferson associated the oppression of the human spirit with the coercions of priests and kings. It was against this tyranny that they raised up the idea of the freedom of the press. It is ironic that their would-be successors have no better use for their liberty than to substitute for the old antagonists the coercions of Mr. Flynt.

A Rake's Progress

MARCH 1979

PREAMBLE

The increasingly dissolute course of American foreign policy makes it difficult to characterize the spectacle of the United States in the world as anything other than a rake's progress. The country exhibits itself in the persona of a profligate heir, squandering his fortune in gambling hells and on speculations in organic farming and utopian politics. Bearing this portrait in mind, I can make sense of the accounts in the newspapers. Otherwise I'm at a loss to know what people mean when they talk about mutual-defense treaties, hegemonies, the China card, and arcs of crisis in Asia Minor and the Persian Gulf. On reading the communiqués from Washington, Beijing, Moscow, and Teheran (together with the supporting sophistry on the editorial pages of the *New York Times*), I see a soft-faced man in a nightclub at 3:00 a.m., earnestly seeking to persuade a bored call girl that he still worries about the higher things in life and that his inheritance has failed to bring him true peace and happiness. Through the dance music I can hear him saying, in a blurred but concerned voice, that he means to do what's right but that this is a much harder thing to do than perhaps the young lady knows. He would have preferred to become a poet or a Protestant minister, or possibly a guitar player hitchhiking across Arkansas with a girl who sings country songs. But his lawyers keep talking to him about the Russians (the boring, tedious Russians, who never laugh at his jokes), and his trust officers keep talking to him about money—about the goddamn price of oil and the second-rate Shah who let him down in Iran, about the Chinese and the Japanese and the Taiwanese and the Vietnamese (all of whom look so much alike that it's hard to remember which ones are floating around in boats), and about the miserable Israelis who failed him in the Middle East.

The persona of the spendthrift heir seems to me appropriate because in 1945 the United States thought that it had inherited the earth. In their earnest and self-righteous innocence, the heirs made of foreign policy a game of transcendental poker, in which the ruthlessness of a commercial democracy (cf., the American policy toward the Plains Indians and the Mexicans) got mixed up with dreams, sermons, and the transmigration of souls. In Europe people may not know very much about foreign policy—as often as not they have no idea what to do about any particular crisis—but at least they can recognize the subjects under discussion. They know enough to know that the dealing between nations is a dull and sluggish business, unyielding in the financial details and encumbered with the usual displays of pride, greed, nastiness, and spite. The Americans, who have little interest in tiresome details, prefer to imagine themselves playing cards with the Devil.

I FIRST encountered the prevailing attitude of mind in the fall of 1957 when, having studied history for a year in England, I returned to the United States with the notion of working for either the *Washington Post* or the CIA. My interest in foreign affairs had been awakened by the Suez and Hungarian incidents of 1956 and by my inability to understand, much less explain to a crowd of indignant Englishmen, the policy of John Foster Dulles. In 1957 the *Washington Post* and the CIA could be mistaken for different departments of the same corporation. Newspapermen traded rumors with intelligence agents, and although the gilding on the Pax Americana was beginning to wear a little thin, anybody who had been to Yale in the early 1950s couldn't help thinking that the totalitarian hordes had to be prevented from sacking the holy cities of Christendom. Failing to find a job with the *Post*, I took the examinations for the CIA. These lasted a week, and afterward I was summoned to a preliminary interview with four or five young men introduced to me as "some of the junior guys." The interview took place in one of the temporary buildings put up during World War II in the vicinity of the Lincoln Memorial. The feeling of understated grandeur, of a building hastily assembled for both a moral and an imperial purpose, was further exaggerated by the studied carelessness of the young men who asked the questions. All of them seemed to have graduated from Yale, and so they questioned me about whom I had known at New Haven and where I went in the summer. I had expected to discuss military history and the risings of the Danube; instead I found myself trying to remember the names of the girls who sailed boats off Fishers Island or who had won the summer tennis tournaments in Southampton and Bedford Hills. As the conversation drifted through the ritual of polite inanity (about "personal goals" and "one's sense of achievement in life"), the young men every now and then exchanged an enigmatic reference to "that damn thing in Laos." Trying very hard not to be too obvious about it, they gave me to understand that they were playing the big varsity game of the Cold War. Before I got up to leave, apologizing for having applied to the wrong office, I understood that I had been invited to drop around to the common room of the best fraternity in the world so that the admissions committee could find out if I was "the right sort."

From that day forward I have never been surprised by the news of the CIA's vindictiveness and inattention. Good, clean-cut American boys, with all the best intentions in the world and convinced of their moral and social primogeniture, must be expected to make a few good-natured mistakes. If their innocent enthusiasm sometimes degenerates into sadism, well, that also must be expected. Nobody becomes more spiteful than the boy next door jilted by the beautiful Asian girl, especially after he has given her the beach house at Camranh Bay, $100 million in helicopters, and God knows how much in ideological support. It is a bitter thing to lose to Princeton and to find out that not even Dink Stover can make the world safe from Communism.

This same undergraduate insouciance has remained characteristic of American foreign policy for the past thirty years. Administrations have come and gone, and so have enemies and allies, but the attitude of mind remains constant, and so does the tone of voice. It is the voice of Henry Kissinger explaining to a lady at a dinner that a nation, like an ambitious Georgetown hostess, cannot afford to invite unsuccessful people to its parties. It is the voice of McGeorge Bundy, who told an audience of scholars in the early 1960s that he was getting out of Latin American studies because Latin America was such a second-rate place. It is the voice of James Reston finding something pleasant to say about this year's congenial dictator, or the State Department announcing its solidarity with Cambodia and expressing only mild regret about the regime's program of genocide.

After 1968 the inflection of the voice became slightly more irritable and petulant. During the early years of the decade the heir to the estate flattered himself with the gestures and exuberant rhetoric appropriate to an opulent idealism. He had access to unlimited resources (of moral authority as well as cash), and he stood willing to invest in anybody's scheme of political liberty. Nothing was too difficult or too expensive;

no war or rural electrification was too small or inconsequential. The young heir undertook to invade Asia and to provide guns and wheat and computer technology to any beggar who stopped him in the street and asked him for a coin. After 1968, when the bills came due and things turned a little sour, the heir began muttering about scarcity and debts, about the damage done to the environment and the lack of first-class accommodation on spaceship earth. Nobody becomes more obsessive on the subject of money than the rich man who has suffered a financial loss. The fellow feels himself impoverished because he has to sell the yacht. President Nixon closed the gold window, and associate professors of social criticism dutifully taught their students that sometimes money weighs more heavily in the balance of human affairs than the romance of the zeitgeist.

Even so, the assumptions of entitlement remain intact. Although feeling himself somewhat diminished (as witness the success of the philosopher-merchants on the neoconservative Right) and somewhat older (as witness the independence on sexual and spiritual rubber goods), the still-prodigal son continues to believe himself possessed of unlimited credit. He is still the heir to the fortune, no matter what anybody says about his horses and dogs, and he can damn well play his game of policy in any way that he damn well chooses. This assumption of grace begets a number of corollary attitudes, all of them as characteristic of a rich man going about his toys and pleasures as of the manner in which the United States conducts its foreign affairs. As follows:

THE WORLD AS THEATER

Children encouraged to imagine themselves either rich or beautiful assume that nothing else will be required of them. What is important is the appearance of things, and if these can be properly maintained then the heirs can look forward to a sequence of pleasant invitations. They will be entitled to a view from the box seats, and from the box seats, as every fortunate child knows, the world arranges itself into a decorous panorama. The point of view assumes that Australians will play tennis, that Italians will sing or kill one another, that Negroes will dance or riot (always at a safe distance), and that the holders of the season tickets will live happily ever after, or, if they are very, very rich, maybe forever. The complacence of this view implies a refusal to see anything that doesn't appear on the program. Nobody imagines that he can be dislodged by a social upheaval of no matter what force or velocity, and it is taken for granted that the embarrassments of death or failure will be visited upon people to whom one has never been properly introduced.

Since the end of World War II the people who make American foreign policy have assumed that the world is so much painted scenery. The impresarios in Washington assign all the parts and write all the last acts. Other people make exits and entrances. Thus President Carter, on the last night of 1977, offered a toast to the Shah of Iran in which he described the Shah as his "great friend" and Iran as an "island of stability" in the Middle East.* A year later Iran was in the midst of revolt and Washington was advising the Shah to abdicate in favor of any government, civil or military, that

---

*It is instructive to quote Mr. Carter's toast at some length because it so nicely illustrates the somnambulism of American statesmen content to see whatever they wish to see. Mr. Carter explained that he decided to celebrate New Year's Eve with the Shah because he had asked his wife with whom she wanted to be on that occasion, and Mrs. Carter had replied, "Above all others, I think, with the Shah and the Empress Farah." The President then went on to say: "Iran, because of the great leadership of the Shah, is an island of stability in one of the more troubled areas of the world. This is a great tribute to you, Your Majesty, and to your leadership, and to the respect and the admiration and love which your people give to you. . . . We have no other nation on earth who is closer to us in planning for our mutual military security. We have no other with whom we have closer consultations on regional problems that concern us both. And there is no leader with whom I have a deeper sense of personal gratitude and personal friendship."

could restore production in the southern oil fields. In 1941 the Soviet Union appeared on the stage in the role of brave friend and courageous ally; six years later, the script was rewritten and the Soviet Union appeared as the villainous *éminence grise*, subverting the free world with the drug of Communism. China remained an implacable enemy of human freedom for the better part of thirty years, but in 1972 President Nixon announced the advent of democracy, and in 1978 President Carter proclaimed the miracle of redemption. Following the example set by the wall posters in Beijing, the American press blossomed with praise for a regime previously celebrated for its brutality. The stagehands of the media took down the sets left over from the production of *Darkness at Noon* and replaced them with tableaux of happy Chinese workers eager to buy farm implements, military aircraft, and Coca-Cola.

In war, Napoleon once said, the greatest sin is to make pictures. But the man who has inherited a great fortune does nothing else except make pictures. Unlike the poor man, who must study other people's motives and desires if he hopes to gain something from them, the rich man can afford to look only at what amuses or comforts him. He believes what he is told because he has no reason not to do so. What difference does it make? If everything is make-believe, then everything is as plausible as everything else. Asian dictators can promise to go among their peasants and instruct them in the mechanics of constitutional self-government; the Shah of Iran can say he means to make a democratic state among people who believe that they have won the blessing of Allah by burning to death four hundred schoolchildren in a movie theater. The rich man applauds, admires the native costumes, and sends a gift of weapons. He believes that, once inspired by the American example, the repentant Asian despot will feel himself inwardly changed and seek to imitate the model of behavior established by Henry Cabot Lodge.

Dictators don't really want to be dictators; they were raised in an unhealthy social environment, and if given enough tractors and a little moral encouragement, they will renounce the pleasures of sodomy and murder. The absurd political presentations that have found favor in Washington over the past thirty years resemble the far-fetched rationalizations with which New York art dealers sell the latest school of modern painting to the nouveau riche. Like the visitors from abroad, the dealers retain a serene and justified confidence in the customer's willingness to be deceived.

THE HABIT OF INATTENTION

The press and the politicians sometimes blame the CIA for being so poorly informed, not only about the events in Iran but also about events in China, Russia, Africa, and Vietnam. The recriminations seem to me unfair. The inattention of the CIA reflects and embodies the carelessness of the society for which it acts as agent. On leaving his club, the rich man never looks behind him to see if the waiter is holding his coat; in much the same way, the United States doesn't take the trouble to notice much of what goes on in the world's servants' quarters. The American press reports news from Africa that deals with disputes between whites and blacks; only large-scale civil wars between armies of blacks deserve mention in the dispatches, and then only if the Russians agree to sponsor one of the contenders. The rich man never knows why other people do what they do because it never occurs to him that they have obligations to anybody other than himself. Few among the nation's more prominent journalists speak or read French. It would exceed the bounds of all decent patriotism to expect more than two or three of them to read or speak Russian, Chinese, or Arabic. The same thing can be said for members of Congress, for Presidents, Secretaries of State, Ministers of

Defense, and almost the entire cadre of people who give shape and form to the discussion of foreign policy. Whenever I remark too loudly on the magnificent displays of American ignorance, somebody who has published an article in *Foreign Affairs* reminds me that the United States is the last, best hope of earth. This is undoubtedly true, but it has nothing to do with the subjects under discussion.

WASTEFULNESS

When President Carter announced the Christmas démarche to Communist China, various mean-spirited critics observed that the United States had failed to gain any specific advantage from the deal. The United States ceased to recognize Taiwan as a sovereign state, abrogated the defense treaty, and agreed to withdraw its troops from the island. In return for these concessions, the Communist Chinese promised to be as friendly as possible and to do what they thought best for the Taiwanese.

The people who object to the slackness of this bargain overlook the rich man's unwillingness to set a vulgar price on metaphysics. The United States habitually makes poor bargains because it feels that it already owns everything worth owning, and so why haggle with the poor little fellows in Asia and the Middle East? Why make unreasonable demands on the Soviets in the SALT negotiations? It is the proof of a rich man's freedom that he can afford to pay an excessive price. It never occurs to him that political economy might be a form of destruction as ruthless although not quite so obvious as war, or that the world is full of hungry people still scrabbling around for anything they can get. The rich man considers it the height of fashion and good breeding to affect an aristocratic disdain for commerce.

Thus a rich nation's portfolio of treaties resembles a rich man's stock portfolio. It is full of issues that he inherited from his grandfather or his mother's uncles, and he has trouble remembering the assets and liabilities represented by NATO, SEATO, CENTO, and God knows how many other shares and securities for which he can't even recall the names. This explains his careless disregard for those countries denominated as allies. To the extent that none of them take precedence over any of the others, they can be bought and sold as the heir feels himself pressed by the need for cash or funds with which to stage an extravagant fireworks display.*

The habit of mind remains firmly ingrained despite the depleted value of the heir's investments. At the end of 1972 foreign banking interests controlled American assets of $26.8 billion; in 1978 the same interests controlled American assets worth $98 billion. During the first five months of 1978 the United States imported machinery and manufactured goods in the amount of $37 billion, as opposed to only $16 billion for foreign oil. The dollar continues to depreciate in the world markets, and American multinational corporations have begun to find themselves surpassed by their competitors in France, Germany, and Japan.

But the rich man intent upon his game of policy impatiently dismisses the accountants niggling at his sleeve. He feels compelled to place another bet in Indochina, this time backing the Cambodians (i.e., the friends of his new partners, the Communist Chinese) against the malevolent croupiers in Vietnam. He wants to make a grand and humanistic gesture in southern Africa, to do something visible and significant in Turkey, to effect a rapprochement in Central America. As recently as last summer, while listening to peo-

---

*Thus the Carter Administration didn't take the trouble to consult the NATO allies about its decision to postpone the deployment of the neutron bomb. In much the same spirit, the Nixon Administration didn't bother to consult with the Japanese in 1971 about the overtures to China, the shift in the monetary system, or the imposition of tariffs.

ple with impeccable credentials discuss the prospects of American diplomacy, I heard a man say that nothing could happen in the world that could affect, in any serious way, the United States. Excepting only a nuclear miscalculation, he was happy to report that the country could consider itself invulnerable.

IMMUNITY

In American military circles, I'm told, it is considered poor form to discuss fortification and the strategies of attrition and civil defense. The whole notion of fortification is seen as stodgy, corrupting, somehow un-American. It brings to mind the depressing memory of stuffy French generals on the Maginot Line in the early weeks of the Second World War. The United States owes it to itself to cut a more dashing figure in the world. Where is the fun in fighting dreary rear-guard actions? The young men in the Pentagon and the military academies speak of forward thrusts, of broad-gauged advances, of assaults and landings and insertions.

All the fine talk conceals an ironic paradox. When it comes down to a question of how to go about these romantic maneuvers, the United States relies less on the daring and intelligence of its commanders than on the superiority of its expensive equipment. It is assumed that the wars will be won by the avalanche of American resources, matériel, production, logistics, and assembly lines—i.e., by the bureaucrats who need be neither impetuous nor brave. The faith in gadgetry and the "tech fix" accounts for the incalculable investment in missiles, bombs, airplanes, and anything else that can be bought in the finest sporting-goods stores. Nobody has the bad manners to insist that strategic bombing has yet to be proved a decisive factor in any of the century's wars. The rich man depends on his technology in the same way that he depends on his trust fund. Even if he makes no effort to think about the great bulk of his capital, it goes about the business of gathering its daily ransom of interest and dividends. The miraculous nature of this contrivance persuades the heir to believe in the divinity of machines.

His unfamiliarity with the effects of a war on his own lands and estates gives him further reason to think that he may have been granted an exemption from the scourges by which less fortunate men sometimes find themselves humiliated. The world is object, and the United States is subject; the fighting always takes place on somebody else's field. The politicians who currently hold office in England suffered the terror of the German bombing; in Moscow the present members of the Politburo watched German tank commanders sight their guns on the spires of the Kremlin. Their peers in Germany, China, Japan, and Italy all carry with them the memory of wives, fathers, brothers, and children killed. But in the United States these are tales that are told. Perhaps this is why the Americans were obliged to push the Vietnamese off the helicopters rising from the roof of the American embassy in Saigon. They hadn't been taught that defeats were as plausible as victories, and so they didn't know how to manage a courageous retreat.

HYPOCHONDRIA

The disease is popular with the rich because only the rich can afford it and because, being incurable, it gives them a constant occasion to talk about themselves. Never before in its history has the United States been so heavily armed a nation, and yet the newspapers and the literary gazettes ceaselessly bring reports of helplessness and alienation, of malignancies in the body politic and the encroaching shadow of Soviet hegemony. The fear of death provides a further excuse for the feverish rates of spending and the extravagant consumption of the estate's assets. Eat, drink, and be merry, for tomorrow we may have to pay two dollars for a gallon of gasoline and give up our chalets in Aspen. Like the society physicians who prey upon the anxieties of dowager heiresses, the learned doctors of foreign policy subtly remind the trembling patient of the illnesses that can befall the unwary traveler in the Third World who strays too far from supplies of safe drinking water.

The symptoms of hypochondria have been chronic since the early 1950s. The moods of euphoria and exultation ("How dare they defy us, those scrawny little peasants in Vietnam?") periodically give way to seizures of doubt and self-reproach. For no apparent reason, the stewards of the American empire suddenly become preoccupied with the phantoms of the missile gap or the energy crisis. Every now and then the consensus of alarmed opinion declares a "year of maximum danger." I have heard this moment in time variously given as 1954, 1962, 1968, 1974, and now—with President Carter's casting around for a credible portrait of himself as statesman and world leader—1979.

The obsession with security corresponds to the desire of the American rich to live in protected enclaves and to escape the filth and nuisance of the world. Howard Hughes ascends to the roof of a Las Vegas hotel, there to keep himself safe from bacteria; Hugh Hefner revolves on a round bed in a darkened room, arranging and rearranging pictures of paradise; Richard Nixon composes his memoirs in the brooding silence of San Clemente; and President Carter retires to the little study next to the Oval Office, listening to Wagnerian opera, checking off his list of things to say and do, communing with his God.

This inward gaze contributes to the poor quality of the reporting from abroad. The diplomats and newspaper correspondents compose pictures that accord with their presuppositions when they signed up for the package tour. They see what they have been told to see (otherwise they wouldn't have been sent), and for the most part they notice that the world is a very poor and undeveloped place, not at all like Greenwich, Connecticut, or Far Hills, New Jersey. They assume that happiness cannot be separated from its natural setting amidst suburban lawns, and this leads them to suspect that the natives are dissatisfied and therefore angry. What man in his right mind would not want to drive a station wagon and ride in triumph through Grosse Pointe? The abyss looms on all sides, at all points of latitude and longitude. By confusing his money with his life, the rich heir imagines himself threatened by enemies of infinite number and variety—by thieves, dictators, IRS agents, hijackers, unscrupulous women, kings, radicals, kidnappers, and nationalist sentiment in South Yemen.

IMPATIENCE

Fortune's child doesn't like to be bothered with details. He never has time to listen to the whole story or to read through the statistical memoranda and the volumes of supporting analysis. He has planes to catch and meetings to attend, and so he expects his advisers to provide him with summaries and conclusions. Unfortunately, this is a habit of mind that obliges him to conceive of foreign policy in extremely simple categories. A nation is slave or free, North or South, in the First World or the Third.

A man who must earn his own fortune learns to make distinctions, and he knows that in all human undertakings, in diplomacy as well as in art or commerce, it is in the details that the issue is decided. So also the man who depends for his livelihood on the animals that he hunts and kills. He studies them with the fondness of a lover, watching them in all weathers, guessing their moods, admiring their grace, following their tracks.

The heir to the fortune hires gun bearers and assumes that all wars will be short. Because he wants to do everything in a hurry and with the minimum loss to his own troops, he relies on the most brutal and undiscriminating means of warfare. In Vietnam the United States couldn't distinguish very clearly between friends and enemies, and so it had no choice but to send the bombers. The soldiers followed the rich man's simple rule of "shooting everything that moves," and the 82nd Airborne Division resolved the political difficulties by defining a Vietcong as any dead Vietnamese.

FAMILY RETAINERS

It is both customary and correct to say that when President Carter arrived in office he knew very little about diplomatic history, political economy, or geography. Had he been asked, prior to his election and without benefit of public-relations counsel, to give the approximate location of Namibia or Romania, I doubt whether he could have come within several hundred miles of a convincing answer. But among American Presidents, at least during their first years in office, the lack of sophistication in these matters is the rule rather than the exception. Who can expect a red-blooded American boy to bother himself with a lot of foreign names? After two years in office, President Ford still had trouble remembering the whereabouts of the Red Army in relation to Poland. Even President Kennedy, who had traveled in Europe and the South Pacific, remained charmingly vague about Asia and Latin America.

Although some schools take more trouble with geography than others, the heirs of the American fortune ordinarily have no occasion to learn much more than the broad outlines of the civilization in which they happen to be spending the money. The better schools also insist that the young men have the good manners to know the difference between a sonata and a logarithm table, but for the most part an American education (at Harvard as well as at the universities of Michigan or California) constitutes a social rather than an intellectual enterprise. It is also a means of acquiring a cash value, comparable to buying a seat on the stock exchange, and it qualifies the recipient for a place in the corporations and the bureaucracies. If the need arises for more refined intellectual goods and services, the heirs to the estate can always hire a Wall Street law firm or "a Jew."

Thus do the tribunes of the people fall like sparrows into the nets of the foreign-policy establishment. For the past thirty years, the trustees of this establishment have been recruited from the banking and legal hierarchies in New York and Washington as well as from the prestigious universities deemed to be sufficiently sound in their distrust of the artistic or political imagination. Although innumerable critics and newspaper columnists have remarked on the primary of this establishment (cf., President Carter's weaning at the dugs of the Trilateral Commission), the term itself causes confusion. The establishment does not define itself in terms of specific institutions, publications, or club memberships. Rather it can be understood as organizational support, of both a financial and an intellectual nature, for the belief in the redeeming and transfiguring power of money. Sums in excess of $100 million have the properties of fairy gold: they can transform apes into men and frogs into princes. It is this doctrine, enforced with the rigor of an ecclesiastical court, that binds together counselors of such otherwise disparate views as Dean Rusk, John J. McCloy, Cyrus Vance, William Rogers, Henry Kissinger, Clark Clifford, Arthur Schlesinger, Jr., McGeorge Bundy, and Zbigniew Brzezinski. These men do not constitute a cabal—it is even probable that they have no wish to form or join an establishment—but because most of the people in the country prefer to avoid the company of foreigners, they achieve their eminence by default.

Perhaps this explains the shoddiness and the timidity of their policies. It is their submission to the rule of money that gives their
advice, no matter what the partisan politics of the moment, its con-
sistency of tone and emphasis.*

In periods of relative optimism and extravagance, when the world
is young and all things seem possible, the family retainers permit the
heir an occasional indulgence or youthful folly. President Kennedy's
advisers made no objection to the assassination of South Vietnamese
Premier Ngo Dinh Diem and allowed him to toy with the hope of
assassinating Fidel Castro. But the heir always likes to think well of
himself, and so when going about these Machiavellian adventures of
state, the family retainers perform the service of doing things in the
heir's name but not in his sight. In this respect they resemble New
York divorce lawyers, who for the sake of the children find it prudent
to blackmail the showgirl wife with photographs of her debut in a
New Orleans brothel. During periods of reaction and constraint the
family retainers warn the heir against doing anything that might
injure the integrity of the trust fund. Thus Mr. Carter's advisers recommend that the United States curry favor with any nation, slave or
free, that can guarantee commodities, raw materials, and markets.

The more desperate the circumstances of the heir, the more likely
that he will be attended by retainers who are themselves consumed
with avarice and ambition. It is the habit of the rich to have enemies
for friends, and so they surround themselves with gossips and hair-

---

*Mrs. Cornelius Vanderbilt in 1960 expressed this principle of American foreign poli-
cy when instructing her niece in the fine points of social politics. "One never meets
Jews," Mrs. Vanderbilt said. The niece reminded Mrs. Vanderbilt that she took tea on
Friday afternoons with Mrs. August Belmont. "Of course," Mrs. Vanderbilt said,
"one chooses who a Jew is." Thus the Carter Administration can decide that the
Nigerian generals have enough oil to exempt them from the status of dictators and
that Mr. Marcos in the Philippines deserves to be paid $1 billion for the use of his
facilities at Subic Bay.

dressers whose sexual sterility presents no obvious claim against the fortune and who take pleasure in contributing to the dissolution of the estate. Similarly, President Nixon employed Henry Kissinger, who seldom bothered to disguise his contempt not only for the Western democracies but also for Mr. Nixon. He told people whatever secret and fantastic truths they most urgently wanted to hear, tapped his associates' telephones with the discrimination of a man making a guest list, and betrayed his nominal friends as blithely as he brought ruin to his enemies. He entered the Nixon Administration in the persona of the faithful squire and left it in the persona of the resourceful manservant, condescending to sell his court memoirs for $2 million. During the televised proceedings of the Republican National Convention in Kansas City in 1976 the camera paused briefly on Mr. Kissinger sitting in the balcony, listening to the speeches with an expression of unconcealed disgust. It was the expression of a fashion designer who has just been told that somebody else will receive the commission to make the dress for the Inaugural Ball.

JEU D'ESPRIT

From time to time the rich man dreams sentimental dreams. He wonders what it would have been like to have wandered as a pilgrim in India or to have composed verses worthy of Lord Byron. Under the influence of this soft and elegiac humor he sometimes builds on his property the equivalent of what the eighteenth-century English nobility described as a folly. Traditionally this was a little gazebo or pavilion with a view of a river or meadow. The heir to the fortune could lean against a marble column, staring into the blue distance and thinking thoughts of the ineffable.

In much the same spirit the United States erected its policy toward Israel. The Middle East wasn't a particularly important place in 1948, and the Jews had been through some pretty rough times at Buchenwald and Auschwitz. Why not, as Nelson Rockefeller might have said, do something nice for the fellas? What did it cost anybody? The United States could admire the pleasing prospect of its conscience stretching into the ennobling spaces of the Palestinian desert.

Besides, Zionist sentiment in the United States was both affluent and politically well-connected. The supporters of Israel could be counted upon for generous campaign contributions and vigorous arguments in the intellectual debates. Everything went well enough for many years, until, in circumstances much reduced, the geologists found oil in a neighboring pasture. Unhappily, the heir needed the money, and his advisers informed him that he would have to tear down his folly and shift the mise-en-scène of his musings to some other pavilion. The heir objected to this, protesting that he had become fond of looking at the little river. But the lawyers were firm and unrelenting. The Arab money from the desert weighed more heavily in the balance than the Jewish money from the sown. Or, as it was explained to me about a year ago by a director of one of the American oil corporations, "Over here at Z—, we get down every morning and pray to Mecca; if necessary we would kiss the ass of every Arab in Riyadh."

SPITEFULNESS AND RAGE

Nothing so angers the rich man as the discovery that his money cannot buy him the world's love and admiration. Being impatient of ambiguity and doubt, he wonders why his fortune doesn't emancipate him from the slings and arrows of outrageous suffering or why, like Shakespeare's Richard II, he must "live with bread like you, feel want, taste grief, need friends." If he gives even $10,000 to a philanthropic charity, he counts upon receiving at least $1 million in services and flattery. President Carter anticipated sustained applause upon the announcement of his opening to China, and when this was not forthcoming he became petulant and sullen.

When things go wrong in the world (i.e., when the painted scenery shifts and moves and comes to life) the rich man casts around for somebody to blame. Characteristically he blames his lawyers and investment managers. Why else does he employ Dean Rusk and Cyrus Vance if they can't straighten out his affairs? How is it possible that all the king's horses and all the king's men cannot put the Shah of Iran back together again? The lawyers and managers in their turn blame one another, as well as inflation, unemployment, and the rising cost of labor. Throughout Washington the bureaucracies ooze whispered recriminations. The White House blames the CIA for the poor quality of the intelligence from Teheran, and the CIA blames the White House for not listening to the early reports of discontent, possibly because Mr. Brzezinski couldn't hear anyone speak ill of his strategic hopes for the Persian Gulf or because he didn't want to think Iran couldn't accept delivery on $18 billion in arms shipments.

The rich man becomes particularly annoyed when he is forced to perceive that he is not behaving decently in the world, that he has associated himself with tyrants and criminals. More than anything else, he expects his money to buy him the illusion of innocence. He resents being told that he might be soliciting the odd $1 billion here and there from people who stand willing to burn and mutilate Jews, or that weapons sold in the world markets fall into the hands of thugs who use them to commit murder. Reports or rumors of these unhappy accidents wound the rich man's self-esteem and cloud the flattering image that he expects to see in the mirrors held up to him by his retainers, his servants, and the press. In the paroxysm of his rage he comes upon the great truth that only the rich and the powerful have rights.* He concludes that other people have failed him, that he has been betrayed by people in whom he placed so much of his trust, and it occurs to him that perhaps other people deserve whatever fate befalls them. The family retainers assemble in comfortably furnished conference rooms to prepare exquisite phrases of regret. They can't quite say that the Jews deserve what they get because Jews are pushy, or that the English lost the empire because they are lazy, or that the French are corrupt and the Latin Americans shiftless and greedy. This is what they mean, but the words don't make a good impression in the newspapers. The lawyers talk instead about treaties, trade balances, and the Arabian oil fields as the wellsprings of the democratic alliance. If there isn't time for the polite hypocrisies, or if the nations in question haven't shown a decent respect for the opinions of mankind, then the rich man simply sends the bombers over Hanoi on Christmas Eve.

ENVOI

In the great game of diplomacy, I don't count myself a professional, or even a particularly well-informed amateur. No doubt I do injustice to some of the American statesmen of the 1950s, and I'm sure that in various aspects of the preceding argument I have oversimplified the matter to the point of parody. Those apologies and qualifications having been duly made, I think it fair to say that the people who formulate the present American policies in the world misunderstand the strength of the American idea. The United States

---

*Justice Felix Frankfurter admirably stated the principle in question when in 1914, as a young lawyer in the War Department, he was asked to research the question as to whether the American occupation of Vera Cruz constituted an act of war. He explained that he didn't need to look up the relevant law. "It's an act of war against a great power," he said; "it's not an act of war against a small power."

remains the most powerful country in the world not because of its wealth or its arsenal but because the Constitution and the Bill of Rights give practical meaning to the possibilities of human aspiration. The society raised up on those foundations allowed men to free themselves from the tyranny of kings and priests. Joined with a democratic form of government, this freedom of initiative gave rise to the enormous expansions, in all spheres of human thought and endeavor, that have both created and defined the United States.

The present generation of would-be statesmen apparently labors under the delusion that the price of liberty, once paid (preferably by a man's ancestors), can be written off as a non-recurring debt. Unfortunately the price of liberty must be paid every day. It requires people to renounce the pleasures of sadistic exploitation and self-aggrandizement and to work instead for the gradual process of evolutionary change. This is never easy, but it becomes all but impossible if people confuse the power of money with the power of the mind and the imagination.

The interests of the United States as a nation do not always correspond to its virtues as a democratic republic; in an increasingly dangerous world, the country sometimes has no choice but to deal with people who couldn't qualify for membership in the Century Club. Dealing with such people is a different thing from enthusing about them with the adulation of gossip columnists. No matter how expensive the barbarian gifts and tributes, and no matter how magnificent the silks and furs, the worship of money binds the worshiper to the past as surely as if he had been buried with the gold in Tutankhamen's tomb. Whenever possible, the United States should ally itself with the evolving future of man's mind, with those forces in the world (ideas, nations, movements, political parties, institutions) that encourage human beings to walk on two feet. Conversely, the country would stand against the forces in the world that require human beings to crawl on the ground like so many humiliated apes. The simplicity of this distinction would oblige the makers of American policy to ask of their allies a different set of questions. The health of a nation's people and the stability of its institutions might come to weigh more heavily in the balance than a shah's capacity to give emeralds to the wives of magazine publishers and oil-company presidents. The more people who become fully human in the world, the more they can do for themselves; the fewer the number of apes, the less seductive the voices prophesying war.

The Arabian Oil Bubble

MAY 1978

In the newspapers lately, as well as in the journals of refined policy opinion, I notice that the promoters of the "energy crisis" have changed their spiel. Instead of talking so much about the failing supplies of hydrocarbons in the world, they have been making more ado about the infamous OPEC cartel. Perhaps this is because enough information has leaked through the mythmaking apparatus of the press to cast doubt on the predictions of the earth's insolvency. The world market at the moment wallows in a glut of crude oil, and every few weeks yet another renegade economist or research institute mentions the abundance of oil and gas reserves. But even the economists who project a condition of surfeit as opposed to one of scarcity quickly recover their sense of patriotic alarm and go on to talk about the sinister conspiracy in the Middle East. About the omnipotence of the cartel all the authorities agree. On Wall Street the bankers sigh and accommodate themselves to the inevitable dominion of the cartel as if it were an obligation pressed upon them by David Rockefeller or the Downtown Association. The politicians in Washington talk about foreigners extorting ransom from the American people, and President Carter raises up both a bureaucracy and a national energy plan to protect the innocence of American enterprise from the capricious despotism of an indolent Arab. This catechism has been so often repeated, not only by government officials and oil-company presidents but also by newspaper columnists and the grand viziers of American foreign policy, that it has acquired the sanctity of dogma. Were it not for the high price of oil in the Persian Gulf, so runs the antiphon in the sacred text, the United States would regain its confidence, restore its credit, rescue its currency, and go forward to its appointment with manifest destiny.

The apparition of an OPEC cabal, unfortunately, has as little substance to it as does the companion stage effect of a world emptied of all its heat and light. The consensus of conventional alarm reminds me of what Stewart H. Holbrook, writing in *The Age of the Moguls*, said about Teddy Roosevelt's theatrical belaboring of the mammoth trusts: "[He] knew a good safe menace when he saw it."

The belief in the cartel's omnipotence serves so many domestic interests that I often wonder what the American managerial class would do without it. If the cartel were everything that people said it was, I would expect to find bankers selling their Long Island estates and moving to Switzerland; I would expect to hear of admirals convening press conferences and leaking to Congressmen confidential documents showing that the United States Navy no longer could guarantee the hegemony of the oceans. I also would expect an atmosphere of anxiety and haste. But instead of this I find people muttering about "the Arabs" and worrying about the regulated price of natural gas, as if they had all the time in the world to consider the fine points of social equity. In Washington the politicians and federal bureaucrats go about the business of commissioning opulent architecture, and in New York nobody thinks to object to the design of yet another glass office building on the ground that it might be wasteful of energy. The dreamlike character of the crisis suggests that to the American managerial class the OPEC cartel subsumes all the ambiguity of human existence into the convenient abstraction sometimes known simply as "them." The working class achieves the same result with diatribes against "the big shots," "the government," or "Octopus Oil."

BEFORE GOING further with this speculation, I probably should explain that I was raised within the bosom of the American oligarchy. Various members of my family have been in various sectors of the oil business since the 1890s, and as I have listened to them talk about their troubles over a period of thirty years, I have understood that the business suffers from a condition of chronic glut. There is always too much oil and gas in the world, and so the problem is always the same—how to restrain the trade. Nobody makes any money unless he can figure a way to control either the production, the distribution, or the price of oil. Old John D. Rockefeller achieved his purpose with hired bullies and a talent for monopoly. His successors, most of them far more timid individuals who have inherited the stewardship of the American hierarchies, take an administrative rather than an entrepreneurial view of the world. Whether employed by banks and corporations or as functionaries within the federal government, they like to think of themselves as gentlemen. They have no particular fondness for colossal profits, which tend to frighten them and to interfere with their affectation of conspicuous frugality. They aspire instead to serve the institutional machinery, to retain those privileges accumulated on their behalf by their primitive forefathers. They look with disfavor upon too much prosperity. Prosperity implies ferment, in the economy as well as in politics; the subsequent disorderliness encourages people to think and to take risks, and this in turn leads downward into the abyss of social change. Although they admire old Mr. Rockefeller's accomplishments, they deplore his methods, and so they prefer to achieve the same result in more decorous ways, either with federal regulation and environmental reform or with a devout belief in such happy accidents of fate as the exhaustion of the earth's resources and the advent of the OPEC cartel.

I will try to be more specific. Having begun to doubt the immaculate conception of the Muslim cabal, it occurred to me some months ago to wonder what would happen if the cabal lowered the price of oil. For all practical purposes the cartel revolves around Saudi Arabia, which produces about 8.4 million barrels a day and has reserves sufficient for another 150 years of extravagant use. The Saudis produce so much oil at so low a cost (30 cents a barrel) that they establish the price of oil in the world market. The spot price of Arabian Light Crude, F.O.B. Ras Tanura, is currently $12.60 a barrel. But what if the Saudis chose to sell a barrel of oil for $6? Certainly they could afford to do so. Money is hardly a scarce commodity in their society; their kings and princes often have said that they would prefer to hold the oil in the ground. If not the Saudis, who then benefits from the high price of foreign oil?

The question is a political one. When a product sells for at least forty times the cost of its extraction, the price no longer has much to do with textbook economics. Over a period of several weeks in the winter of 1978 I raised the question with a number of people in New York and Washington who have a financial interest in sustaining the fiction of perfidious Araby. Without exception they looked upon the possibility of a break in the Saudi price as being destructive of their own interests. Although they thought that the United States as a whole would benefit from a cheaper price, they could foresee nothing but panic and confusion among their institutional confederates in the Department of Energy, the State Department, the international banks and oil companies, even the charitable foundations and the environmental organizations. Or, in the words of an investment banker familiar with the mechanics of oil and gas deals: "If you ask me that question on the record, then I have no choice but to say, 'Yes sir, we have a terrible energy crisis, and the Arabs are awful people.' Off the record I can tell you that we have no crisis, and that the Arabs are doing us a service. If they cut the price, people would start going out of windows."

Like the other people to whom I put the same question, he offered a partial but fairly impressive list of American interests that find it convenient to languish under the tyranny of the OPEC cartel. As follows:

1. The international oil companies. Ever since OPEC quadrupled its price in 1973 the energy companies have reported steady gains in both income and government subsidy. The Saudis make the market price, and by so doing they perform the function of the old Texas Railroad Commission.

2. The financial institutions, primarily the banks and the insurance companies that underwrite explorations as well as the construction of pipelines, tankers, ports, and refineries. The investment of large sums of money calls forth correspondingly large commissions and fees. Without the OPEC cartel the Alaska pipeline might not have been built in such expensive haste. The pipeline cost $8 billion, and much of the money was paid to American corporations.

3. Any company, institution, or syndicate that has invested substantial sums in the development of exotic fuels or alternative energies. As has been noted, to the Saudis it doesn't make much difference whether they sell a barrel of oil for $12 or $6. But to anybody who hopes to make a profit by extracting energy from shale, tar sands, uranium, or liquefied natural gas (all of which imply production costs equivalent to between $10 and $20 for a barrel of oil) the guarantee of a high market price presents itself as a sine qua non.

4. The environmental movement. If the Saudis lowered the price of oil, the stock market probably would rise and money would find its way into equities and into the hands of the citizenry. As every environmentalist knows, the citizenry cannot be trusted. People who believed themselves suddenly affluent would go around buying vulgar consumer goods with which to desecrate the landscape. The high price of foreign oil inhibits not only the building but also the conception of industrial development on too large and too indecorous a scale. It contains the suburbs, stalls the construction of highways and chain stores, obstructs the restoration of cities.

5. The sutlers and camp-followers selling their goods and services in the Persian Gulf. The Pentagon sells arms; the banks and financial institutions arrange expensive financing; other people sell real estate, computers, and political influence. In 1977 the United States reported a trade deficit of $26 billion and paid $42 billion for foreign oil. Even so, the United States reported a favorable balance of payments with Saudi Arabia.

6. The coal industry and its union. President Carter's energy plan recommends a conversion of oil-fired plants to coal, but if fuel oil were to become less expensive than coal, then the miners, no matter what their new contract says, could look forward to an extended period of unemployment.

7. Consultants and energy specialists with a fixed investment in what they have said. Together with their attendant databanks and research institutes they offer advice, information, and analysis (much of it useless except in the papier-mâché world of contrived crisis) to both government and the energy companies.

8. "The crisis industries." The arms merchants and the alarmist factions of the media have a considerable interest in preserving the belief that the United States wobbles on the precipice of defeat. Without the apparition of an insidious cabal they would have trouble

selling their lines of goods to the Congress and the Book-of-the-Month Club. The cabal thus contributes to the well-being of the defense industry and its associated unions as well as to the circulation of the *New York Times.*

9. Politicians. The energy debate dwells on unknowable mysteries and thus bears a fortunate resemblance to a debate about the existence of God. The politicians can wax eloquent on a subject about which they need know nothing. Their theological discussions allow them to avoid or postpone the temporal matters of race, poverty, crime, and justice.

10. Exporters of manufactured goods. The weakness of the dollar, brought about in part by the imbalance of payments, gives an advantage to American goods competing against the exports of Western Europe and Japan.

11. The art and real-estate markets. The high prices paid for furniture and paintings, as well as for coins, sculpture, and houses in East Hampton, presume a rising rate of inflation. If the cartel collapsed, the oligarchs who bestow tax-exempt gifts on museums and universities would lose not only the advantage of immense deductions but also the corresponding sense of their own worth.

THE INTERESTS enumerated in the foregoing list all belong predominantly within the private sector of the economy. They dwindle almost into insignificance when compared with the advantages that accrue to the federal government. The specter of a cabal, and of the sudden darkness that would descend on the United States if the Arabs were to embargo their shipments of light, supports the government's discovery of "an energy crisis" and lends credence to the need for a huge bureaucracy through which the government can award the political dispensations of money and fuel. The Saudis now hold currency reserves estimated at more than $60 billion. Of this sum about $30 billion has been invested in U.S. government notes (Treasury bills and bonds), and another $20 billion has been invested in Eurodollars or in the paper offered by American corporations. The arrangement constitutes an ingenious variation on the old colonial trade. The money leaves the private sector of the American economy (i.e., gets taken out of the hands of the spendthrift and irresponsible natives), passes through the wastes of the Arabian desert (enriching the caravan of middlemen, brokers, consultants, arms dealers, et cetera), and so returns to Washington. Thus does the government use the supposedly infamous cartel to finance its debt and manage the transfer of wealth within its own society. If the triangular trade happens to increase the rate of inflation, well, from the government's point of view, inflation also has its uses. Citizens give over more of their money in taxes, and the increased uncertainty in the economy calls forth demands for more bureaucracy with which to protect the innocent tribes from the rapacity of such imperial agents as Octopus Oil and the OPEC cartel. The Saudis invest their money in the United States as a form of Danegeld. The splendor of their tribute stills the voices of doubt and conscience. It also buys the protection of the American military machine against the possibility of reckless aggression from Israel and the Soviet Union. To the Saudis, who apparently take as literal-minded a view of religion as does President Carter, the United States stands as a bulwark not only against atheism and Communism but also against the forces of social change.

I concede that the government might not know exactly how or why all these pleasant things get done. If too many people took the trouble to wonder how the system works, they couldn't play their parts within it. To imagine an American conspiracy would be as foolish as to believe in the vast powers of the OPEC cartel. As noted earlier, I don't think of the American oligarch as a rapacious man; I think instead of a man perpetually anxious, of Joseph Conrad's "flabby white devils" in Brussels sending Kurtz to look for ivory at the headwaters of the Congo. I think of men who don't want to make trouble, who would make a deal if necessary with any retired whore or fledgling dictator who offered them a concession in a bordello or the television rights to the making of a coup d'état. Give them their percentage and promise them peace in their time, and they will smile and bow and sing a national anthem. The decay of American enterprise clearly cannot be discussed at the Council on Foreign Relations, much less in the newspapers, and so the crisis must be blamed on somebody else, preferably a foreigner. Enter the damnable Arabs. The media find this convenient partially because they also stand within the American oligarchy and partially because they cannot bear to make princes of darkness of figures so obviously bourgeois as government bureaucrats and the presidents of oil companies. How much more satisfying, to both the aesthetic and the theological senses, to imagine a satanic Arab in a robe, wandering the world in a 747, sipping sweet coffee, fondling French women or small boys, playing baccarat for enormous sums while toying with the vague notion of destroying Western civilization. To the economic intellectuals, the Arab cabal appears as a deus ex machina. It explains the otherwise inexplicable conundrums of the international economy, and it redeems, as if by an act of God, all previous theories and predictions that have been proven so fatuously wrong.

Best of all, the invention of a cabal makes a trivial melodrama of what otherwise might be perceived as the terrifying prospect of a world increasingly crowded with nuclear weapons and populated by people who are angry, poor, ignorant, and hungry. If everything is a crisis, then nothing is a crisis; and the more enormous it can be made to seem, the less needs to be done about it. The American oligarchy can postpone the difficult business of thinking about what would happen if the supply of Middle Eastern oil suddenly were to become unavailable, and it can reduce the complexity of history to the size of a commodity speculation. In the meantime, the aura of crisis flatters the vanity of all concerned. The managerial class has lost so much self-esteem in the past generation that it must be pleasant for people to imagine themselves once again in the presence of momentous events.

JUST AS the mythmaking about the Arab cartel obscures the nature of the understanding between the United States and Saudi Arabia, so also does it obscure the nature of the partnership between Octopus Oil and the federal government. The gigantic institutional and financial combinations, in both the public and private sectors of the economy, honor one another's interests and recognize one another's prejudices as universal laws. From what I have read of the Saudi princes, they appear to have much in common with the moneyed oligarchs in New York and with the feudal bureaucrats in Washington. None of them likes to take risks. If the possibility of intellectual freedom threatens the safety of Islam, so does the emergence of unregulated markets threaten the banks and the government agencies. The weakness of the dollar discourages expansion in the domestic economy and reduces the pressure of competition from abroad. If the stock markets atrophy, and if the common people can be made to see that their venturesome impulses bring them nothing but debt and taxes, then perhaps they will come to feel grateful for the protection of their institutional overlords.

As Saudi Arabian wealth becomes increasingly necessary to the American economy, I expect that it will lead to the further degradation of those people who think of money as an elemental force of nature. I sometimes wonder what it must be like for an American civil servant or foundation official, earning even as much as $75,000 a year, to spend his days tagging along behind a Saudi prince. What self-defeating fantasies of political and sexual conquest must trouble the poor fellow's thoughts while riding the evening train to Oyster Bay.

The contrived mechanism of the Arab ascendancy constitutes a bear raid on the American economy and the democratic idea. As with all bear raids, the advantage falls to the already rich. The available wealth accumulates in a small number of fabulous hoards—with the Saudi royal family, the international financial institutions, the federal government. Measured over a short period of years, the lack of enterprise sustains the illusion of peace. But what happens when the capitalist princes can think of nothing else to do with their barbarism except to turn it inward, upon themselves? The sheen of money, like the ornamental engraving on Renaissance cannons, deceives them into thinking that they can escape the savagery of war.

Notes on the View from 43,000 Feet

AUGUST 1978

For the past few months I have been making notes on the feeling of dread that seems to afflict so many of the officials and quasi-officials who conduct the national debate and formulate the public policy. I think of them as belonging to an equestrian class (of lawyers, government functionaries, journalists, academics, corporate and foundation hierarchs) that sustains itself by substituting words for things. They have a faith in abstraction, and I think that they believed until quite recently that their abstractions more or less accurately represented the world of events. But since the election of President Carter I notice that they have begun to lose confidence in their epistemology. I cannot say that I blame them for this, but their panic and anxiety set a poor example for the people whom they would lead and instruct. They remind me of first-class passengers traveling in an airplane at an altitude of forty-three thousand feet, careening through the upper air at greater and more efficient speeds, but knowing nothing of aerodynamics and wondering if something might be wrong with the engines.

They exist in a suspension of time and space, afraid of an environment they didn't make, feeling themselves always and unjustly (i.e., through no fault of their own) besieged by risk. The stewardesses do everything possible to conceal the risk, to soothe the passengers, and to persuade them that nothing unpleasant can happen to them. The passengers remain unconvinced. They know that the plane sustains itself by unnatural means and that only a few feet away from them the immense forces of the universe shriek like banshees along the wings.

Their fearfulness is not easy to describe. Although I can sense it almost as if it were a palpable thing, I'm not sure that I can make it visible. The following set of notes deals with aspects of what I take to be a shriveling of the American spirit and the loss of courage on the part of people in perpetual flight.

In the intellectual amphitheaters people take elaborate pains to obscure the meaning of what they say and write. They might be proven wrong by events, and in the meantime they do not want to give offense. Who knows what is going on in Libya or Washington? Who knows what politician will be elected to what office, or what dictator will surround what palace with whose tanks? The man who hopes to keep open all his options for money and preferment does well to say what he thinks everybody else is saying. The debate minces along like a dog on a leash.

ON A plane coming east from Houston at the end of May I found myself looking at the design of the Mississippi River and thinking about the deceptions implicit in the view from forty-three thousand feet. At that height the landscape dissolves into lines on a map, and for a moment I could imagine that I was looking at what the equestrian class likes to call "the big picture." The topography of Arkansas presented itself in the form of an abstract painting about which I could make the kind of critical analysis practiced by literary critics and Presidential advisers. Everything seemed so easy to perceive and understand. I could distinguish between the straight lines of man's invention and the soft, alluvial shapes of the ancient floodplain; farther to the east I could observe and categorize the changing texture of the land as it shifted into forest and the Appalachian Mountains. Given the advantages of height and speed, I could believe that I knew as much about Arkansas as the poor souls obliged to build the roads or work the farms that I perceived as pretty diagrams. The geometric clarity of the view reminded me of *Time* magazine and the idiot omniscience of the media, of earnest men gathered around conference tables, busily dividing the world into free-fire zones and spheres of economic interest. I remembered a prominent journalist telling me that one underdeveloped country was like any other underdeveloped country. He spoke of them as if they were stage sets against which it might be possible to play out the dramas of geopolitical theory and ambition.

But if I turned away from the universal truth that shimmered in the far distance, what remained? I was left with the equally seductive image of my own face in the window. At forty-three thousand feet the middle distance disappears, and I could choose between the broad perspective so beloved by makers of public policy and the narrow reflection of self so much beloved by the human-potential movements and the legions of soi-disant revolutionaries trying on the Halloween costumes of social and political dissent. I thought of the books written to be admired by a small circle of critics in New York, of people "getting into their own heads," "doing their own things," going on journeys to India to "make a movie of my philosophy." The mirror provides them with a world as malleable as the one seen through the blue distance, a world in which they arrange and rearrange the precious objects of their experience.

But it is the middle distance that is the locus of human society and the human family, of art and government and other people. No wonder the United States has so much trouble with its politics and its attempts at literature. Instead of using the imagination as an instrument through which to perceive and understand the world, the equestrian class uses it as a means of escape. Nobody has any interest in the middle distance. Since World War II, parliamentary politics has fallen out of fashion together with any and all writing that seeks to describe social reality. The politicians promise to restore the faithful to never-never land; the novelists and academic historians amuse themselves with theory and metaphor.

WHY, THEN, despite the most elaborate precautions, do so few people ever feel really safe? The society is obsessed with security in all its declensions—security police, national security, risk-free foods, and political pamphlets. Even the word *risk* (together with words like *additive, artificial, plastic,* and *exposure*) has come to connote something awful.

The equestrian class prefers to live in enclaves—in heavily guarded apartment buildings, in suburbs protected by discriminatory zoning laws, in sealed-off atmospheres of gigantic bureaucracies and corporations, in what was the air-conditioned lunar module of the American military command in Vietnam. These environments resemble the enclave of the plane at forty-three thousand feet. Either the plane falls down or it doesn't. The passengers have no use for courage or compassion. Like humor, the human virtues belong to the middle distance, to the realms of imagination and feeling in which people have something to do with one another. The man in the plane, like the child in the nursery, remains dependent on mysteries about which he knows nothing. No wonder the poor soul feels so constantly threatened by a nameless dread. He can no more rid himself of his unconscious fear than can the man who thinks too much about the prospect of thermonuclear war. Either the world dissolves or it doesn't; in the meantime there isn't much the man on the plane can do about it except to listen to the music and sign petitions.

The well-bred passenger, of course, can complain about the champagne. He proves his moral sensitivity by showing himself capable of being blistered by a rose leaf. This is equivalent to the earnest convocations sponsored by the Trilateral Commission, at which people express their alarm about Africa and their concern for civil rights in Chile or Cleveland. How else can they demonstrate their courage except by worrying about all the things that could go wrong? The substitution of sensibility for action disguises the fact of one's helplessness.

JUDGING BY what I can read of the public record, in the autumn of 1979 the American equestrian class has become enthralled with the romance of failure. President Carter drags himself around the country like a dying king in an old play, weighed down with grief, blaming himself (as well as the oil companies, the American people, his Cabinet secretaries, the Arabs, and the weather) for the misfortunes that have befallen the Republic.

The peasantry in Iowa produce record harvests of corn and soybeans, but on suburban lawns in California and Connecticut the capitalist nobility walk solemnly to and fro with glasses of iced gin in their hands, gesturing vigorously in the direction of the yacht club, bemoaning the ruin of the currency, and worrying about the lack of leadership among their public and domestic servants. Nothing works anymore, they say; the world has gone awry. The Russians have acquired a more impressive collection of weapons than the one purchased by the curators at the Pentagon; in the Third World ruffians leap and dance; at Burning Tree the caddies have raised their fees.

The more I listen to these sorrowful recitations the more I think of heirs to comfortable fortunes who delight in the display of their weakness. Self-blame constitutes an exquisite and expensive form of self-praise. No matter how severe the adjectives, the conversation remains fixed on the subject of supreme interest and importance. The American press never asks, "How do the Germans and the Japanese manage their economies? What can we learn from their example?" Such questions would distract the attention from the American self. During the present debate on the Strategic Arms Limitation Treaty nobody mentions the difficulties confronting the Soviet Union—its prisons, its dwindling oil reserves and inadequate production of wheat, the unhappiness of its citizens, and the chance of nationalist uprising among the many peoples yoked together by a frayed ideology.

For the past eighty years all the best people have complained of neurotic disorders. The doctrines of modernism substitute art for religion, and the lives of the saints (Joyce, Pound, Van Gogh, et al.) demonstrate the relation between neurosis and genius. The acknowledgment of weakness therefore becomes a proof of spiritual refinement, something comparable to a house on the beach at Malibu or a feather boa bought at an auction on behalf of public television. The neurosis distinguishes its possessor from the anonymous crowd of stolid and capable citizens who endure their lives with a minimum of self-dramatization. Who pays attention to people who don't make piteous cries? Who wants to pay $100,000 for the movie rights to their chronicles of marriage and divorce? Who bothers to take their photograph for *Vogue*?

It is the fear of not being noticed that prompts so many people (among them President Carter) to make so fatuous a show of their defects. Mr. Carter puts his whole heart into proving himself weak and effeminate, and by so doing he seeks to make himself charming.

His weeping confessions aspire to the romance of fan magazines. Like the frequently divorced lady met in a bar at Miami Beach, who whispers the secrets of her self-indulgence and her depravity as if these confidences enfolded her in the cloak of the Queen of the Night, Mr. Carter imagines himself so glorious that anything that impairs his perfection must be thought of as monstrous.

Even when he had been deprived of his kingdom, which he had let fall into disorder by reason of his extravagance and indecision, Shakespeare's Richard II believed himself omnipotent. He imagined that spiders and heavy-gaited toads would rise up to strike down Bolingbroke's rebellion. What was so hideous about his humiliation was the fact that the indignities of hunger, politics, and death routinely visited upon lesser human beings could in turn be visited upon the majesty of an anointed king.

So also the American gentry, who still believe that they command the tides. They cannot bear to blame the cost of gasoline on their changed circumstances or the shift of the political balance in the world, and so they blame their own lack of attention. This is much more flattering and allows them to preserve the illusion that the rest of the world plays a supporting role in the melodrama of the American self.

NOBODY LIKES to discuss the loss of the Vietnam War or the failure of Keynesian economics. Once the war had been lost it became implausible, as well as impractical, to talk about the imperial projections of American power. The United States found itself much weakened, both in terms of its own courage and in terms of the way it was perceived by the rest of the world. Mr. Richard Nixon and his liberal critics had their own reasons for choosing to portray themselves as pitiable and self-pitying giants. They made a show of weeping great, sad tears to demonstrate their appreciation of what they believed to be their country's peril. To their embarrassment and surprise they found that their respective audiences accepted their performance as truth rather than illusion.

The talk of an "energy crisis" conceals an arrangement that works tolerably well (profitable for the wrong people, perhaps, but still profitable) and that reflects, with the degree of accuracy customary in dealings between nations, the balance of military and economic force that prevails in the world. Certainly it is preferable to buy the oil, even at preposterous prices, than to go to war for it. This cannot be satisfactorily explained to the lady of reduced means, and so the press thunders against satanic Arabs, environmental ruin, and the earth's insolvency. In these matters the press resembles the faithful butler who remains on the premises to reassure the lady of the house that none of this could have been foreseen and that it certainly isn't the family's fault. My goodness, Madam, it isn't like the old days, is it?

THE PRESENT stewards of American government and opinion, like the inheritors of great fortunes, feel themselves dependent upon a mechanism that they do not care to understand. They resemble passengers on the afterdeck of a luxurious yacht, hoping to God that somebody knows how to steer the thing and meanwhile telling each other frightful stories about radical politicians, Soviet generals, Greek upstarts, and dead gulls floating on the waters of Puget Sound.

Throughout the 1960s the most diligent advocates of the environmental movement tended to possess substantial wealth and property. Their expressions of concern about the natural world had a way of sounding like the pleasantries of landowners asking tenant farmers about this year's rain. Their earnestness invariably reminded me of a lady who once was nearly stabbed to death on a beach at East Hampton. From the deck of a glass house, at about noon on a Sunday in August, the lady noticed a company of fishermen dragging a heavy net through the surf. It had taken them six hours to set and haul the net, but the lady apparently wasn't aware of their labor or their need to sell the fish for something so loathsome as money. The piteous sight of so many fish gasping on the sand moved her to politics. Arming herself with a garden shears, she rushed forth to cut the net. The man who told me the story described the lady as "chic, but obviously committed to a cause." One of the younger fishermen, not yet wise in the ways of the world, had to be restrained from driving a knife into her stomach. In resort towns the local residents and the summer people seldom understand one another's motives, and I concede that the lady with the cause presents a fairly extreme example of the fearfulness that sustains so much of the prevailing confusion. The point to bear in mind is her dramatization of her own innocence. Presumably she didn't object so much to the killing of fish (later that same evening I doubt whether she had much difficulty eating the cold salmon); she objected to bearing witness, and therefore becoming an accomplice, to the killing. As long as the fish were killed in cold and distant seas she could pretend that they arrived on her table of their own free will. So also with many of the people who protest the building of nuclear power plants in their townships or states. If the plants cannot be built in New Hampshire, then the power companies have no choice but to build them at a further remove, usually in communities that need the additional tax revenue and thus find themselves too poor to expect anything but a steerage passage on Spaceship Earth. Like the lady in East Hampton, the innocents of Seabrook, New Hampshire, can find uses for heat, light, and electricity, but they do not want to bear the burden of its manufacture.

THE ENVIRONMENTAL movement has accomplished many good and extraordinary things, and I do not mean to quarrel with its obvious benevolence. Mankind inflicts catastrophes upon the natural world, and if these can be avoided or made less terrible, then the earth must profit from the better management of whales, of trees, of people. But in its more militant and evangelistic phase the environmental movement tends to speak in the voice of a doom-ridden preacher. This is the voice that so often governs the making of laws and regulations meant to impose a code of ethics on swinish louts who don't know what's good for them. The preachers take pleasure in their contemplation of the world's demise. They present visions of boiling rivers and pestilential cities, of dead seas and decaying oceans, of nuclear clouds seeping across suburban New Jersey and the skies black with pollution. Few among them make mention of man's courage and resilience, or of nature's capacity to recover from calamity. In March 1977, the natives of Eniwetok returned to the atolls on which a sequence of nuclear bombs had been exploded between 1948 and 1958. They found a profusion of life, birds everywhere, the fish and corals restored. Nor could the assisting biologists find any evidence of mutation, even among the descendants of the rats who had buried themselves in holes at the time of the explosions and so had survived through twenty-four generations.

The more I listen to talk of dying seas, the more clearly I can hear the wheezing of an old man in an old house, believing that if he must die, then the world must also die. He confuses man's creativity, which is always wasteful and dangerous, with the intolerable stupidity of anybody who threatens to interfere with the status quo. Such a man fears not only the Faustian but also the Promethean instinct in man.

Two or three days after Mr. Carter delivered his first energy message to the Congress I had occasion to listen to several New York editors talk about the "moral imperative" of energy conservation. In their enthusiasm they confused the lost American frontier with an advertisement for Marlboro cigarettes. None of them seemed to know that the frontier was defined by its ignorance and by its cruelty. "We can be like the pioneers," somebody said, "husbanding our resources and wearing sweaters."

Everybody present had acquired a comfortable inventory of possessions; they had learned to drive European cars and to live in a frugal manner in Westchester County; they had read Cousteau and they worried about seals. And yet suddenly, in the midst of their newfound asceticism, here were all these wretched poor people, not only in the United States but also in the godforsaken barrios of the Third World, crowding out of nameless slums, taking up space on the roads, having the effrontery to want things they ought not to want. Costly and unnecessary things that required precious energy to build and maintain. Why couldn't they understand how much better off they were without portable radios? Didn't they know that automobiles don't bring happiness? How could they be so foolish as to want to give up a view of the Caribbean (admittedly a view from a slum, albeit a picturesque slum) for such a paltry thing as a television set?

The man who grows up with the wilderness knows with Ecclesiastes that there is a time to live and a time to die. But the urban environmentalist, accustomed to the wonders of modern technology, thinks of the natural world as if it were a complicated machine. He worries that if too many people mess around with it (particularly poor and illiterate people who haven't read Alan Watts), then the machine will break down. If the machine breaks down and nobody knows how to fix it, then he will die.

When reading through the proofs of the energy crisis I sometimes think that the authors of the reports and studies mean to tell me of their lost childhoods. Somehow they find themselves less rich than their fathers before them, and so they assume that the whole world must be falling apart. Nothing will ever be so good again as it was that summer at the seashore before the war. If only they were rich enough to pay for all the means of recovering energy from the earth (rich enough to extract oil from shale and tar sands, or to make solar engines the size of Los Angeles), why, then, there would be no reason to be afraid of death because even Death, a poor and straggling figure, could not gain admittance to the palace.

WHO CAN speculate about the causes of the present loss of courage? It is easy enough to mention the loss of the war in Vietnam and the bitter disappointments of the 1960s, a decade in which so many had been encouraged to expect so much. Possibly the level of anxiety has to do with the emptiness of American education. The schools teach children little or nothing about their own bodies. People graduate from college knowing nothing about biology and nutrition. Nor do they learn much about technology. No wonder they believe in quacks and astrology. The so-called liberal-arts education achieves the effect of alienating the graduate from what he has been told is reality.

I suspect that much of the present anxiety has to do with the habit of living in time present. So few people have any sense of history. Thus they lack proportion, and they also lose their sense of humor. I associate both losses with the end of World War II and the beginning of the age of American empire. Before it became an imperial nation the United States could rely on the sardonic wit of Mark Twain, Dorothy Parker, James Thurber, Artemus Ward, Robert Benchley, and H. L. Mencken. Hiroshima and the Cold War made it difficult for the newly seated equestrian class to laugh at itself. People took themselves very seriously indeed (as how could they not when the fate of mankind depended upon them?); they had a use for entertainment, not for humor. With the ascension of John Kennedy the rest of the world began to fade and dissolve into the lines on a brightly colored map. All history prior to the founding of Camelot receded into the mists of romantic legend.

But the more that people bind themselves to the dimension of time present, the more threatening the world becomes. Every edition of the news brings word of disaster or the threat of disaster. The Soviet Union adds to its store of weapons, and a drought in California inspires reports of famine and plague. In the East the rain brings little succor because it washes the land with carcinogens. Travelers returning from Africa or the Middle East think themselves less perceptive, less deserving of respect if they fail to bring back proofs of Soviet conspiracy and rumors of World War III. The world changes so fast that the perceived risks reach catastrophic levels. This induces widespread feelings of suspicion and resentment. People become paranoid, believing that their happiness and well-being is being subverted by the active intervention of unknown agents. They find it hard to believe that other people have their own reasons for doing whatever they do, but they don't care, much less think about, what effect their actions might have on innocent bystanders.

The more that one is reminded of one's mortality, the more this must be denied; the more complicated and threatening the world becomes, the more that people must insist that it is simple. Thus the general retreat into the caves of superstition and the closets of fantasy. To wandering saints and evangelicals the faithful pay higher prices than they pay for foreign oil. They initiate themselves into the mysteries of cult religions and supernatural diets. They take up jogging and hope that if they run far enough and fast enough they will outdistance the black hound, death. President Carter talks to God; the Hilton hotel chain requires the candidates for its management and training programs to take instruction from the apostles of the Maharishi Mahesh Yogi. I have heard of doctors who go among the ranks of corporations, marking (as if with a piece of chalk) those executives whom they judge doomed to die by heart attack.

The press, of course, profits from the fearfulness and ignorance of its audience. So also the government bureaucracies and the entrenched commercial interests. It becomes prudent to merge existing companies rather than to undertake new ventures. The emphasis shifts away from the creation of goods and ideas to the marketing of goods and ideas already acceptable to large numbers of people. This contributes to the ascendancy of the bureaucrat—i.e., the man who explains, categorizes, and passes judgment as opposed to the man who makes, builds, and invents. The government assumes the robes but not the authority of the medieval church, and its labyrinthine regulations serve the same purpose as religious observances. People devote more and more of their time to these observances (i.e., filling out federal forms); the money spent making these offerings (comparable to the sums collected for the stained-glass windows at Chartres) last year amounted to $36 billion.

PEOPLE WHO build and make things accept risk as a necessary condition of doing business. The heirs to the fortune imagine that they can avoid risk, as if, like politics, it were an artificial additive. Thus the pretense that foundations, Presidential commissions, and universities constitute sanctuaries beyond the corruption of politics.

Unfortunately, no matter what the faith healers say, the law of the conservation of risk suggests that it can be deferred or displaced, not excluded. A man maybe can choose which death he wants to die, but this is not the same thing as proclaiming himself immortal. The United States might think itself rich enough to neglect the development of speculative research and nuclear energy, but the rest of the world is not yet inclined to take so exquisite a view of things. Even now the United States imports not only raw materials but also technology from abroad.

Over the past twenty years the American bourgeoisie has noticed that otherwise profitable or patriotic acts have unpleasant or unforeseen consequences. The corporations prosper, and the arms merchants sell their goods to illiterate tyrants, but the whales languish, and somebody always gets killed or sent out to sea in a boat. This disturbs people who do not wish to have anything to do with killing or, to put it more precisely, who like to think that any killing done on their behalf remains safely in the past—buried with the glorious dead who paid their debts to the future at Concord, Gettysburg, Château-Thierry, and Guadalcanal.

The resistance to risks of all kinds and degrees testifies to the much magnified fear of death. The national obsession with health (cf. the princely sums spent on jogging and diets as well as in the hospitals and research laboratories) reflects the refined sensibility of people grown too delicate for the world. The prompters of the public alarm observe that with enough effort it is possible to avoid a specific risk (death by asbestos poisoning, say, or lung cancer caused by cigarettes), and so they go on to assume that with even greater and more expensive efforts they can escape all risks and death itself will be denied credit at the better department stores. Thus the country squanders fortunes on quack doctors and federal safety regulations. Sooner or later a lady with a charge account at Bloomingdale's will bring a lawsuit against the sun.

It never occurs to the heirs of the American fortune that if they neglect to save their money, then the miracle of their unearned income must necessarily fade and diminish. Nor does it occur to them that if they shrug off the burden of political power, which entails the cost and nuisance of maintaining fleets and armies, then they will be unable to buy goods in the world market below the prices paid by Ecuador. They complain about the insensitive delay of the bureaucracy in Washington, but it never occurs to them that the government moves so slowly because it has been asked to do so much.

The sense of human possibility expands and contracts like the beating of the human heart. The nineteenth century took pride in the march of learning and the advance of the intellect; the twentieth century shrinks from these campaigns because the vanguard keeps sending back reports of weird monsters and deadly amoebas. The exaggerated claims of the early 1960s give way to exaggerated doubts; absurd confidence relapses into absurd cowardice. In 1962 everybody had power; in 1979 nobody has power. The feverish market in stocks, which reflects a belief in a limitless future, gives way to the feverish market in gold, which reflects a belief in imminent ruin.

IF AMERICANS have learned anything in the past twenty-five years, they have learned that everything connects with everything else. Every triumph of medicine or biology brings with it the corollary news that yet another substance or bodily malfunction, heretofore unknown, tends to kill people. A man feeds a raisin to a fish, and seven years later in the South Atlantic calamity overtakes the unsuspecting krill. Decisions made for partisan political reasons in a Washington basement result, nine years later, in the massacre of 3 million Cambodians.

Even as medicine extends the life span, so also do people feel themselves more expendable. They accept the doctrines of progress and the perfection of the self as product, and so they expect to be superseded. Having become defensive about their transience and about the smallness of their achievement, and having lost the connection between time past and time future, they come to think of themselves as being no more substantial than a summer fruit fly. The less valuable they become in their own estimation, of course, the more useful they become to the people who would reduce them from citizens to subjects.

The Leisure State

NOVEMBER 1977

More often than usual this fall I have heard it said that the United States is a wasteful place. The people who remark on this state of affairs invariably intend a moral judgment. They mention the consumption of paper napkins and automobiles, the surfeit of melons, and the expense of television programming; from these or similar observations they conclude that wastefulness is an evil thing, somehow associated with sloth, gluttony, and pride. Unless they can be forcibly restrained, they go on to say that if only enough Americans would stop wasting so many precious resources (oil, money, space, light, air, schoolchildren, porpoises, et cetera, et cetera) then all would be well, and the high-minded folk in the community could go about the business of building the Utopia they had seen advertised in a religious tract.

I never know what to say to such people. In what country do they imagine themselves resident? How is it possible that they can have failed to notice the importance of waste and futility to the American way of life? They condemn the general extravagance, but they seldom take the trouble to notice that their own professions and livelihoods (not to mention their social or spiritual ambitions) stand on the bedrock of wasted effort. Newspaper editorialists ignore the lavish use of paper in their own publications; oil-company presidents say nothing about their manufacture of plastic containers; Congressmen dedicated to social reform fail to observe that it costs about $750,000 a year to maintain them in office.

The superfluity of complaint this fall prompted me to read Thorstein Veblen's *Theory of the Leisure Class.* Although I had seen the book referred to almost as often as Tocqueville's *Democracy in America,* I had not read it, and for this failure I owe the reader an apology. Not having read Veblen deprived me of a perspective that might have clarified a good many of the confusions and absurdities that provide the stuff of the American comedy. Having read the book, I find it even more difficult to understand the present clucking and prattling about waste and wastefulness. In 1899 Veblen explained the social imperatives that enforce the task of conspicuous consumption on a hapless populace. Given the foolishness of a society that defines the possession of wealth as a meritorious state, even a critic of that society has no choice but to give an "unremitting demonstration of the ability to pay." An impoverished critic clearly cannot hope to acquire a reputation for truth, honor, or justice.

Veblen defines waste as that which doesn't contribute to the community of human life or human well-being. He concedes that the task of consumption might seem pleasant to the man who undertakes it, as well as profitable for the man who makes a market in toys and luxuries, but the ceaseless round of consumption does nothing to advance the cause of human freedom.

People dedicated to the frenzy of consumption engage of necessity in a predatory habit of life and look about them with a narrowly self-regarding habit of mind. Both of these attitudes Veblen found characteristic of the leisure class, i.e., of people devoted to the worship of money and enthralled by a belief in magic. The admired figures in such a class exhibit their prowess by means of inflicting injury, either by force or by fraud, on their competitors. The aptitude for acquisition stands as the definitive measure of self-esteem.

Much to my sorrow, I can find no fault with Veblen's principal observations. I cannot see that the passage of time has done much to ameliorate the force of his argument. The social imperatives have become both more insistent and more pervasive. What was true of a relatively small class of people at the turn of the century has become true of the society as a whole. The leisure class has become the leisure state. As the nation has prospered, the leisure class has multiplied and increased, assuming unto itself what formerly might have been identified as its subservient or ancillary classes. The regime of status now counts among its adherents not only Veblen's captains of industry but also a vast horde of government officials, lawyers, journalists, politicians, bureaucrats, and academicians. The stores and advertisements bulge with superfluous goods. In an age of mass communications the precept and example of the higher social orders (what Veblen called "the radiant body") transmit themselves more readily to the aspirants in the lower orders, and so larger numbers of people consume a larger number of goods as proof of their decency, worth, and good reputation.

Veblen arrived at his theory by contemplating the folly of private individuals. He drew his examples from the lives of the capitalist princes who held sway in Newport or Saratoga and who concerned themselves with oysters, fêtes, horses, parrots, clothes, sporting events, coaches, and dogs. As the wealth of the country has been transferred into institutional or bureaucratic treasures, so also has the citizenry at large come to adhere to the canons of reputable waste. The burden of conspicuous consumption has been shifted from the private to the public sector, and this entails the slight revision of some of Veblen's theory. As follows:

CLEANLINESS

Veblen discussed the fanatic insistence on cleanliness in the context of clothes and bodily health. Under the rule of money, appearances obviously become paramount, and a threadbare coat testifies to the presence of a nasty man. The immaculate condition of one's clothes also indicates an exemption from any useful or productive labor that might bring about a soiled or disheveled appearance.

Transposed from the private to the public sector, the insistence on cleanliness explains the present concern for the environment. Only a nation possessed of immense wealth can afford to scrub dirt out of the air. In the realm of foreign policy, the corollary belief that poverty implies spiritual contamination governs the American attitude toward the Third World.

HONORIFIC DISSIPATION

The leisure class looks upon displays of indulgence as proofs of a man's ability to sustain losses inconceivable to lesser mortals. Veblen described drunkenness as an honorific occupation.

The same principle accounts for the extravagance of the 1960s. Not only the war in Vietnam but also the self-annihilation of the Woodstock generation testified to the greatness of a state that could afford such princely gestures.

PERSONAL SERVICE

Veblen confined his remarks to the household apparatus, to women and domestic servants. Together with the wife (considered in her capacity as sumptuary object) the legions of domestic or body servants perform the tasks of vicarious leisure. They consume the master's goods as proof of the master's ability to maintain them. The less that is required of them, the more eloquently they argue their master's wealth and prowess. Mostly they devote themselves to elaborate punctilio, which offers further proof of their master's greatness because the consumption of trained service obviously entails a larger expense than the consumption of untrained service.

The surfeit of goods eventually made it necessary to establish a higher order of servant who could assist with the task of consumption and thus uphold the standards of pecuniary decency. As the society as a whole has come to embody both the attitudes and the habits of the leisure class, the individual employers have been replaced by institutional employers. The conditions of service remain as before.

The society does itself honor by employing a retinue of bureaucrats at all levels of government who do nothing but read the newspapers. The habitual idleness of union members (trained service as opposed to untrained service) testifies to the magnificence of American enterprise. The *New York Times* gives evidence of its greatness by assigning Harvard graduates to run errands, and the charitable foundations accomplish the same purpose by awarding large amounts of money to scholars who present inane proposals in unintelligible prose.

CHILDREN

Among the leisure class Veblen remarked the disinclination to bear children. The necessities of raising children interfere with the spending of money on oneself. This truth has made itself apparent to the population at large. As more and more people have entered the leisure class, the markets in narcissism have prospered, and the national birthrate has declined.

CONSPICUOUS CONSUMPTION

Veblen used the phrase to describe the consumption of objects (ornaments, weapons, cakes, polo ponies, et cetera) as well as the consumption of people's time and effort (amusements, rituals, devout observances). He made the further point that the canon of honorific waste requires the mark of superfluous expense. Goods that do not give evidence of wastefulness (either in the cost of their manufacture or the futility of their purpose) must be counted as inferior.

Transposed into the public sector, this principle explains, among other things, the cost of government. In precisely the same way that a Tiffany box adds luster to the beauty of a diamond tiara, the cost overrun for a nuclear submarine guarantees its intrinsic worth.

DEVOUT OBSERVANCES

Veblen counted devout observances as one of the four occupations, together with government, sports, and war, that the leisure class deems appropriate to its magnificence. All other forms of labor appear menial and therefore ignoble. This distinction remains in force, with only slight modifications as to what constitutes the civil religion. In 1899 Veblen could still offer the example of church services, but in the course of the past eighty years the sacerdotal offices have passed into what was once the secular realm. The most expensive debates in any age resolve themselves into the question, Why do I have to die? In the late nineteenth century this question still could be addressed by clergymen. The events of the twentieth century have referred the question to the politicians, who have access to the teleological weapons, and to the scientists, who perhaps will discover the secret of immortality. The aura of divine immanence thus shifts its light from cathedrals to universities, research centers, and government agencies. God continues to be imagined as a rich man and heaven as a country estate on the order of Pocantico Hills, but the forms of ritual require a profession of faith in democracy, liberal social theory, the freedom of the press, and scientific truth. The people employed to celebrate these rituals acquire the stature of an ecclesiastical class. In large part this accounts for the enormous expenditure of money on tracts, studies, reports, and legislation embodying the principles of social justice.

The money once invested in the adornment of cathedrals now supports the manufacture of nuclear weapons. The government comforts itself with a defense establishment that stands as the wonder of the age. The weapons will prove to be inadequate in the event of a nuclear war, but the building of the arsenal becomes a form of religious art. The twelfth century squandered its substance on stained glass; the twentieth century prefers the imagery of technology, and the most beautiful images are those that instill the illusion of omnipotence. The twelfth century discovered a reflection of God's judgment in the facade of Chartres Cathedral; the twentieth century looks for the face of God in the smooth surfaces of an ICBM.

PETS

In the late 1890s a man might squander a fortune on the breeding of racehorses, but in the late 1970s so many people can afford to do the same thing that the enterprise fails to meet the condition of honorific waste. As the burden of conspicuous consumption shifts from a few individuals to the society as a whole, the keeping of pets transforms itself into the maintenance of celebrities. The amplification of the media allows more people to imagine themselves owners of statesmen, talk-show hosts, and movie personalities. The cost of maintaining Frank Sinatra or Henry Kissinger exceeds what even John Jacob Astor could have afforded to pay for a racing stable, but as the expense has been diffused through larger segments of the population the leisure state can pay for even more exotic species and grotesque effects.

DRESS

Observing the similarity of dress worn by women, priests, and domestic servants, Veblen suggested that each of these costumes was an insigne of leisure, attesting to the indolence of the wearer and thus to the wealth of the master. So also the present fashion that encourages men to dress like women and to spend comparable amounts of money for cosmetics. A state that can afford to dress so many men in the costumes of futility obviously must be very great.

ARCHAISM

As leisure and wealth sift downward, neither attribute serves as a definitive mark of the highest pecuniary grade. Veblen made reference to this devaluation in what he called "the physiognomy of goods." People on the upper tiers of the hierarchy avoided vulgar displays in favor of crude and rustic effects. They bought handicrafts and books sewn together with clumsy stitching and printed on heavy paper in archaic typefaces.

The most striking elaboration of this principle in the modern era has to do with the more truculent expression of feminism. The educated classes encourage women to revert to the primitive forms of matriarchy. This also satisfies the demand of honorific dissipation by proving that the state can afford to support not only indolent servants but, even more expensive, declared enemies.

CONSPICUOUS LEISURE

Even in Veblen's day, ostensibly purposeless leisure had begun to lose its value as a demonstration of the ability to pay. The man who appeared at a golf club or class reunion had to give an account of the time that he invested in other pursuits. He couldn't simply say that he had been sitting in a chair for a matter of days or months. Thus the obligation to speak with some degree of knowledge about antique furniture, the breeding of greyhounds, or the study of defunct languages. The more useless the occupation in question, the more credit accrued to his account. A knowledge of medieval Latin commanded more respect than a knowledge of contemporary Italian.

Under the imperatives of the leisure state, the consumption of leisure expresses itself most satisfactorily in the resort to committees, boards of directors, and ornamental commissions. A man who can say that he has attended meetings at the Aspen Institute or the Council on Foreign Relations attains a higher caste of reputability than the man who has been traveling on a cruise ship or going to business conventions. This is because an invitation to Aspen implies a much larger waste of time in the acquisition of the necessary connections and the reading of turgid discussions about the condition of the NATO alliance.

JOHN F. KENNEDY

Veblen's *beau idéal.* He consumed the best of everything the society had to offer and employed the most exquisitely trained and therefore the most expensive servants. Who else could afford to hire the dean of Harvard College as a footman? So gracefully and so enthusiastically did Mr. Kennedy consume the products of the society (women and ideas as well as houses and celebrities) that he restored to the magazine advertisements a sense of redeeming social purpose and gave to money the luster of something new.

Guests of the Management

JULY 1979

As an editor subject to the mails, I have the chance every morning at ten o'clock to confront the spectacle of my own ignorance. I am sure that the same opportunity presents itself to people
in other professions, but in a magazine office the encounter takes
place with a degree of punctilio. On any given day I no sooner sit
down at my desk than I am likely to find myself in the company of at
least five periodicals (three of them on political affairs, the others
treating of environmental matters and weapons systems), two books
as yet unpublished (one of them about the du Pont family, the other
about molecular biology), a newsletter sent by a gloomy political
economist in Washington, a public-opinion poll describing the
national attitudes toward lesbians and the presidents of oil companies, three reports from charitable foundations (about the meager
levels of federal money available to the arts), and at least twelve
manuscripts, solicited and unsolicited, whose authors in their
accompanying letters assure me that they have discovered, among
other items of interest, the secrets of Chappaquiddick and the universe. Although I count myself a reasonably well-educated man, I
cannot hope to make sense of so many different arts and languages.
I look at this juggernaut of words, and I wish I knew of a dictionary

in which I might look up the necessary translations—of economics into physics and back again into politics—or where I could find the literary synonyms for the equations of chemistry.

If I had lived in Paris in the thirteenth century, or in London in the eighteenth century, I might have been able to find a sage who could have provided me a coherent vision of the world in which I happened to be resident. Walking with the students of Aquinas across the river from Notre Dame, or with the members of the Royal Society of which Isaac Newton was president, I could have listened to them resolve the dissonances between appearance and reality in the harmonies of the age. Although proved wrong by subsequent discoveries (by Copernicus's observations and Einstein's theories), for the time being, and within the gravitational fields that held together the particles of science and philosophy, they could have explained the laws of motion and the origins of light.

But in the city of New York in the year 1979, close by the media installations of a society that likes to think of itself as the wonder of Western civilization, with whom can I walk along the embankments of the Hudson or the Harlem River and expect to hear anything but the dreary recitation of an aesthetic or political grievance? Who can draw a sufficiently large and imaginative paradigm from the systems of relation seen by Darwin, Einstein, and Freud? Who can make me perceive that nature is not static or immutable, that every particle of matter (whether contained in the girders of a bridge or the circulation of the blood) takes part in the ceaseless round of birth and death? Who can make me see that not only the surface but also the substance of things consist of restless movement, that everything collides and dances with everything else, and that I can define myself as a sequence of coordinates plotted as infinitesimal moments on the graph of space and time? Who can make me see these things and then organize them in the form of art, government, and morality? What modern novelist understands the scale of nature as a landscape in which all organic being (presumably the human sexual expressions as well as the wings of butterflies) fits together in dependent equations?

ABOUT THE courage and exuberant energies of the society at large I have not the slightest doubt. The country possesses so many genies of technology that even the government's swarm of clerks cannot keep accurate records of all the people following the tracks of electrons, experimenting with the properties of hydrogen, observing the permutations of cells. The nation's research vessels voyage in the reaches of deep space, sending back photographs and radio transmissions from the other side of Mars; its scientists make their bows every year in the Nobel Prize lists, and its armorers tinker with weapons of teleological magnitude. The United States counts among its citizens people who have been as expensively educated as any people in the history of the world. The available statistics suggest that they make reckless use of the national museums and libraries, pursuing lines of inquiry of which the authorities undoubtedly would disapprove.

Occasionally I have the chance to spend an afternoon in a research laboratory, and although I seldom understand the whole of the supporting lecture, I form an impression of people intensely excited by their journey toward the horizons of the human mind. I sense something of the same adventurous spirit among the freebooting lawyers in both the public and the private service who, over the past thirty years, have shifted the balances of wealth and politics in the United States almost as carelessly as if they were moving pieces on a chessboard. Over a desk in Washington I talk to a Congressional assistant who thinks of rewriting a tax or labor law in a way that will transform the lives of as many as 40 million people, and I am reminded of the high-energy physicist who flings together atomic elements in the hope of achieving temperatures of 40 million degrees. Or again, in the company of tax accountants and arbitrageurs, I cannot help but be impressed by the rigor of the conceptual imagination that goes into the making of stock swindles and bank frauds, by the almost polyphonic combinations required to merge corporations, and by the capacity for abstraction that can make visible the transposition of money through five currencies and seven tiers of taxation.

Why then does so little of this creative force show up in the poor and timid stuff sold in such stupefying volume under the label of contemporary American literature? The trade and university presses produce more than forty thousand titles a year, and yet, judging by the shoddiness of the merchandise, the curiosity and judgment of the literate audience continue to decline. I don't know how else to account for the superstitious confusion that fell like a sorcerer's cloak over the accident at Three Mile Island. In all the clamor of frightened voices, of politicians summoning press conferences and newspaper correspondents filing communiqués from Armageddon, the consensus of alarmed opinion could agree upon nothing except that a demon had been let loose upon the earth. Comparable levels of superstition befuddle the public conversation on almost all subjects complicated enough to admit of ambiguity and a second opinion. In a country that declares itself educated, how is it possible that for ten years the Hooker Chemical Company in northern New York could poison the water of the Love Canal without thinking it worth the trouble or the expense to inform the people living in the neighborhood that their children stood the chance of being born deformed? Why did nobody inquire about the drainage, or, if they did inquire, why couldn't they do so in the language of science rather than in the rhetoric of politics? Just as the mind and body of a child can be deformed by ignorance and greed, so also the mind of a country can be destroyed by the numbing effect of a literature shaped not by the dreaming mind but by the worship of money.

I SOMETIMES wonder why so many writers of my generation and acquaintance regard themselves as tourists traveling in an alien wilderness. If they could be asked to fill out a passport stating their metaphysical country of origin, I suspect that it would never occur to them to give their nationality as American. Instead, they would identify themselves as Catholics or southerners, as utopians or counterrevolutionaries, but always as discerning visitors from a better world (frequently confused with their childhood), passing through town on their way to Europe or Los Angeles or the English department at Yale. Those among them who write novels feel obliged to devote the first few hundred pages to establishing their provenience, as if their lives might be evaluated as objects of art.

Their detachment from the native anthropology is partly a matter of literary convention. The modernist doctrines taught in the schools over the past twenty or thirty years require the writer with pretensions to sensibility to conceive of the world as a metaphor. James Joyce proved that it is impossible to know anything other than oneself, and so the society at large remains at best a fiction. Any description of the theoretical construct known as "the real world" can be left to the journalists and Harold Robbins. The authors of detective novels might still take the trouble to explain the workings of an automobile or a weapons factory, but the writer who aspires to keep company with the immortals learns to affect a well-bred disdain for commerce and trade. He achieves his effects in the precious metals of symbolism. Language becomes an end in itself, the imagination a vehicle for escaping reality rather than a means of grasping or apprehending it.

For as long as I have been going to the *levées* of the New York literary salons I don't think that I have met more than two or three people who know much about the specific weights and measures of economics, medicine, history, law, finance, physics, or human anatomy. Even reading in these subjects apparently has become distasteful, as if they constitute too ominous a reminder of the world's rigor and contingency. A few weeks ago I spoke to a critic who reported that he had seen a child drown in a flood. The child's death impressed him as being faintly vulgar. Not so much frightful or shocking as a transgression against the canons of good taste. He went on to explain that what has become inconceivable for both the writers and readers of "serious" fiction is the possibility of anybody becoming implicated in the realm of action. Even the smallest of actions might prove catastrophic—if not to oneself then possibly to a cousin or a newt—and so it is best to do nothing at all. The characters define themselves by virtue of their moral and aesthetic attitudes and by the mutual recognition (or, more often, nonrecognition) of states of refined feeling.

A second reason for the general dissociation from the American experience has to do with the difficulty of finding an audience for literature. The existence of a literature presupposes a literate and coherent public that has both the time to read and the need to take seriously the works of the literary imagination. The United States hasn't had such a public since the victory of World War II. The society lacks a common agreement as to its history, its character, and its hope for the future, with the result that the arts in all their forms and expressions have disintegrated into as many fragments as the sciences. Instead of one public there are many publics, each of them speaking in code and all of them advancing the causes of political or emotional faction. The solipsism of American writing in the present generation argues not so much for the lack of literary genius as for the loss of a national theater of ideas in which writers (as well as painters or chemists or politicians) can perform the acts of the moral or artistic imagination. Nobody can decide whether these acts should be performed on a stage, in pantomime, or on a trapeze. In place of a theater of ideas the cultural impresarios provide buildings designed by I. M. Pei; they resolve the aesthetic dilemma by booking into the arena any act that can draw a crowd. The rules of egalitarian protocol forbid them from making invidious distinctions among poets, magicians, and performing bears.

In nineteenth-century England Charles Darwin could expect *On the Origin of Species* to be read by Charles Dickens as well as by Disraeli and the vicar in the shires who collected flies and water beetles. Dickens and Disraeli and the vicar could expect that Mr. Darwin might chance to read their own observations. But in the United States in 1979 what novelist can expect his work to be read by a biochemist, a Presidential candidate, or a director of corporations; what physicist can expect his work to be noticed, much less understood, in the New York literary salons? To an editor the absence of a theater of ideas raises questions about the lines of reasoning that can be taken for granted among his prospective subscribers. What allusions, classical or otherwise, will be accepted as safe or intelligible? Who can be counted on to recognize the tone of irony?

No wonder the bookstores resemble circuses and fairs. The thousands of books so gaudily tricked up on the shelves, each of them possessed of a voice (either human or recorded), compete among themselves in the wheedling din of Gypsy fortune-tellers, of jugglers and acrobats clamoring for a few coins amidst the harsh cries of money changers, animal trainers, herbalists, cooks, sorcerers, augurs, gamblers, military captains, whores, thieves, merchants, dealers in horses and religion.

As the book business comes to resemble journalism, so also do the publishers come to resemble the editors of Sunday newspaper supplements. They hope to catch the falling stars of a popular or academic fashion, and they seldom have the time or the inclination to sustain their interest in a property that takes much longer than a few months to write, publish, and sell to a reprint house. The more careful an author's thought and the more complex his argument, the smaller his chance of big-time success. Not enough people will understand what he's trying to say. If this year's fashion has it that the United States has fallen into moral disrepair, then the publishers can hawk the bad news until the fashion changes, whereupon, next year or the year after, they can bring out the revisionist news that the United States is really a very nice place, much befouled by ungrateful intellectuals and in need of the restorative elixirs of another war. If managed correctly, both announcements can sell fifty thousand copies in hardcover and five hundred thousand copies in paperback.

I can guess well enough the motives of the authors and the publishers in making a market for their goods, but the question remains as to why people buy the stuff. Any diatribe against the venality of the publishing business must collapse under its own ponderous moralisms unless it takes into account the problem of audience. If I can imagine a New York publisher, chagrined and penitent, confessing to the sins of greed, I also can imagine the publisher saying that even if he published a decent book there would be nobody to read it. Who would believe the advertising campaign?

ALTHOUGH I have spent the better part of twenty years in and around the New York literary bazaar, I have come across only a small number of people who can talk about any particular book at convincing length. Yes, they have read the reviews in the gazettes (usually with feelings of envy and spite), and yes, they can quote the price at which an author's reputation was trading last week on the literary exchanges, but of the book itself, of what the author actually said or didn't say, they have nothing more than a polite impression. They assimilate books in order to have an opinion, but they do not enjoy the act of reading, which, as every critic knows, interrupts the perfect contemplation of oneself. When writing reviews the critics tend to award their most fulsome praise to those writers whom they least fear—to the brilliant young novelist in the provinces who quite obviously will never write a second novel, to the reliably mediocre historian who can be counted upon for a vote in next year's prize committees, to the feminist poet who will think that she has been praised for her craft and sullen art.

Outside the circle of the literary salons I have noticed a comparable lack of interest in the book itself. A majority of people apparently buy books because they think they already know what's in them. They have seen the author on a television talk show, or they have come across his name in a gossip column, and so, once having bought his book, they have no reason to read it. The book furnishes a room, and after a decent interval the man who owns it comes to imagine that he knows the author well enough to drop his name in a conversation about God or capitalism.

The American is an enterprising fellow who will take elaborate precautions against the embarrassment of being left alone with his thoughts. Rather than sit and look idly at the sky he will run twelve miles in the rain; on weekends in the country he arranges as many picnics and sporting events as might be necessary to prevent him from being surprised by an uninvited silence. Perhaps the publishers do him a service. By printing so many books of so little worth they raise up a parapet of words that protects the buyer from the onslaughts of consciousness. I suspect that quite a large number of people buy books because they think of them as amulets and charms. To the extent that they feel threatened by the world (by government, hydrogen bombs, terrorists in airports), they seek to make it trivial. The publishers oblige them with the political romances of Theodore White and Arthur Schlesinger, Jr., and with the long letters from summer camp written by such gifted and salacious youths as John Updike and Philip Roth. The books enjoy the fluttering acclaim of the critics, and their shallowness has a soothing effect on the buyer, suggesting in their flattering way that the world, as Joseph Alsop once remarked, consists of no more than two hundred people (presumably resident and nonresident members of the Cosmos Club in Washington) who administer the laws of gravity.

Americans tend to prefer the uses of power to the uses of freedom, and the heirs to the great fortune that fell to their lot in 1945 assumed that they had inherited not only the goods and chattels of the earth but also the spoils of intellect accumulated over centuries in the vaults of Western civilization. They wished to acquire and consume the products of the artistic imagination (somewhat comparable in the general conception to a vineyard in Bordeaux), and they had neither the patience nor the need to experience art. The study of literature, like that of any other art, offers as its reward freedom of mind and spaciousness of thought. Neither of these possessions makes much of a show in the world, and for the most part they are thought to be superfluous. Freedom, like reason, is a privilege conferred at birth, merely another of the things inherited with the Purdy shotgun and the house in Maine, and therefore not something to worry about. People excited by power can make a more satisfactory display of their newfound sensibility by going to the opening of the opera at Lincoln Center, by collecting the season's new paintings as they would collect the season's new clothes, by gorging themselves on words.

In nineteenth-century France the newly enriched bourgeoisie

crowded into the restaurants invented for their amazement (as well as in the hope of returning them to penury), and there, complacent under the chandeliers, they professed themselves duly astounded by the sauces of Escoffier. They took the food extremely seriously, solemnly digesting the most expensive trifles, not daring to express a naïve opinion for fear of making some atrocious blunder in the presence of the waiters. The same air of heavy significance distinguishes the *nouveaux littéraires* ennobled in their hundreds of thousands by university degrees in the past thirty years, solemnly consuming the *rôti de Barth,* the *mousse au Sontag,* and the *prix fixe* offered by the Book-of-the-Month Club. Rather than be proved ridiculous by what the critics might say in the *New York Times,* the clientele makes itself sick on fantasy and nihilism in cream.

WHEN TAKEN together with the precepts of modernism and the fugitive character of the audience for literature, the complexity and size of the American experience further encourage the literary professional to adopt the pose of a tourist or exile. How can the poor fellow possibly illuminate a society of which he has seen so small a part? In what language or tone of voice can he address a minister of state, a financier, or a nuclear physicist?

Prior to the twentieth century, the bulk of the world's literature was written by men who had some knowledge of business or the state. I think of Sophocles and Thucydides (both of them military commanders), of Seneca, Cicero, and Caesar (all politicians), of Montaigne, Bacon, Donne, Pascal, Fielding, Gibbon, Burke, Jefferson, Franklin, Tocqueville, Trollope, Stendhal, Lincoln, Huysmans, Marx, Bismarck, Keynes, Cavafy, de Gaulle, Malraux, Churchill, and Freud. The enormous wealth of the United States has made possible the existence of a verbal class that need do nothing but produce objects of language as ornate, and often as lifeless and heavy, as the jeweled chalices and gold figurines contrived for the greater glory of medieval popes. Organized into subsidiary guilds, the members of this class talk chiefly to themselves—weapons analyst to weapons analyst, historian to historian, public relations counsel to public relations counsel, lawyer to lawyer, novelist to novelist, and so forth through the hierarchy of intelligible discourse. The guild makes a profession of reading books and forming opinions; it feeds off itself, writing about the act of writing, producing commentaries on commentaries.

Every now and then I go to one of those melancholy seminars at which, almost continuously for twenty years, the well-known authors of the moment ask one another ponderous questions about the fate of American letters. Everybody talks about the transmigration of the American novel, about the quality of truth to be found in journalism, about the decay of criticism. When listening to the set speeches I ask myself who reads the novels of Norman Mailer except the people who have reason to write about the novels of Norman Mailer. Is it conceivable that the physicists at the Livermore laboratories look to the stories of John Updike to inform their speculations about the nature of the universe, or that Cyrus Vance, en route to yet another disappointing exchange of views with an Islamic tyrant, rummages through the novels of William Styron in the hope of finding some hint as to the purpose of diplomacy?

The questions reduce themselves to absurdity, and the writers of the present generation, well aware of the absurdity, come to think of themselves as guests of the management. What else can a poor scribbler do but sing and dance and play with the toys of words? Joseph Heller makes bleak jokes about the inanity of Washington, D.C., because he has no choice in the matter. Knowing nothing about why or how the government functions, he makes a virtue of necessity and presents his ignorance as wit. Other writers seek to curry favor with their unseen hosts by transforming themselves into clowns or prophets, offering parodies and self-parodies, never knowing what will endear them to the audience behind the screen—an audience that, for reasons unstated, may or may not be amused. Thus the vogue for autobiographies on the part of so many writers still in their twenties or thirties. Surely the managers must also have been children once; surely they will listen to the confessions of a young girl's youth and early sorrows. Although brought to the highest pitches of sentiment by the women diarists, the genre also embraces the novels of middle-aged English professors. Even at the age of forty they send postcards from Europe or academia. Being observant lads, they notice sexual comings and goings in the dormitories or on the lawns, and somewhere in the drunken summer darkness they're sure there lurks the answer to Donne's question about who cleft the devil's foot. But they still don't know what Daddy does when he gets off the train in New York or Washington, or how he gets the money that pays for the divorce lawyer, the new bicycle, or the library's complete edition of Proust.

Or consider the novels purporting to bear witness to the Vietnam War. Those I have read eloquently convey the emotion of combat but nothing about the density of warfare or the ambiguity of command. The war, like everything else, has become a metaphor. It takes place in the timeless present of a medieval morality play or the romances of J.R.R. Tolkien. Unlike Tolstoy writing about the Napoleonic wars, or Robert Graves writing about World War I, the American writers on Vietnam cannot render the historical coordinates of a specific time and place. They have gone off on an ill-conceived summer vacation: the experience proved to be unpleasant, but as to how or why they got there they have heard only rumors.

NEWTON'S THIRD Law of Mechanics holds that every action engenders an equal and opposite reaction, and perhaps this explains the timidity of contemporary American writing. The more alarming the threat or rate of change, the more insistent the denial of change. Over the past thirty years the novelists have joined together with professors and the journalists to assure their audiences that nothing has changed, that everything remains as it was in Weimar Germany when Bertolt Brecht first discovered greed and fascism. The American novel's descent into the maelstrom of the twentieth century can be measured by the distance between Melville's Ishmael and Mailer's Sagittarius. The histories of the 1920s and 1930s record that large crowds awaited the publication of a new novel by Hemingway or Fitzgerald or Dos Passos with a feeling of eagerness and anticipation, apparently in much the same way that people stood around newspaper kiosks in nineteenth-century Moscow, waiting for the next installment of *Anna Karenina* or *The Brothers Karamazov.* I find this incomprehensible. Within my lifetime I can remember nothing of a comparable excitement attending the publication of a novel by an American author. The publishers make the usual breathless announcements, seconded by the floor walkers touting the books in the literary reviews, but the novels seldom justify the squandering of so many expensive adjectives.

The literary guilds take no pleasure in the advancement of the mind—an enterprise they regard as both dangerous and unnecessary—and their torpor suggests an analogy to Roman literature in the first century A.D. Roman eloquence was never so prized as when it ceased to have any public meaning, and in the first century of empire the Romans contented themselves with the polished rhetoric in which they could see reflected their own dignity and grandeur. Remarking on the lack of curiosity among the Roman equestrian classes, H. G. Wells described it as a phenomenon "more massive than their architecture." The Romans had little interest in the world of which they were landlords, and they made no important discoveries in medicine, astronomy, or geography. As is customary with his-

torical analogies, the parallel is not exact. The American upper middle classes (i.e., the readers and writers of books sold for $15) have
a fondness for technology and a touching faith in the wonders of
applied science, but they betray the Roman lack of curiosity in matters of human character and the evolution of the human mind.

The impressive failures of American journalism over the past thirty
years follow from its unwillingness to recognize as legitimate any truth
that cannot be reduced to number and weight. The country already
has set forth on the quadrennial hue and cry of a Presidential election, but if the press pursues its usual courses, the electorate will discover as little as possible about the character of any of the candidates.
For the next fourteen months the newspapers will conduct polls, and
the newspapers will confer grades and prizes upon the candidates, as
if rewarding grammar school students for their rote memorizations of
"the issues." At the end of the campaign the country will be left with
slogans and phrases, all of them as empty as the headquarters of the
losing candidate through which the television cameras will follow the
melancholy flight of balloons. In the way that the press chose to
ignore for twenty years the pathological disfigurement of Richard
Nixon, so also it continues to hide from itself what it doesn't want to
know about Senator Edward Kennedy, as well as the distressing flaws
of character in Mr. Carter's family and privy councillors.

Unless the journalist first translated himself into sycophant he had
trouble gaining access to the more obscure levels of authority. Who
would talk to the fellow except in lies and half-truths? Certainly not
newspaper publishers or network executives; nobody in the investment banks, the Pentagon, the influential law firms, the White House,
or the corporations. The journalist could choose between writing
vicious gossip or the authorized biography. Both commodities sold on
large volume, and for a period of ten or fifteen years nobody bothered
to wonder about the consequences of so threadbare a discourse.

During the 1960s the so-called new journalism briefly replaced the so-called old journalism, and for a period of some years the leading lights of the age spoke of "non-fiction novels" and the "first drafts of history." The new journalism flattered the envious ignorance of both the *nouveaux riches* and the *nouveaux littéraires*. The adepts of the art made mockery of established institutions, and by so doing they comforted an audience obsessed with the great questions of status and that wanted to know, above all else, that it had no reason to feel inferior in the presence of its betters. The new journalism relied on a simplistic morality and described a world without ambiguity, in the Day-Glo colors of David Halberstam and *Time* magazine. The technique worked reasonably well on the margins of the society, among Hell's Angels and show-business celebrities, on tour with politicians, Jackie Onassis, and other journalists. The technique didn't work so well among people who didn't need the publicity. The present impatience with the press reflects the general disappointment with the inability of the press to comprehend, much less accurately describe, the energy crisis, the nuclear accident at Three Mile Island, the Arab ascendancy, or the indebtedness of New York City—i.e., anything more complex than an exchange of news between two celebrities seated on a peak in Acapulco.

If neither writer nor reader wants to make the effort of imagination necessary to align his accounts of the world with even the little that he can perceive of its reality, then he remains suspended in a state of artful innocence. The condition resembles the dynamic passivity of the rich. Transported from place to place at high speeds, talking incessantly about their acquisitions and travel arrangements, the American upper middle classes devote their energies to questions of technique and to the relief of boredom. A writer like Theodore White in the political balcony, or William Styron in the grandstands of sensibility, admirably exemplifies the prevailing habit of mind. On the assumption that they received their systems of ideas with the tickets of admission, they have no further cause to think. Thus they can concentrate their attention on the logistics of getting inside the White House, on the excitements of riding around in airplanes with the candidates or collecting news of the Holocaust, on the ceaseless repetition of gossip and the description of scene. But when, after prodigious labor, they find themselves in the presence of John F. Kennedy, or confronted with the implacable evil of Auschwitz, they can think of nothing to say. They have no idea what any of it means, only that it is there and somehow very, very important, and very, very glamorous or very, very sad.

Together with the rich, the *nouveaux littéraires* have seen everything once. They can afford not to look too closely at the spectacle under consideration because they assume that there always will be something else to look at—another Presidential candidate or victim of repression, another opening night or sexual revolution in California.

Like the heirs to a great fortune, the contemporary American writers do not dare to think that they can improve upon the miracle wrought by the Founders. They content themselves with fitting out safaris and hunting expeditions (e.g., moving the television cameras around the world in pursuit of a white gorilla or a Presidential candidate) or with the toys and puzzles of literary experiment. Having inherited the national faith in technology, they imagine that they can find their way out of their boredom by means of mechanical contrivances (cf. the elaborate word games constructed by Messrs. Gass, Pynchon, and Coover), and, like the outrageous child in the nursery with a chemistry set, they take an infantile delight in setting off tiny explosions. They have a talent for ingenuity rather than originality, for the visibly clever rather than for the invisibly profound.

To THE extent that the writers of the present generation feel themselves intimidated, impotent, or enraged, their vision of the world tends to narrow and shrivel. In modern fiction, as in modern paint-ing or television, the techniques of abstraction (i.e., of making the part a surrogate for the whole) reduce the scale of conception to an oblique fragment of talk between two or three characters on an empty stage. The writers produce miniatures, and the painters work within the limits of minimalist art. Their ambition becomes as small as the coteries that make up their audiences. In the less-crowded space of the nineteenth century, Dickens and Balzac could project their characters in rounded, rather than flat, dimensions, populating their scenes with human figures instead of with symbols. To the modern writer this would be too frightening. The world seems so huge and so full of terror that it becomes necessary to reduce it to a model or a toy; to concede too much reality to a character unlike oneself might result in a diminishing of self, and this alarms peo-ple—not only novelists but also evangelists and corporation presi-dents. Thus the protagonists of both fiction and the higher forms of corporate advertisement resemble the authors of the play within the play, pitted against gigantic grotesques, no more believable than the balloons and floats dragged into the Rose Bowl on New Year's Day.

Rather than being ashamed of their ignorance, the literary guilds take a perverse and willful pride in what they regard as their spiritu-al cleanliness. When pressed for further explanations on this point they rely on the familiar mythologies of the romantic artist warring with the Philistines. This is mostly nonsense, but it provides a con-venient excuse and allows both writer and reader to maintain the belief in their mutual and perpetual innocence. If they remain igno-rant of the evils abroad in the world (choosing to see them as sym-bols and abstractions instead of as specific cruelties inflicted on specific individuals for specific reasons), so also they can disclaim any responsibility for the casualty lists. None of it is their fault. The guests of the management complain about the accommodations, the service, and the dance music, and in a society that doesn't want to look under the rock of its motives, the complaints go by the name of social criticism.

As the guests feel themselves increasingly superfluous, their complaints become increasingly strident, and, in the absence of anything better to do, they concentrate their attention on the debased romantic notion of the literary personage as celebrity. As recently as the early twentieth century an author's life, no matter how bizarre, was not the stuff of gossip. The literary man, still living in the country of which he was a citizen, had it in mind to become a substantial member of society and, if necessary, to carry forward the affairs of the state. Huysmans was employed as a police official, Trollope as a postal inspector. But who can imagine John Gardner as a civil servant, or Thomas Pynchon conducting an embassy to the Afghans? The modern author has become the most extravagant of his own characters, the persona most self-consciously and lovingly conceived. Truman Capote gains more stature by virtue of publicly describing his love affairs than he does by the private act of writing books; Norman Mailer stabs his wife and enhances his reputation as an author of sensitivity; Gore Vidal loses an election for the U.S. Congress and remarks that he might have become President of the United States if it were not for "this fag thing." Lesser figures acquire luster by parading naked in the streets, wandering in India, or writing reviews of the sexual performance of their dead or famous paramours. The author who would be king achieves expression in his life rather than in his art; each new book becomes a further dramatization in the theater of self.

The emphasis on celebrity results in a cultural postponement of adulthood that corresponds to the biological postponement of death. Writers flattered for their celebrity receive the praise bestowed on children. The critics comfort them with effusive adjectives in the same way and for many of the same reasons that parents admire the daubs on the walls of a nursery-school art exhibit. They praise the talent and intent rather than the accomplished task, and this results in the euphoric infantilization of the New York literary salons. For the time being, at least, the gifted children can play the game of let's pretend and vent their rage on the conspiracy of grown-ups that makes all those dangerous mistakes with foreign policy and nuclear energy.

It is a commonplace to say that the fault is to be found in the times, that the triumphs of democracy and modernism have necessarily brought about the debasement of art and the failure of education. This seems to me a poor argument. The times, like all other times, can be said to be the best of times and the worst of times. The play of ideas is never easy, seldom popular, and always regarded with suspicion by the established order. In the literary bazaar the pride of place customarily falls to knaves and fools, as witness Balzac's description of the milieu in the Paris of the 1830s or George Gissing's account of the same milieu in London of the 1880s.

No law of nature holds that a society must come forward with works of the literary imagination. Through long periods of its history the world has gotten along very well indeed without writers of enduring consequence. The Byzantine empire lasted for nearly one thousand years, content with its genius for bureaucracy, dress design, church liturgy, and political assassination. Nor did the Hellenistic world have much use for poets and dramatists. It was a civilization that made great improvements in mathematics, technology, and the architecture of country houses.

But if it is no disgrace for any country at any particular time in its history to fail to write a literature, it is also a matter of some interest in a country that possesses the power to poison the earth and yet possesses neither the desire nor the courage to know itself.

The Retreat from Democracy

DECEMBER 1977

As often as not these days I run across people who seem to think that democracy is a peaceful idea. They talk about the incessant disagreement within the society as if it somehow did violence to the laws of nature. Having observed that the United States cannot provide all of its constituencies with enough of everything (water, education, justice, appearances on the Johnny Carson show), they worry about riots in the streets. The other afternoon, at a conference of public-spirited citizens, I met a woman who recently had discovered that the setting aside of land for a bird sanctuary in Massa-chusetts would entail the loss of tax revenue for a township that already could not afford to maintain its schools. The news disturbed her. She had been encouraged to think of democracy as a pastoral; it alarmed her to learn that civil rights could interfere with property rights, that the common interest occasionally required the suppression of a private interest. She talked a good deal about personal liberty and the freedom of expression. After listening to her discuss these subjects for the better part of an hour, I had the impression that she imagined the democratic idea to be something easy, quiet, orderly, and safe.

Democracy is none of these things. It assumes conflict not only as the normal but also as the necessary condition of existence, and it defines itself as a continuing process of change. Change implies movement, which implies friction, which implies unhappiness. The structure of the idea resembles a suspension bridge rather than an Egyptian tomb. Its strength, which is the strength of life itself, depends upon stress and the balance struck between countervailing forces. The idea collapses unless the stresses oppose one another with equal weight—unless enough people have enough courage to sustain the argument between government and the governed, between city and town, capital and labor, men and women, matter and mind. Transposed into the biological realm, the democratic idea corresponds to the process of evolution, which also expresses itself in the transitory nature of its forms and which, like democracy, offers no permanent coalitions. In the economic realms the stability of the nation depends upon a balance between the confusions of money and the clarity of mind. Hardly anybody likes to admit that the soaring achievements of the Western mind spring from the same soils that nourish the lush flowerings of corruption and greed. On the one hand the capitalist system implies the exploitation of any available weakness; on the other hand it encourages the freedom of thought and experiment. The two genies emerge from the same bottle, simultaneously and without benefit of ideology. In November of 1975, in the same week that the usual gang of public officials was rounded up on the usual suspicions of fraud, seven Americans received the Nobel Prize.

Over the past twenty years, the more rigorous interpretations of democracy have fallen out of popular favor. For the most part they have been replaced by sentimentality and nostalgia. A considerable number of people have been persuaded to think of democracy as a summer vacation or as a matter of consensus and parades. In the ensuing confusion they come to imagine that the United States constitutes a refuge and a hiding place from the storm of the world. The general eagerness to avoid making trouble results in the intimidation of the American mind. The retreat appears to be taking place across a broad front, in both the intellectual and political sectors of opinion.

A few weeks ago in the *New York Times* I noticed an article by a professor of American history at Harvard who announced "the irrelevance of the past." He had abandoned the hope of teaching his subject because he found little purpose in it. He had discovered, together with everybody else in the country over the age of twelve, that times changed and horsemen passed by. This made the professor sad. He wondered what was the point of holding up the example of the eighteenth and nineteenth centuries in the United States, an age that the professor associated with abundance, to students living in the twentieth century. The latter-day students lived in what the professor conceived of as an age of scarcity. It didn't occur to him that his students had paid a tuition of approximately $7,000 a year to listen to his lesson of despair or that the abundance of the eighteenth and nineteenth centuries was available to only a privileged few.

The professor, unfortunately, speaks with what appears to have become the voice of conventional authority. I hear the same melancholy statements not only in academic quarters but also from book publishers and presidents of corporations. They find no practical value in the study of history, particularly if it cannot be made to serve the interest of tomorrow's stock market quotations.

Within a week of reading the professor's report from Cambridge I read a corollary item in the paper about the absence of speculative research in the sciences. Between 1965 and 1976 the federal investment in such research dropped from $126 million to $29 million. Fewer patents were being awarded to American inventors, and fewer American scientists were publishing research papers. What little research was still being done tended to be subservient to a military or industrial interest.

If speculative research produces nothing but dangerous or irrelevant equations, and if history constitutes nothing more than a tale that is told, then what is the point of assigning significance to objective fact? Everything becomes relative, a matter of opinion and interpretation. The reporting of the news becomes an allegory or a mystery play. A few numbers remain convincing (among them the Nielsen ratings, the tabulation of the public-opinion polls, and the price of Saudi Arabian oil), but, for the rest, what does it matter if people believe what they want to believe? Who can possibly know what the Communists have in mind, or how a nuclear holocaust might come to pass? Edward Teller might know what he's talking about, but so might the astrologer on East Fifty-second Street or the Mexican child who beheld a vision of the Holy Virgin walking on a mountain in Sonora.

Superstition. The courage of the human mind always presents itself as an affront to whatever idols have been set up as the local godhead. But people who have lost faith in themselves, who no longer possess their own history or trust to their own experiments, no longer can summon the courage to imagine their own future. They subside into a state of holy dread, waiting for signs and portents, seeking to make peace with anybody who will promise them another twenty minutes of life and the pursuit of happiness.

The President of the United States consults with the Lord about the decisions of State and informs the faithful that they must preserve their meager stores of light against the coming of the dark. If this means paying ransom to our Arab benefactors, then we have no choice but to pay the ransom, and be careful to say nothing about extortion.

The perception of the world as a barren heath (known chiefly for war and the threat of war, for famine and the threat of famine) makes it convenient to pronounce the world an illusion. The decay of the temporal order provides the spiritual order with proofs of its dogmas and creeds.

Once man has been recognized as unremittingly corrupt (destroying the wilderness, building machines, wasting resources, lapsing into greed and cruelty), then it becomes necessary to remove him from the administration of the state. This results in the pretense that conflict doesn't really exist, that even the most stubborn and irreconcilable differences can be resolved by committees of impartial experts. The state must remain as innocent as an unreclaimed swamp, and this requires removing the political motive (i.e., the corrupt or human motive) from all decisions of national consequence. The procedure is analogous to that of the early church fathers who amputated their genitals in order to rid themselves of temptation.

If a price can be set on the worth of a man's labor but not on the worth of his dreams or his hope of the future, then the mainspring of democratic capitalism must contain the tension between the pressure for social justice and the inertia of greed. The shifting weight in this balance sustains as fair and equitable a redistribution of wealth as seems to me possible in a society that tries to make an equation between creativity, profit, and survival. The election of each new administration, sometimes even the election of a new chairman to the House Armed Services Committee, gives rise to the creation of new wealth.

The confusions of wealth make themselves most plainly visible among people who believe in the omnipotence of money and who therefore lose the capacity to think. I suspect this is what happened to Richard Nixon. He had become so stupefied by the aura of money that he couldn't destroy the tapes of his White House conversations, probably because he thought that they might represent, if properly edited and advertised, another $1 million. Although I feel sympathy for the man distracted by the promise of money, I become depressed or uneasy if required to stay long in his presence. The feeling has nothing to do with moral precepts. In the greenhouse atmosphere of inanimate wealth, my mind begins to sag with the heaviness of sleep. It isn't a matter of place. The arrangement of horses and lawns, or the Impressionist view of the summer sea, doesn't necessarily preclude the hope of consciousness. Neither is it a lack of cunning or connections. Somebody always knows somebody who owns something, whether a football team, a corporation, or an island in the Bahamas. The befuddlement of the rich follows from their single-minded staring into mirrors. Beneath the surfaces of their talk I sometimes hear, as if from an ominous distance, something akin to a thin and paranoid music, a sound like the rattling of bones or the voice of the former Shah of Iran explaining to a newspaper correspondent his reasons for having bought weapons worth $15 billion in the past four years. "The defense of Iran," said the Shah, "is above even history and time. The arms I choose. All systems I choose." Or it is a sound like the rustling of leaves across stone courtyards, the whispering advice of McGeorge Bundy saying to President John Kennedy that the United States might do well to assassinate Fidel Castro. Or it is the testimony of Charles Francis Adams, who, in the latter half of the nineteenth century, spent twenty years in the railroad business, finding and losing fortunes. In the heyday of American capitalism he had known the great men of the period (Gould, Morgan, Hill, and their confederates), and he regretted having made their acquaintance. "Not one that I have ever known," he said, "would I care to meet again, whether in this world or the next; nor is one associated in my mind with humor, thought, or refinement." The names change, and so does the line of goods, but the vacuity remains.

The dehumanizing effects of capitalism become more vicious as they become separated from the exuberance of the dreaming mind. The builders of the American railroads presumably had a vision of a continent drawn together by lines more palpable than those found on any of the known maps. The contemporary evidence suggests that their descendants no longer have the energy to conceive of anything but their own safety. Their crimes have a sallow and diminished aspect, as if it was all they could do to steal a few thousand dollars from the corners of a bureaucracy. Like the ministers of the Ford Foundation, they seem to dwindle into the personae of courtiers or shuffling clerks, doing whatever anyone asks them to do in exchange for the prerogatives of office. What impressed me about the Watergate scandal was the pettiness of it. In decorous conference rooms of the so-called Establishment these days, whether in the universities, the banks, or the departments of government,

I have the uneasy feeling that it is the money which owns and uses the people rather than the people who use and own the money.

THROUGH THE long chains of political and economic causation, whether it is a matter of kings levying taxes for their murdering crusades or Senators Hubert Humphrey and Howard Baker timidly accepting gratuities from the Gulf Oil Corporation, the strand of the profit motive weaves itself into the thread of human destiny as inextricably as molecules of DNA. If it is possible for Harold Geneen to earn $750,000 a year as president of ITT, or for the *New York Times* to pay $500,000 for the syndication rights to Richard Nixon's memoirs and then resell those rights for a reported $1.25 million, then it must be required of somebody else to live with the rats in a Brooklyn slum. We are all of us caught up in the same net of circumstances from which only the more inventive impulse of the capitalist genius can rescue us. This is an unfortunate and no doubt primitive state of affairs, and I wish that it were not so, but I don't know how to avoid the recognition of it. The moralists in the press who mumble about the quasi-religious foundations of a free society remind me of the spokesmen for the business interests who believe that their products appear in the retail stores as if by virgin birth. They forget that if people take seriously the guarantee of their inalienable rights they have no choice but to fight for the truths they hold to be self-evident. Like the totalitarian or religious systems of thought, they would have me believe that the slaughter doesn't exist, that people somehow conduct themselves according to the movements of stars or political abstraction. Their hypocrisy obscures the dynamic as well as the tragedy of the capitalist balance. The best that can be done is to ameliorate the slaughter, but this is difficult to do if the scribes and the pharisees insist that capitalism brings nothing but gladness to the hearts of the people obliged to obey its rules.

Over a long enough period of time, possibly through the slow evolution of the next eight or nine generations, people might think of a way to relieve themselves of the rule of money. They might learn to exchange property as lightly as they exchange remarks about the nuclear holocaust, and their inherent worth might come to be traded in a market of good intentions. But for the time being I don't see how the conflict can be resolved. The attempts to break it by force or subversion, either because it has become embarrassing to the fastidious ministers of the state or because it does not lend itself easily to the language of ideological doctrine, seem to me comparable to the building of guillotines.

TO A greater or lesser extent we are all greedy and frightened children, and if the possession of money comes to mean the difference between life and death, then how is it possible to blame people for whatever they do to obtain it? The history of American business is shot through with incidents of theft, graft, and fraud. The revisionist historians who delight in the obviousness of this, and who seek to make of their discoveries a theory of consistently evil intent, neglect to mention the other genie in the bottle. There is also the history of American invention in the arts and sciences. The two traditions oppose each other, and to ignore the competition between them is to belittle the striving of the human spirit. Although a capitalist society pays huge sums of money for the popular imitations of art or truth, it seldom can recognize, much less reward, its greatest genius. It allows people to stumble into visions of their own truth because it considers such visions irrelevant. In a totalitarian society the lines of intellectual inquiry threaten to expose the fiction of the state and therefore lead inevitably to the offices of the secret police; in a capitalist society they lead into the obscurity of a small room where Herman Melville sits writing prose or out onto the waters of Great Peconic Bay, where Einstein drifts in a sailboat and wonders about the refraction of light.

Given the American capacity for transforming anything and everything into an article of merchandise, nobody can escape the seductions or the intimidations of money. That so many people refuse the offers and resist the threats testifies to their larger understanding of the character of human life. They make their choices not so much on moral grounds as on the basis of empirical observation, because the obsession with money, as witness the long and unhappy life of Howard Hughes, reduces a man to the gibbering sycophancy of a frightened ape.

The Ten Commandments stand as the precursor to Magna Carta and the Bill of Rights. The mind tries to free itself from the confusions of murder and lust because it seeks the greater excitements of courage, faithfulness, truth, and love. The lesser excitement of money becomes clear in the perspective of time. Who can remember last year's tycoon? Who can name the ten most powerful men in St. Joseph, Missouri, in 1845? When I read the annual lists of names published in the pages of *New York* magazine ("The Power Brokers," "The Men Who Really Count," et cetera) I think of the patrons and donors disguised as Magi who stand around in the foreground of Renaissance religious paintings. They peer at the Madonna with the same anxious obscurity of Henry Kissinger staring into the camera of a photographer from *Women's Wear Daily*. They have paid for the space, and they hope to be introduced to the best people in heaven.

Over the course of time it has been the power of the spirit and the imagination that has shaped the clay of civilization. The greatness of man expresses itself in the force of mind, in Bach's music or Shakespeare's plays, in the art of da Vinci, the physics of Newton, or the theories of Marx. Money follows with the baggage, traveling among camp-followers and putting up the tents. It can maintain the status quo, whether of tyranny or democracy; it can gild markets or temples, employ four hundred thousand automobile workers or Benvenuto Cellini, buy Panama or *Aristotle Contemplating the Bust of Homer*. It is a power worth having, but without the greater power of thought it amounts to little more than the temporary ascendancy of a bully.